MANAGING GOD'S BUSINESS

From his own work as a priest in the Church of England and his interest in the theory and practice of the management of religious and faith-based organizations, Malcolm Torry has written a significant contribution to the field. I warmly commend this book to leaders and led, to those who often work against the odds, but most of all to the ordinary people (lay and ordained) who manage God's business in their corner of this world.

Extract from the Foreword to *Managing God's Business*
by Wesley Carr, Dean of Westminster

Leaders and managers of religious and faith-based organizations grapple daily with management challenges which are very different – and often more demanding – than those faced by their counterparts in private companies or public sector agencies. This ground-breaking book offers them – for the first time – the intellectual tools that can help them understand the complexities of their role and get to grips with the challenge of Managing God's Business.

Colin Rochester, Director of the Centre for Nonprofit and
Voluntary Sector Management, Roehampton University, UK

Religious and faith-based organizations constitute a large and important group of organizations. This is the first book to study systematically their characteristics and the distinctive challenges they pose to the people managing them.

Malcolm Torry discusses how to define religious and faith-based organizations, how to study them, and the secular context in which they operate in Western Europe and the USA. There are chapters on congregations, denominations, governance, membership, the clergy, leadership, and religious and faith-based organizations' relationship to civil society. The book relies on research-based literature and case studies and contains full bibliographies, making it an essential tool for anyone studying this important new field.

*Dedicated to those religious and faith-based organizations
which I have had the privilege to serve*

Managing God's Business

Religious and Faith-Based Organizations and their Management

MALCOLM TORRY
Roehampton University, UK

ASHGATE

Published by
Ashgate Publishing Limited
Gower House
Croft Road
Aldershot
Hants GU11 3HR
England

Ashgate Publishing Company
Suite 420
101 Cherry Street
Burlington
VT 05401-4405
USA

Ashgate website: http://www.ashgate.com

British Library Cataloguing in Publication Data
Torry, Malcolm
   Managing God's business : religious and faith-based organizations and their management
   1. Religious institutions – Management 2. Nonprofit organizations – Management
   I. Title
   206.5

Library of Congress Cataloging-in-Publication Data
Torry, Malcolm, 1955-
   Managing God's business : religious and faith-based organizations and their management/by Malcolm Torry. – 1st ed.
      p. cm.
   Includes bibliographical references.
   ISBN 0-7546-5159-2 (alk. paper)
   1. Religious institutions – Management. I. Title.

   BL632.T67 2005
   206′.5–dc22

                                                            2004013982

ISBN 0 7546 5159 2

Typeset by Tradespools, Frome, Somerset
Printed and bound in Great Britain by Antony Rowe, Chippenham, Wiltshire

Contents

List of Figures

Foreword

All of a sudden, so it seems, you cannot move anywhere in the churches without being confronted by issues of management. Books abound, though often more about leadership. Leadership is seen as being essentially good, personal, charismatic and like Jesus. Management is more suspect, something to do with bureaucracy and dullness, the unnecessary institutional aspect of churches, often treated as the opposite of mission. Many offer practical advice on how to lead churches. Few have written at all about management.

Malcolm Torry's book is different. From his own work as a priest in the Church of England and his interest in the theory and practice of the management of religious and faith-based organizations, he has written a significant contribution to the field. It is largely based in the literature, with extremely full bibliographies. But he also brings in his own experience from time to time. His basic proposition is that religious and faith-based organizations are essentially voluntary and therefore possess particular and distinctive characteristics. This obvious point is increasingly overlooked by the churches, but is a necessary insight to retain in today's over-professionalized world and church.

The distinction between religious and faith-based organizations is not very familiar. 'Faith-based' organizations range from a small local community development project through to something vast and international, such as the Red Cross. He also writes on management questions such as congregations and how they work; the governance of religious organizations; religious organizations as an element in civil society; and leadership. On all of these issues, both old and new, Malcolm Torry throws fresh light garnered from his extensive reading.

It is always dangerous to say 'never', especially in the life of a church. Most of a church's activities and structures, although dated, have seen it through change. 'Good enough' is ample precedent. However, today's Church of England has created a structure more unsuited to its task than ever before. Yet many religious organizations and faith-based organizations still manage to flourish, and their work, in spite of increasing government involvement, remains voluntary and religious.

The author follows these trails and in so doing offers a coherent, but not universal, understanding of the place of religion in contemporary Western society. Few, if any, will have read widely on something like this. But he does much of the preliminary work for us, and leaves all religious people and indeed volunteers with much to think about and many things to reconsider.

I warmly commend this book to leaders and led, to those who often work against the odds, the therapists and others who listen to them, but most of all to the ordinary people (lay and ordained – but differentiated, too) who manage God's business in their corner of this world.

Wesley Carr
Dean of Westminster

Acknowledgements

There are many people who have contributed to the writing of this book. The first person to thank must be Margaret Harris, then at the Centre for Voluntary Organisation at the London School of Economics and now Professor of Voluntary Sector Organisation at the University of Aston, who supervised the research which led to the publication of *Managing Religious and Faith-based Organisations: A Guide to the Literature*. I was subsequently invited to join the Centre for Nonprofit and Voluntary Sector Management at the University of Surrey Roehampton as an honorary research fellow, and I would like to thank the Centre's staff and students and particularly Colin Rochester, the Centre's Director, for supervision, encouragement, and much reading of drafts. Helen Cameron, of Oxford Brookes University, also read a draft, and I thank her for the useful comments she made; and I would also like to thank Sarah Lloyd at Ashgate and Ashgate's referees for encouragement and practical suggestions for improvement of the text. Much of the book was written during the period January to March 2003 when I was a guest of St John's College Cambridge, and I would like to thank the Master and Fellows of the College for electing me a Fellow Commoner for that term and for hospitality in previous years and subsequently. For permission to take study leave for those three months I would like to thank the Bishop of Woolwich, the Rt Revd Colin Buchanan; and I must also thank those members of the Parish of East Greenwich who took on additional responsibilities while I was away, to say nothing of my wife, Rebecca, and children, Christopher, Nicholas and Jonathan, for managing largely without me for three months.

This book is firmly based on the research literature, but some of what it contains (and particularly the case studies) is based on my own considerable experience in the field. So I would finally like to thank all those people, impossible to number, with whom I have worked so happily in religious and faith-based organizations.

The Study of Religious and Faith-Based Organizations and their Management

In 1995 a conversation took place at the London School of Economics between myself and Dr Margaret Harris, with whom I was studying for the MSc degree in Social Policy. *Why* were Archdeacons in the Church of England going to Business School to take MBAs? – for religious organizations are not commercial organizations. So where *could* those managing religious and faith-based organizations go for guidance on how better to manage them? Where *could* Rabbis and Ministers go to gain a better understanding of their organizations and thus be able to contribute better to their development? For religious organizations are not commercial or public organizations, and even if they are voluntary organizations they are not like most other voluntary organizations. Whether you look at their memberships, their paid servants, their structures, or their values, they are different: they are a category of their own, and a most interesting category because every member of it is unique – there appears to be no religious organization the same as any other. And then there are those organizations which lie between religious organizations and secular organizations (church schools, housing associations founded by churches, homes for the elderly run by Jewish charities, and so on); and these too seem to have characteristics of their own, and some of those characteristics are recognizable as the characteristics of religious organizations. So it did appear to be rather important that people managing religious organizations should be able to study *religious* organizations, and not some other sort.

The Bishop of Woolwich granted me a month's study-leave, which I used to survey the research literature available on the nature and management of religious and faith-based organizations. Dr Harris supervised the project. During that month and subsequently I read several hundred books and articles, and the result was a fairly slim volume, *Managing Religious and Faith-Based Organisations: A Guide to the Literature*, published in 2000 by the University of Aston, at which Dr Harris had by then become Professor of Voluntary Sector Organisation. The volume was slim because, although there is a growing literature on religious organizations, there is relatively little research-based literature directly relevant to the management of religious and faith-based organizations.

Following the publication of the bibliography, Colin Rochester, at the University of Surrey's Centre for Nonprofit and Voluntary Sector Management, invited me to work as an honorary research fellow with the Centre. The aim is a programme of teaching and research on the management of religious and faith-based organizations, and this book is the first product of our collaboration. It is work in progress, and will, we hope, stimulate further research and reflection. It will also form the basis for a course to be taught at the Centre. And it will delineate an emerging new field: the study of religious and faith-based organizations, and their management.

(I use the word 'field' loosely here, to mean a category of organizations to be studied, in this case religious and faith-based organizations. Strictly speaking it should be called a subfield, for it is a category within the category of voluntary organizations – which is itself a subfield of the field of organizations. By the end of the book the reader might decide that religious organizations possess a sufficient number of distinctive characteristics for them to count as a field in its own right, and similarly with faith-based organizations.)

The History of Religious Organizations

In prehistory society was simply religious, and the whole community would normally be a religious association. As societies developed more structure the community remained religious: thus in the Hebrew Scriptures Moses' organization of Israel during their desert wanderings is the organization of a religious organization – but we begin already to see the development of distinctively religious organizations within a wider community in the building of the tabernacle and the establishment of its priesthood. (I here make no judgment on the historical accuracy of the accounts in the first five books of the Hebrew Scriptures, or on the date of their composition.)

This situation persisted right up to the Enlightenment (1650–1750), with the whole of society normally being regarded as religious, but with specifically religious organizations (particularly the religious orders in the West) representing the religious aspect of society.

It was the Enlightenment which changed all that. With the development of explicitly secular disciplines with no positive relationship with the Church (a process given early momentum by Reformation religious breakaways from the Catholic Church in Europe), and subsequently with the emergence of secular states in France and North America, the sacred and the secular evolved different discourses – and different organizations. Thus churches, synagogues and mosques came to be understood as religious organizations within an essentially secular society, suggesting that there are clear boundaries between the organization and wider society – though, as we shall see when we study the concept of membership in relation to religious organizations, boundaries are frequently by no means clear, suggesting that either the organization is secular as well as religious, that society is religious as well as secular, or both. The absence of a clear boundary between the sacred and the secular is also suggested by the existence of 'faith-based organizations': organizations firmly related to a religious tradition but which do not have religious activity as their primary aim. Such organizations occupy a social space between religious organizations and secular organizations, and deserve a treatment of their own.

We are thus left with a complex situation: religious, secular and faith-based organizations existing in a society more or less secular, with faith-based organizations sharing some of the characteristics of religious organizations and some of the characteristics of secular organizations. The historical process that gave rise to this is depicted in Figure I.1.

The Emergence of the Study of Religious Organizations

The secular and religious discourses which emerged during the Enlightenment often related to each other, but they were different and were felt to be different. The sciences took their own areligious path, and the social sciences set out to study religious activity as one human activity amongst others, with Durkheim's work on different rates of suicide in Protestant, Catholic and Jewish communities a hundred years ago being a particularly important stage in this development. Weber's work on authority-types relied heavily on the study of

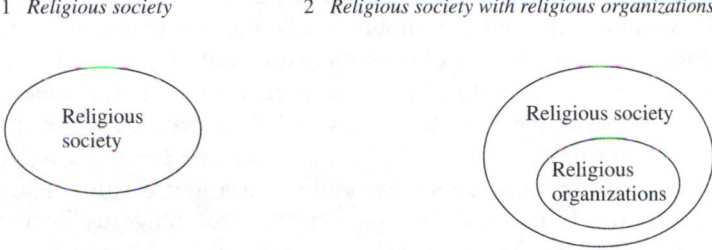

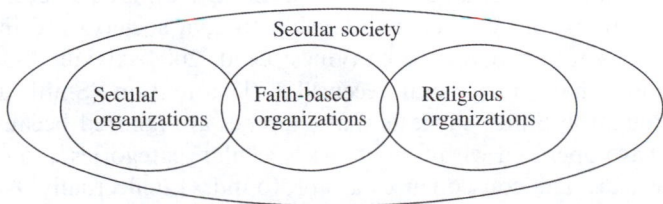

Figure I.1 **The historical process from society as religious to a secular society containing religious and faith-based organizations**

ancient societies, and, whilst the theory is still very usable, its roots lie as much in the past as in the present. So it is to Troeltsch and Niebuhr in the 1920s that we look to find the beginnings of our own emerging field: the study of specifically religious organizations. The employment of social scientific method within a secular society containing religious organizations is what gave us Troeltsch's distinction between churches and sects (Troeltsch 1911; Gill 1996) and subsequently Niebuhr's description of the denomination (Niebuhr 1929). There are certainly connections between these religious organizations and the societies in which they are set, but there are also boundaries between the organizations and the wider society.

Both in the UK and in the USA the study of organizations and then of voluntary organizations (particularly at Brunel University and subsequently at the London School of Economics) has enabled the question to be asked: What is a *religious* organization? The deepening secularization of our society, charted recently by Callum Brown in his *The Death of Christian Britain* (Brown 2001), has made this question both more askable and more important. We are now more aware than ever that there are secular organizations, that there are religious organizations, and that there is a category in between called 'faith-based organizations'; and that there are connections between these organizations and also important differences between them.

So what is now required is a study of religious organizations as religious organizations, and of faith-based organizations as faith-based organizations, and all of them in the context of a secular society.

And it is important that we should study these organizations, not only because they have meaning for their participants, but also because they are an important element of civil society, because religion is a live issue, because relationships between the faith-traditions and thus between those traditions' institutions matter more than ever before, and because there is a lively debate about the relationship between science and religion and because, if religion is its institutions (as I try to show), then a study of religious institutions is important to this and other wider debates.

So why hasn't there been the same kind of study of religious and faith-based organizations as there has been of commercial and public organizations and of secular voluntary organizations? Whilst in the USA there has been some study of congregations and of their relationship to civil society, and in the UK of congregations for their own sake (Guest et al. 2004: xi–xiii, 1–38), religious organizations have in general received little attention (Smith 1983; 1984). David Houghton Smith suggests that churches are ignored because the social sciences have operated with 'sacred' and 'secular' categories and concentrated on the secular. The consequences are profound: 'Intellectually, both religious research and voluntary action research suffer from and are stunted in their growth by their mutual lack of scholarly interaction and consequent lack of cross-fertilization of concepts and generalizations' (Smith 1983: 299; 1984: 15).

He calls for comparative studies, particularly in relation to participation in organizations, and for scholarly interaction which would enable practitioners to benefit from conclusions drawn from study of organizations different from but in some ways similar to their own. Voluntary action research could give to religious organizations better understandings of themselves, and secular organizations could benefit from religious organizations' experience. Smith calls for a new 'ecumenism' between related research areas, and he makes some practical proposals.

But there is another reason, too, for comparative neglect of the management of religious and faith-based organizations, and that is because those with positions of responsibility in religious organizations tend to be trained for their roles in theological colleges or similar, and these organizations see themselves as having a primarily theological task, with the organizations which their students will serve being regarded as theological realities related to an underlying theological position rather than as the heart of the matter. If we were to ask why religious organizations are not the focus of attention, we might find ourselves suggesting that this might lead to comparative study in relation to other types of organizations, which might bring into question the religious nature of religious organizations, and thus the religious nature of everything else on the curriculum: but this is to hypothesize. There *has* been research conducted on theological colleges (for example, Williams 1994), but this has been mainly on how *they* change as institutions. It would be interesting to see the results of research on how and why theological colleges choose their curricula, and on the effects of choice of curriculum on the students and on the organizations which they go on to serve.

It would also be interesting to see research on how and why theology is studied in universities, for it is normally studied within a humanities faculty, thus distancing it from any study of organizations, of management and of the social sciences, all of which normally go on within a science faculty of some kind. This is probably another reason why there has been so little study of religious and faith-based organizations and of their management.

And all this matters. It is important to study the management of religious and faith-based organizations because if they are going to serve their participants and if they are going to contribute to relationships between the faiths and wider society, then they must be well understood and well managed.

'Management'?

But this raises two important questions: Is the notion of 'management' sufficiently clear to enable us to study it? And is 'management', an activity developed in a largely secular sphere, appropriate to religious organizations?

According to Selznick, 'management' suggests 'rational, efficiency-minded, goal-driven organization' (Selznick 1992: 289): that is, an administrative rather than a political activity. 'Ends are characteristically taken as given, and every act is justified by the contribution it makes to those ends. All else is a distraction' (ibid.: 290). Employees, students, tourists and soldiers are 'managed', that is, they 'are expected to defer to legitimate authority, having agreed beforehand to subordinate their own preferences and suspend their own judgments, within more or less well-defined limits. So long as those limits are respected, the managers can take obedience for granted' (ibid.: 290). But nothing is ever quite so simple, and all organizations, throughout their structures, experience competing goals and values and changing goals and values, meaning that any organization is in fact 'an open system with uncertain and ever-changing boundaries' (ibid.: 290): and such an organization needs 'governance' and not just 'management'. 'Governance takes account of all the interests that affect the viability, competence, and moral character of an enterprise ... The broader the organization's goals, the more leeway it has in defining its mission, the more requirements there are for winning co-operation, the more fully the lives of participants are lived within it, the more important does governance become' (ibid.: 290). Organizations with committed members and with less easily definable goals are like communities, suggesting to Selznick that there is a spectrum, with the 'organization' at one end, the 'community' at the other, and 'institutions' of various kinds in the middle, which in turn suggests that, if for the organization management is what is required and for the community governance is needed, then institutions require management and governance to coexist and interact. In the examples from the USA which Selznick studies he finds that, whilst some decisions are mainly managerial and some are mainly governmental, many are a mixture of the two: and 'the continuities ... are always troublesome' (ibid.: 291).

As we shall see, in religious organizations goals are generally obscure and contested, and also, as we shall see, members experience a variety of motivations. This suggests that governance is what is required rather than management, and that where management and governance function together the combination will be 'troublesome'.

So why continue to use the term 'management' if governance is what is required? Because the distinction between 'management' and 'governance' which Selznick employs, whilst being useful analytically, doesn't reflect normal English usage. The *Chambers Twentieth Century Dictionary* includes 'to deal tactfully with', 'to contrive successfully', 'to be able to cope with' amongst the definitions of the verb 'to manage' and 'skilful treatment' amongst those of 'manager'. I would go further. Now that 'management' is a term employed in relation to voluntary organizations, organizations which are often as much 'community' in nature as they are 'organization', governance functions are understood as part of the task of 'management'; and now that commercial and industrial enterprises are regarded more as communities with conflicting goals than they once were, in these institutions too 'management' implies governance. In this sense it is appropriate to speak of the management of religious and faith-based organizations.

This understanding of 'management' gives a useful context to Richard Roberts' question as to whether 'management' is appropriate to religious organizations, and in particular to the Church of England. He identifies 'managerialism' as one of the products of the Thatcher, Major and Blair years: 'What emerges is a primal antithesis, not between property owners and the propertyless, but between managers and the managed' (Roberts 2002: 59). Management has become a religion (Pattison 1997), and management in the sense of control has indeed infected many areas of social life, and particularly politics (Roberts 2002: 65). In his study of recent changes in the Church of England he finds appraisal of performance, benchmarking, mission statements, and middle managers whose task it is to secure the conformity of the front-line operatives, the clergy, to the organization's goals, as the organization seeks to gain control over an 'other', the 'customer' in the pew (ibid.: 188). In Roberts' view, 'the *uncritical* incorporation of managerialism within the Church of England amounts to a betrayal' (ibid.: 64) which endangers individuals' souls and the human community.

The 'management' which Roberts seems to have in mind is that which Selznick discusses: 'rational, efficiency-minded, [and] goal-driven' (Selznick 1992: 289), an administrative rather than a political activity. But if our definition of 'management' includes governance when we apply the word to organizations which are essentially communities, then we *ought* to discuss the management of the Church of England and of every other religious and faith-based organization.

Our aim in this book is to discuss the management of religious and faith-based organizations to enable practitioners in those organizations (and they *are* organizations) to manage them appropriately: not uncritically to employ types of management employed in other types of organization, but to ask precisely what kind of management is needed in this particular type of organization. By doing this we shall delineate a new field of study: the management of religious and faith-based organizations.

The Future of the Study of the Management of Religious and Faith-Based Organizations

There are now plenty of opportunities to study the management of voluntary organizations (at the Centre for Civic Society at the LSE, at the University of Aston, at the University of the South Bank, at the Centre for Nonprofit and Voluntary Sector Management at Roehampton University and elsewhere), but no opportunity yet for the same kind of in-depth study of religious and faith-based organizations. It is to that process that this book hopes to contribute.

The field requires:

1   teaching (in order to promote informed debate, to develop skills, to develop the field, and to identify new areas for research);
2   research (especially now, as most of the small amount of research literature available is old; and especially in the UK, as most of the research literature available is from the United States, where the religious scene is very different);
3   consultancy (there is some consultancy available, but it is not always research-based); and
4   literature and other resources to support educational efforts.

To all of these tasks this book is intended as a contribution.

A Presupposition and Its Consequences

The basic presupposition underlying this work is that religious and faith-based organizations are mainly voluntary organizations and that they are voluntary organizations with characteristics all of their own. The consequence of this presupposition is that these organizations need to be studied as a category of their own, and that only literature based on research on religious and faith-based organizations will be directly relevant. Literature based on research on other types of organizations (and particularly the now substantial literature on voluntary organizations) will be useful insofar as it applies, and a judgment will need to be made in each case as to whether it applies or not.

As we shall see when we ask the question as to how religious and faith-based organizations should be studied, our basic presupposition means that ideas and theories found helpful in studying organizations in general and voluntary organizations in particular will be found helpful here – provided we recognize that bodies of theory might need to be adapted if they are to be applied to religious and faith-based organizations. We shall employ two bodies of theory found helpful in studying organizations generally: Weber's three authority-types – the bureaucratic, the traditional, and the charismatic (Weber 1922: 6ff.); and Etzioni's compliance structures – the coercive, the normative, and the utilitarian (Etzioni 1980: 88ff.). We shall find helpful two bodies of theory developed mainly to explain the evolution and behaviour of voluntary organizations: Chapin and Tsouderos's theory on how voluntary organizations formalize as they grow (Chapin and Tsouderos 1956: 342ff.), and David Billis's theory, which explains the behaviour of voluntary agencies lying between the associational and the bureaucratic world's (Billis 1993: 160ff.). In relation to religious organizations, important explanatory frameworks will be Troeltsch's distinction between a sect and a church (Troeltsch 1911; Gill 1996; Moberg 1970) and Niebuhr's extension of the categorization to the threefold church, denomination and sect (Niebuhr 1929).

An essential piece of theory is secularization theory. This is important because the secularization of society and of religious and faith-based organizations has had a considerable impact on these organizations' behaviour. There has been much debate over whether secularization is mainly about ideas or mainly about institutions, and the importance of this debate to our study means that the idea is given the whole of Chapter 3. As a working definition I shall take 'secularization' to mean: 'The drawing apart and declining integration of religious and secular institutions and their personnel' – thus making 'secularization' part of a process of diversification and change rather than a process somehow separate from everything else which is going on in society.

What this book will *not* do is discuss in detail the theologies of religious traditions and ask how these relate to the traditions' organizations. This is not because this isn't a fascinating aspect of the field: it is; but it is a large and complex aspect and would warrant a book of its own, not least because it would need to begin with a consideration of whether or not theology is a science and of how theological discourse relates to the discourses of the social sciences.

Applying the Theory

The aim of the book, and of any subsequent programme of teaching and research, is to study research results (*both* that described in the existing literature and that arising from fresh studies inspired by the opening up of this new field), and to employ the research in the development of usable theory (and here bodies of theory from other fields will be useful, but new theory might also be helpful, as will appear in Chapter 9 on the clergy). The theory developed will then be applied to case studies which might give some insight into situations which those involved in religious and faith-based organizations might face.

So this book is not a manual for those managing religious and faith-based organizations. Every organization is different (and this is probably more true of religious and faith-based organizations than it is of any other type), so every organization must be treated separately. But the body of theory developed should help participants to understand their own organizations better and thus to manage them more appropriately.

Future Development of the Literature on the Management of Religious and Faith-Based Organizations

In a new field boundaries will not be clear, and precisely what is relevant will be a matter for debate. In preparation for the writing of the bibliography *Managing Religious and Faith-based Organisations: A Guide to the Literature*, the literature of a variety of fields was studied: that of the management of voluntary organizations, that of the sociology of religion, and various others. What is now required is an even broader search of existing literature, together with the undertaking of new research where there are gaps (as there are many), so that a field of literature called, say, 'Religious and faith-based organizations and their management' might emerge. We are particularly in need of case studies. In this book two organizations will appear occasionally: the Church of England and the South London Industrial Mission. This is because the author has been employed by the Church of England for over 20 years and knows it well; and because his doctoral thesis was on the practice and theology of the South London Industrial Mission, for which he worked from 1983 to 1988. There are a few substantial published case studies of congregations and their activity (Ammerman et al. 1997; Becker 1999; Harris 1998; Heskins 2001; Hopewell 1987), but more are needed; and as far as we know there are no substantial published research-based studies of faith-based organizations (though we are open to correction here, of course).

We are also in need of literature in English on religious traditions other than the Christian. In my research for *Managing Religious and Faith-based Organisations* it was relatively easy to find research literature on Christian organizations (though some of it was rather dated), more difficult to find literature on Jewish organizations (though possible to find literature on their clergy and on Jewish faith-based organizations), and far more difficult to find material on any other religious tradition. In this multicultural and multifaith age it is essential that this deficit be repaired: religions are their organizations and for religious traditions to understand each other they will need to understand each other's organizations, something that only high-quality research literature will enable to occur.

An Overview of This Book

The first chapter is about defining religious and faith-based organizations. It studies different ways of forming definitions and concludes with working definitions of religious organizations and faith-based organizations.

Chapter 2 asks how we might best study religious and faith-based organizations in order to give us tools to use as we undertake our own studies of the field, while Chapter 3 is a thorough discussion of the concept of 'secularization' and of the consequences for religious and faith-based organizations of the secularization process.

The congregation is the fundamental religious organization, so Chapter 4 asks how congregations function and how they change. The next chapter, Chapter 5, understands churches, sects and denominations as federations of congregations, and studies how they function. Chapter 6 is a substantial chapter on the governance of religious organizations, and in many ways is the heart of the book.

In Chapter 7, faith-based organizations are described as lying between religious organizations and secular voluntary organizations, and some of the consequences of this location for their management are discussed. Then Chapter 8 asks what 'membership' means in religious organizations, and finds the concept rather more difficult than we might have expected.

The position of the clergy is a unique facet of religious organizations, and so Chapter 9 discusses how the clergy function. Next, Chapter 10 explores the nature of civil society and the problems facing it, and asks how religious and faith-based organizations fit into it. Finally, Chapter 11 discusses how leadership might best be undertaken in religious and faith-based organizations. And the concluding chapter is precisely that.

It will be clear from this introductory chapter, and it will be clear once the end of the book is reached, that much is still vague and uncertain, that the boundaries of the field are unclear, and that future directions are by no means obvious. This is to be expected: for here we are dealing with an emerging field, and to develop it into an ordered, well-taught, well-discussed and well-researched field is our task. And it is an important task because, as Geertz suggests, 'religion is sociologically interesting not because … it describes the social order (which, in so far as it does, it does not only very obliquely but very incompletely) but because, like environment, political power, wealth, jural obligation, personal affection, and a sense of beauty, it shapes it' (Geertz 1975: 119). If an essential element of religion is its organizations then those organizations are interesting not just for their own sake but because of the way *they* shape our social order.

But we shall not be studying religious organizations simply because they are interesting. We shall be studying them because these organizations *are* managed and because they could be managed better. (In Wuthnow's phrase, these organizations 'produce the sacred' (Wuthnow 1994: 2), and production needs to be planned.) 'Pastors are trained to be in contact with the sacred, meeting houses are constructed to provide a place for the gods to dwell, publishing companies print and distribute the Bibles we read, even our private meditations may be performed with a background of recorded music' (ibid.: 2) – and every aspect of the life of a religious or a faith-based organization is planned, whether this be done well or badly. Whilst this book won't tell its readers precisely how to manage their organizations, it will, I hope, enable them to think about their organizations' management in a more informed manner and thus be able to work out for themselves how to improve it.

References

Ammerman, Nancy Tatom, et al., (1997), *Congregation and Community*, New Brunswick, New Jersey: Rutgers University Press

Becker, Penny Edgell (1999), *Congregations in Conflict: Cultural Models of Local Religious Life*, Cambridge: Cambridge University Press

Billis, David (1993), *Organising Public and Voluntary Agencies*, London and New York: Routledge

Brown, Callum G. (2001), *The Death of Christian Britain: Understanding secularization 1800–2000*, London and New York: Routledge

Chapin, F.S. and Tsouderos, J.E. (1956), 'The Formalisation Process in Voluntary Associations', *Social Forces*, **34** (4), May, 342–44

Etzioni, Amitai (1980), 'Compliance Structures', in Etzioni, Amitai and Lehman, E. (eds), *A Sociological Reader on Complex Organisations*, 3rd edition, Austin, Texas: Holt, Reinhart and Winston, pp. 87ff.

Geertz, Clifford (1975), *The Interpretation of Cultures*, London: Hutchinson

Gill, Robin (ed.) (1996), *Theology and Sociology: A Reader*, new and enlarged edition, London: Cassell

Guest, Mathew, Tusting, Karin and Woodhead, Linda (eds) (2004), *Congregational Studies in the UK: Christianity in a Post-Christian Context*, Aldershot: Ashgate

Harris, Margaret (1998) *Organising God's Work: Challenges for Churches and Synagogues*, London: Macmillan

Harris, Margaret and Torry, Malcolm (2000), *Managing Religious and Faith-based Organisations: A Guide to the Literature*, Birmingham: University of Aston Business School

Heskins, Jeffrey (2001), *Unheard Voices*, London: Darton, Longman and Todd

Hopewell, James F. (1987), *Congregation: Stories and Structures*, London: SCM Press

Moberg, David O. (1962), *The Church as a Social Institution*, Englewood Cliffs, New Jersey: Prentice Hall

Moberg, David O. (1970), 'Theological Position and Institutional Characteristics of Protestant Congregations: An Exploratory Study', *Journal for the Scientific Study of Religion*, **9**(1), 53–8

Niebuhr, H. Richard (1929), *The Social Sources of Denominationalism*, reprinted Gloucester, Mass.: Peter Smith, 1987

Pattison, S. (1997), *The Faith of the Managers*, London: Cassell

Roberts, Richard H. (2002), *Religion, Theology and the Human Sciences*, Cambridge: Cambridge University Press

Selznick, Philip (1992), *The Moral Commonwealth: Social Theory and the Promise of Community*, Berkeley: University of California Press

Smith, David Horton (1983), 'Churches are Generally Ignored in Contemporary Voluntary Action Research: Causes and Consequences', *Review of Religious Research*, **24** (4), 295–303

Smith, David Horton (1984), 'Churches are Generally Ignored in Contemporary Voluntary Action Research: Causes and Consequences', *Journal of Voluntary Action Research*, **13** (4), October–December, 11–19

Troeltsch, Ernst (1911), *The Social Teaching of the Christian Churches*, vol. I, reprinted London: Allen and Unwin, 1931

Weber, Max (1922), 'The Three Types of Legitimate Rule', in Etzioni, Amitai and Lehman, E. (eds) (1980), *A Sociological Reader on Complex Organisations*, 3rd edition, Austin, Texas: Holt, Reinhart and Winston

Williams, Rhys H. (1994), 'Organizational Change in Theological Schools: Dilemmas of Ideology and Resources,' *Nonprofit and Voluntary Sector Quarterly*, **23** (2), Summer, 123–37

Wuthnow, Robert (1994), *Producing the Sacred: An essay on public religion*, Urbana and Chicago: University of Illinois Press

Defining Religious and Faith-Based Organizations: and Defining Them as Voluntary Organizations

Religious and faith-based organizations form a sizeable proportion of organizations in the UK and other European countries, and possibly an even larger proportion in the USA; they make a distinctive contribution to civil society; and they are now particularly important for the part they will play in enabling people of different faiths and of different ethnic groups to relate to one another and to society as a whole. It is therefore vital that such organizations should be studied and understood – and, if we are to study organizations in the category 'religious and faith-based organizations', it is important to know which organizations are in that category and which are not.

A subsequent question which I shall tackle is that of the relationship between definitions of 'voluntary organization', 'religious organization' and 'faith-based organization'. It is important to do this because the ways in which we define and study religious and faith-based organizations will depend largely on how we answer the question: Do religious and faith-based organizations belong to the voluntary sector?

Two Ways of Defining

Ludwig Wittgenstein suggested the image of 'family resemblances' to describe the relationship between one use of a word and another (Wittgenstein 1967: §§ 66f.). To suggest a core definition of a word is simply to add yet another member to the existing 'family' of meanings. This rather suggests that we shall never formulate a tight definition of 'religious organization', 'faith-based organization' or 'voluntary organization', as whenever we use these terms in new contexts they take on new meanings and new connections with other words. But we do need to try to define categories for the purely practical reason that it is helpful to generalize and we need to know what we can generalize to and what we can generalize from. If we want to know how to manage better a particular organization then we shall seek out other organizations which we can label as the same type of organization. This requires categorization, and it requires definitions of categories.

The 'classical' way of defining a category is to propose a list of characteristics. Those entities which possess the characteristics are in the category, and those entities which do not are not: so a square is a rectangle because it has four sides and opposite sides are parallel. But for anything other than simple cases of definition this strategy quickly breaks down because there are frequently cases where we cannot determine whether the entity concerned is in the category or not. Thus, if to be a 'bird' something needs to fly, then an ostrich is not a bird and a bat is.

Eleanor Rosch (Rosch and Lloyd 1978; Rosch 1999) has suggested that categories are not the clear-cut things we often think they are, and that it is often not the case that entities are either in the category or not in it; and neither is it the case that entities belong equally. Thus a robin is more a bird than an ostrich is, and a bat is on the boundary of the category.

Rosch points out that in the real world we define categories in terms of prototypes and then decide whether something is in the category by asking how similar it is to the prototype. Mark Johnson (Johnson 1993) has successfully used this means of definition to give a coherent account of how we categorize actions as moral or otherwise: we have in our minds a prototype lie and we then ask whether other actions are more or less like it; and (of particular interest to us) Anthony Freeman (Freeman 2002) has employed the same method to define 'Church'.

Defining Religious Organizations

The first problem we face when defining 'religious organization' is a problem with the definition of 'religion'.

Durkheim defines religion as 'a unified system of beliefs and practices relative to sacred things, that is to say, things set apart and forbidden – beliefs and practices which unite into one single moral community called a Church all those who adhere to them'. A 'Church' is essential to the definition because religion is 'a collective thing' (Durkheim 1915: 47) which connects practices and ideas together 'to classify them and systematize them' (ibid.: 429). Geertz suggests a similar definition:

> Religion is 1) a system of symbols which acts to 2) establish powerful, pervasive, and long-lasting moods and motivations in [people] by 3) formulating conceptions of a general order of existence and 4) clothing these conceptions with such an aura of factuality that 5) the moods and motivations seem uniquely realistic. (Geertz 1975: 90)

In his *The Oxford Dictionary of World Religions*, John Bowker (1997: xv) lists a variety of definitions of religion, suggests that 'we can recognize a religion when we see one because we know what the many characteristics of religion are; but we would not expect to find any religion which exhibited all the characteristics without exception' (ibid.: xxiv) and follows that with: 'Religion is a risk of intolerance, cruelty, bigotry, social oppression and self-opinionated nastiness' (ibid.: xxiv). David Ray Griffin suggests this: A 'full-fledged religion' is 'a complex set of beliefs, stories, traditions, emotions, attitudes, dispositions, institutions, artistic creations, and practices – both cultic and ethical, both communal and individual – oriented around the desire to be in harmony with an ultimate reality that is understood to be holy and thereby to provide life with meaning' (Griffin 2001: 12). The introduction of a bibliography on *Managing Religious and Faith-based Organisations* (Harris and Torry 2000) begins: 'This Guide has its origins in our own quest for research-based literature which could help us to understand the organization and management issues faced by religious and faith-based organizations – primarily congregations, denominations and religious-based voluntary and non-profit organizations.' So is a for-profit Christian radio station a religious or faith-based organization? On Griffin's definition: is humanism a religion? And Marxism? And National Socialism?

For any definition based on a list of characteristics, there will be people who will disagree with the list, there will be entities we might want in the category but which don't fit the criteria, and in this case there will be entities which do fit the criteria but which we might not wish to call a 'religion'.

A second problem with defining religious organizations is that the notion of 'religious' is not related to the notion of 'religion' in any clear-cut way. An attitude or an action might be thought 'religious' without being related to any particular religion; and religions frequently give rise to actions and attitudes which we might not wish to call 'religious'.

A third problem is that we have to choose whether a 'religious organization' is to be defined as an organization related to a religion or as an organization which has religious characteristics: and the lists of characteristics of these two kinds of organization will be different. (A meditation group might be a religious organization on the latter basis but not on the former).

A fourth problem related to the classical method of definition is that we shall have to decide how many 'religious' or 'religion' characteristics an organization will need to have if it is to be counted as a religious organization. The fewer characteristics we require the more organizations will be religious organizations; but the more we employ the more we shall be sure that there will be little controversy over whether the organizations picked out by the characteristics are in fact religious organizations.

It might be better to do what we do in fact do, and pick a prototype. Christian congregations, synagogues, Sikh and Hindu temples, and mosques, are religious organizations (and Jeavons is right to suggest that they are the only unambiguously religious organizations; Jeavons 1998). So the British Humanist Association might be a religious organization, and Tate and Lyle is not one. By comparing other organizations with those organizations which are undeniably 'religious organizations' (with the two words always taken together, as religious organizations might not always be religious on the basis of some definitions of that word) we can decide whether they are at the centre of the category, whether they are to some extent religious organizations, whether they belong on the boundary of the category, or whether they are not religious organizations at all. By doing this we shall be doing what Peter Clarke and Peter Byrne invite us to do and operate a 'family resemblance' strategy for defining religion and religious organizations (Clarke and Byrne 1993).

I suggested that the first problem we face when defining 'religious organization' is the definition of 'religion'. An alternative strategy is suggested by the mention of institutions and practices in Durkheim's and Griffin's definitions of religion, by Alata's definition of religion as a 'way of life' (Alata 1977) and by Bruce's decision to ignore inner spiritual states because they are so difficult to study and instead to define religion in terms of individual and group behaviour (Bruce 1995: vii). In the same way, we could define religion in terms of institutions and their members' activity, thus obviating the need to define 'religion' at all because religion then *becomes* religious organizations and their memberships.

Defining Faith-Based Organizations

We experience the same problems with faith-based organizations as we experienced employing the classical method of definition with religious organizations. By 'faith' we might mean either a particular 'Faith' or a faithful attitude of some kind; and we shall then need to ask to what extent an organization is influenced by that Faith or that faith. For an organization to be 'based' on a faith could mean either that a particular Faith or kind of faithfulness provides some of its values, or we might mean that it is closely governed by that Faith's religious organizations.

But a problem we face when we attempt to employ a 'prototype' definition is that 'faith-based organization' is relatively recent terminology which was specifically invented to denote organizations influenced by Faith-traditions but not to the extent of being religious organizations: that is, a religious organization's main purpose is religion (although we might have cause to question this once we begin to discuss the sociology of religious organizations) and a faith-based organization has another main purpose but is strongly influenced by a religious tradition or by a religious organization. The recent genesis of the terminology means that it is not easy to pick a prototype or prototypes, as the choice of a prototype relies on a history of custom and practice; and the history of this particular terminology means that a definition in terms of characteristics is imposed on us from the beginning and to seek other means of definition will not be to define correctly or usefully.

The only solution is to employ both methods of definition, with the classical definition suggesting prototypes, and the prototypes then being used to decide which other organizations we admit to the category and to what degree we admit them – with our decisions always being tested against the classical definition of the category.

A Church of England school is thus a faith-based organization, as its main purpose is education but it is significantly influenced by the Christian tradition; and a Christian radio station might be a religious organization or a faith-based organization – but probably not both, as the definition of a faith-based organization as an organization the main purpose of which is not religion is likely to preclude a faith-based organization from being a religious organization (though not necessarily, of course, if we employ the prototype method of definition for religious organizations and not a strict list of criteria which includes the criterion that an organization is a religious organization only if its main purpose is religion). The South London Industrial Mission (SLIM) is supported by Churches and its staff are mainly clergy, but only careful examination of its activity could decide whether it is a religious or a faith-based organization. (We cannot discuss motivation very easily as only observed behaviour is available to us.) SLIM has done, and still does, education, networking, pastoral care and welfare work. It does very little worship, prayer or evangelism. It might be faith-based in the sense of faith-influenced, but it is not religious. (It might also be closer to the Kingdom of God than many religious organizations, but that is a different debate.)

Of interest on the boundary between faith-based organizations and other organizations are faith-based organizations which are becoming secularized (Demerath et al. 1998: part V; Stone and Wood 1997) – a process which Swartz sees as inevitable (Swartz 1998), but which is never complete, because differences remain between organizations which were once faith-based and those which never were (Cormode 1998; Grønbjerg and Nelson 1998). Thus an industrial mission which takes on more and more secular activities does not necessarily become secular if its motivation and support-structures remain church-based (Torry 1990); and a Jewish elderly care home which has few Jewish staff is never entirely secular (Harris 1997).

So: a housing association recently founded by a group of churches is likely to be a faith-based organization; a housing association founded some time ago by a group of churches might or might not be a faith-based organization; and neither a congregation nor British Airways is a faith-based organization.

It might be that the best way to envisage the situation is as a spectrum, with religious organizations at one end and secular organizations at the other. Faith-based organizations will then be found between the two end-points, either nearer to the 'secular' end, or nearer to the 'religious' end, or somewhere in the middle (see Figure 1.1):

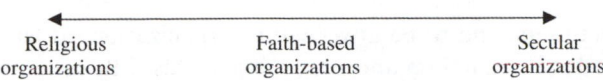

Figure 1.1   **A spectrum of organizations**

Thus we shall expect faith-based organizations to have some characteristics like those of religious organizations, and some characteristics like those of secular organizations. We might locate a Church of England Voluntary Aided School nearer to the 'religious' end of the spectrum than a Voluntary Controlled School, because in the former case the parish and the Diocesan Board of Education provide more governors than in the latter case; but both will be quite close to the 'secular' end, because the local education authority pays the staff and the government sets the curriculum. And there will be movement along the spectrum: a housing association might start off quite close to the 'religious' end, and might then slowly (or maybe even rapidly) migrate towards the secular end as it relates more closely to secular bodies and consequently changes to become more like them.

An interesting question, of course, is whether there is such a thing as a 'religious organization', for *all* organizations are to some extent affected by other organizations. Simply to discuss the 'management' of religious organizations is to relate religious organizations to secular organizations, because they too are managed; so perhaps all we've got are faith-based organizations. But congregations the main purpose of which is worship *are* different from other faith-connected organizations, and, as we shall see, they exhibit particular characteristics all of their own. So for the time being, whilst we recognize that creating a firm boundary between religious and faith-based organizations will not always be easy – is a Diocesan office, for example, a religious or a faith-based organization? – we shall retain the distinction as a working hypothesis.

Defining Voluntary Organizations

There is now a long history of the study of voluntary organizations, and so a considerable literature on their definition.

In 1948, Beveridge recognized that not all of the activity of voluntary organizations was being carried out by volunteers, but did expect the organizations' modes of birth and of governance to be voluntary, that is, 'free and independent' (Beveridge 1948: 150) – and since then an important means of defining 'voluntary organizations' has been to determine the extent to which an organization is 'voluntary'. Voluntary organizations have founders, governors (trustees, management committee, and so on), staff (paid and/or volunteer) and users, and to be a 'voluntary organization' at least the current governors need to be voluntary and, according to David Billis, to have the power to close the organization down (Billis 1993: 234). Lester Salamon offers a longer list of defining features: the organization must be formal, private, non-profit distributing, self-governing and 'voluntary' 'to a significant degree' (Salamon and Anheier 1993: 537f.). But the problem with such a definition is that it either leaves out organizations which some practitioners or academics would include in the category 'voluntary organization' or it includes organizations which we might not wish to include – and the above cluster of definitions includes Trades Unions, a class of organization usually treated as a category of its own.

A second cluster of definitions is what I would call 'negative' definitions, that is, a list of features which 'voluntary organizations' do *not* have. Dobkin Hall defines a voluntary organization as one which undertakes tasks which neither the State nor for-profit organizations are willing or able to fulfil (Dobkin Hall 1987: 3), David Mason, in order to draw conclusions about how to manage voluntary organizations and for-profit enterprises, lists 14 differences between the two (Mason 1984), and Margaret Harris offers as a definition 'that area of organized activity which is neither the commercial, for-profit sector, nor the public, governmental sector' (Harris 1990: 126).

The search for a positive classical definition has led to study of what I would call the 'location' of voluntary organizations. David Billis discusses their sociological location (in the 'associational' sphere and in the areas of ambiguity between the 'associational' and the 'bureaucratic' worlds; Billis 1993: 134); Hansmann and Weisbrod locate them in the economic space in which information failure makes it difficult for for-profit organizations to operate (Hansmann 1988: 29; Weisbrod 1988: 6) or in which nobody else provides for minority needs (Weisbrod 1988: 25); Etzioni locates voluntary organizations in the political space in which status groups try to influence society (Di Maggio and Anheier 1990: 141f.); and Rob Paton locates them in a matrix of organizational types (between 'the public sector' and 'the natural economy' and alongside 'small businesses'; Paton 1991: 5f.). Such 'location' definitions do indeed tell us important things about the histories of voluntary organizations and about their relationships with other sectors, but they tell us little about what they are and even less about what they *do* – which is why a 'functional' definition is often employed. Charles Handy, amongst others, divides voluntary organizations into those offering mutual support, such as Gamblers' Anonymous; those undertaking service delivery, such as Relate; and campaigning organizations, such as CND (Handy 1991: 13). Kendall and Knapp add categories of 'individual advocacy' and 'resource and co-ordinating' to this list (Kendall and Knapp 1995: 68). Such categorization helps our understanding of the sector but it cannot stand alone as a definition of voluntary organizations because there are many organizations in these categories which are by no means 'voluntary'.

Rob Paton's definition introduces another approach: The 'social economy' (an American term close to our 'voluntary sector') is 'the small or medium-sized value-based organization founded on commitment (arising from devotion, compassion, enthusiasm, solidarity, defiance, etc.) and working for a common or public benefit' (Paton 1991: 7). There *is* always some commitment based on a value-system underlying voluntary sector activity, but there is in the National Health Service (NHS) and in other public sector organizations too – so, even though this definition points to something important about voluntary organizations, it cannot function on its own as a defining feature of the voluntary sector. Lohmann's slightly different version of the 'common benefit' definition excludes such public bodies as the NHS: he defines the voluntary sector by employing the concept of 'the commons': 'a sector characterized by participation, shared purposes and resources, mutuality, and concern for fairness' (Lohmann 1992: 319), and he draws an analogy with the village common (ibid.: 318). It is surely of interest that this definition would include trades unions in the sector.

Di Maggio has pointed out that government funding of organizations causes 'isomorphism', that is, a self-understanding by a group of organizations that they are in the same 'industry' (for example, social care) and a consequent professionalization of activity and growing similarities between organizations in the 'industry', whatever their origins or histories. Thus public sector organizations and organizations that were originally 'voluntary' can come to look very like each other (Di Maggio 1983: 147ff.; Di Maggio and Anheier 1990: 154), and we are left asking whether there is anything very distinctive about voluntary organizations after all. By raising the question of whether 'member-benefit' organizations belong amongst voluntary organizations or in a category of their own, David Horton Smith (Smith 1991: 137ff.) sets us this question: If the boundary of the category 'voluntary organizations' is so insecure, can we properly define such a category? (Incidentally, Smith locates churches in the member-benefit sector. This is a misunderstanding of churches and of the complex motives of people who belong to them, for the belonging is frequently intended as a contribution to the church's outward-looking activity.) Rather than speaking of 'the voluntary sector, it might be better, as Marshall suggests, to speak of 'a multiplicity of voluntary sectors' (Marshall 1996: 52): a religious sector, a philanthropic sector, a community sector and an informal sector. And similarly, in the American context, van Til suggests that, rather than speaking of the 'not-for-profit' sector (for many not-for-profit organizations are in fact operating as large tax-exempt businesses), we should speak of a 'third space' within which there is a variety of types of organization (van Til 2000).

Defining a category of 'voluntary organizations' is looking rather more difficult than we might have thought it was going to be. However, if we turn to the prototype approach to definition, we find that there is sufficient agreement about which organizations are voluntary organizations and which are not for scholars to be able to examine members of the category and discover a number of frequently occurring features. Margaret Harris offers a list of these which includes volunteering, structures which match values, multiple goals, rapid change, and multiple accountabilities (to funders, users, members, and so on; Harris 1990: 134f.). Rob Paton discusses the diverse roles which many organizations undertake, the resulting tensions, and the consequent complexity of managing voluntary organizations (Paton 1991: 11); and David Billis follows his discussion of the ambiguous location of voluntary agencies with an exploration of the ambiguity of statuses within them – for a member of the governing body might be a user, and a founder might be a staff member (Billis 1993: 164). Thus complexity, tensions, and constant structural and role revision, are widespread features of organizations in the category – particularly now that statutory funding often comes with contractual obligations which might conflict with an organization's original goals (ibid.: ch. 13). Similar organizations in the sector share similar problems (Blau and Scott 1963: 43), and a particularly widespread problem is the tension experienced when a self-help group becomes a service-provider, employs staff (Billis 1993: ch. 10), and finds that the 'bureaucratic' and 'democratic' organizational models have to be operated together (Billis 1993: ch. 11; 1991). The process of 'formalization' might be a general one (Chapin and Tsouderos 1956: 344), but there are always decisions to be taken about direction, and the outcome of change can be either death or survival and growth (Wertheim 1976: 4ff.) – revealing another important feature of voluntary organizations: their vulnerability to changes in government policy (Billis 1993: 231), to the cutting off of grants for political reasons (Brenton 1985: 94), to Charity Law's broad definition of 'political activity' (ibid.: 98), and to *increased* funding, which might jeopardize the character of the organization (ibid.: 207). (Ostrander, however, disagrees with an apparent consensus here and suggests that increased government funding gives voluntary organizations the option of stepping up their advocacy for a strong welfare state and does not necessarily jeopardize their independence or their original goals; Ostrander 1989: 39, 42.) The successful management of change is a challenge facing all voluntary organizations, and uncertainty about the future of funding, about changing relationships with government and about revision of legal and regulatory frameworks adds to this problem (Lewis 1995: 159). Innovation remains a characteristic shared by many voluntary organizations (Handy 1995), as is a distinctive management ethos which coheres with organizations' foundational goals (Paton 1991: 10) and a continuing strong commitment to the disadvantaged (Salamon 1993: 37).

The boundary of the category *is* debatable, fuzzy and fluid, but it is still meaningful to use the concept 'voluntary organization', and by that term we generally seem to mean an organization which exhibits some or all of a list of characteristics (but without implying that every voluntary organization exhibits all of those features). The concept is also meaningful because there are agreed prototypes: Oxfam, Age Concern, the Scout Movement, and the local community newspaper. The relative robustness of both prototype and classical types of definition in the case of voluntary organizations might suggest that, in a mature field, we are likely to find a sufficient understanding of the characteristics of organizations and a sufficient consensus about which organizations are in the category to ensure that the two methods of definition are likely to give very similar answers to the question as to which organizations are in the category. Moreover, because a large number of characteristics are considered when membership of the category is decided, the classical method might in this case be as capable of creating a structured category as is the prototype method.

Voluntary, Religious and Faith-Based Organizations

By their definitions, the categories of religious and faith-based organizations will rarely overlap (though such organizations as local authority-funded Muslim schools might be in both categories in relation to different aspects of their complex activity). Clearly, most religious and faith-based organizations are also voluntary organizations – though not all, as a Christian TV channel in the USA might be a for-profit organization, and Church schools might or might not be voluntary organizations. (As far as I know, whether voluntary aided schools should be counted as voluntary organizations is a debate still waiting to happen.) One interesting phenomenon is religious and faith-based organizations' reluctance to count themselves as voluntary organizations – there are only a handful listed amongst the 2600 members of the National Council for Voluntary Organisations (National Council for Voluntary Organisations 2002: 26ff.) – and an equal reluctance amongst those who study the voluntary sector to include religious organizations in their studies (Smith 1983; 1984). (In David Knoke's major study of collective action organizations in the USA there isn't a single mention of a religious or faith-based organization; Knoke 1990.)

But the number of religious and faith-based organizations which are not also voluntary organizations is likely to be small, which suggests that our understanding of religious and faith-based organizations will rely heavily on our understanding of voluntary organizations, and that if we are seeking better ways to manage religious and faith-based organizations then we shall have much to learn from good management practice in voluntary organizations (Bemrose 1996).

But, as we have seen, religious and faith-based organizations are robust categories of their own (and I hope that Beckford would recognize that we have now gone some way towards responding to his suggestion that this still needs proving; Beckford 1985b). While the listing of characteristics might not be the best way to define the categories, once the categories are defined by the prototype method or by an amalgam of the prototype and classical methods, characteristics of the organizations in the categories can be listed – and relationships to religious traditions, activities, ideas and attitudes will be seen to influence heavily the character and activity of this category of organizations. Religious and faith-based organizations will therefore need to be understood as religious and faith-based organizations, and not simply as voluntary organizations; and the study of their management will be the study of the management of particular institutions to which lessons learnt in other voluntary organizations might not necessarily apply.

Demerath and Schmitt (1994) have shown that secular and voluntary organizations have religious aspects and vice versa, that religious categories have properly affected the study of all organizations, and that religious and secular organizations have much in common: bureaucracy, nontangible goals, nontangible means, cultural primacy (as opposed to organizational necessities being regarded as primary), the expression of anti-organization ideologies, the constraints of relations with the organization's history, dependence on leaders, taken-for-granted-ness (by society and members), local/national dissonance, boundary constraints, and cultural power used as a political weapon. As far as they are concerned, the reason for studying religious organizations and faith-based organizations is because they are the 'foundries' of other voluntary organizations and therefore need to be understood if other voluntary organizations are to be understood; and as far as Yinger is concerned, we should study religious organizations because religion has a role in society and thus to study religious organizations is to study society (Yinger 1957).

The definition of religious and faith-based organizations is the first step in the fulfilment of a variety of connected tasks: the mapping of the fields; study of the organizations and of their management; analysis of the findings; and the dissemination of a deeper understanding of these organizations and of related proposals as to how such organizations might be better managed.

We have made a start, but only a start, on the definition of these organizations. There is much still to be done.

References

Alata, Syed Hussein (1977), 'Problems of Defining Religion', *International Social Science Journal*, **29** (2), 213–18

Beckford, James (1985b), 'Religious Organizations', in Hammond, Philip E. (ed.), *The Sacred in a Secular Age: Towards Revision in the Scientific Study of Religion*, Berkeley: University of California Press, pp. 125ff.

Bemrose, Chris (1996), 'The Church as a Voluntary Non-profit Organisation', in Nelson, John (ed.), *Management and Ministry*, Norwich: Canterbury Press, pp. 111ff.

Beveridge, Lord (1948), *Voluntary Action: A Report on Methods of Social Advance*, London: George Allen and Unwin

Billis, David (1991), *Sliding into Change: The future of the voluntary sector in the mixed organisation of welfare*, working paper 14, London: London School of Economics/Centre for Voluntary Organisation

Billis, David (1993), *Organising Public and Voluntary Agencies*, London: Routledge

Blau, Peter M. and Scott, Richard (1963), *Formal Organizations: A Comparative Approach*, London: Routledge and Kegan Paul

Bowker, John (ed.) (1997), *The Oxford Dictionary of World Religions*, Oxford: Oxford University Press

Brenton, Maria (1985), *The Voluntary Sector in British Social Services*, London: Longman

Bruce, Stephen (1995), *Religion in Modern Britain*, Oxford: Oxford University Press

Chapin, F.S. and Tsouderos, J.E. (1956), 'The Formalisation Process in Voluntary Associations', *Social Forces*, **34** (4), May, 342–4

Clarke, Peter and Byrne, Peter (1993), *Religion Defined and Explained*, Basingstoke and London: St Martin's Press / MacMillan

Cormode, D. Scott (1998), 'Does Institutional Isomorphism Imply Secularisation?: Churches and Secular Voluntary Associations in the Turn-of-the-Century City', in Demerath et al. (1998), pp. 116ff.

Demerath III, N.J. and Schmitt, Terry (1994), 'Transcending Sacred and Secular: Mutual benefits in analyzing religious and nonreligious organizations', in Bromiley, David G., Greil, Arthur L. and Robbins, Thomas (eds), *Religion and Social Order*, vol. 4, Greenwich, Connecticut: Jai Press

Demerath III, N.J, Hall, Peter Dobkin, Schmitt, Terry and Williams, Rhys H. (eds) (1998), *Sacred Companies: Organizational Aspects of Religion and Religious Aspects of Organizations*, New York and Oxford: Oxford University Press

Di Maggio, Paul (1983), 'State Expansion and Organizational Fields', in Hall, Richard H. and Quinn, Robert E. (eds), *Organizational Theory and Public Policy*, London: Sage

Di Maggio, Paul, and Anheier, Helmut K. (1990), 'The Sociology of Nonprofit Organisations and Sectors', *Annual Review of Sociology*, **16**, 137–59

Durkheim, Emile (1915), *The Elementary Forms of the Religious Life*, London: George Allen and Unwin

Freeman, Anthony (2002), 'Sister Churches and Sisters in the Church: How do we think about such things?' *Modern Believing*, **43** (1), 11–21

Geertz, Clifford (1975), *The Interpretation of Cultures*, London: Hutchinson

Griffin, David Ray (2001), *Reenchantment without Supernaturalism: A Process Philosophy of Religion*, Ithaca and London: Cornell University Press

Grønbjerg, Kirsten A. and Nelson, Sheila (1998), 'Mapping Small Religious Nonprofit Organizations: An Illinois Profile', *Nonprofit and Voluntary Sector Quarterly*, **27** (1), March, 13–31

Hall, Peter Dobkin (1987), 'A Historical Overview of the Private Nonprofit Sector', in Powell W.W. (ed.), *The Nonprofit Sector: A Research Handbook*, New Haven: Yale University Press

Handy, Charles (1991), 'Types of Voluntary Organisations', in Batsleer, J., Cornforth, C. and Paton, R. (eds), *Issues in Voluntary and Non-profit Management*, Harlow: Addison-Wesley.

Handy, Charles (1995), *The Empty Raincoat*, London: Arrow

Hansmann, Henry (1988), 'Economic Theories of Nonprofit Organisations', in Powell, W.W. (ed.), *The Nonprofit Sector: A Research Handbook*, New Haven: Yale University Press, pp. 28ff.

Harris, Margaret (1990), 'Working in the Voluntary Sector', *Work, Employment and Society*, **4** (1), 125–40

Harris, Margaret (1997), *The Jewish Voluntary Sector in the United Kingdom: its role and its future*, London: Institute for Jewish Policy Research

Harris, Margaret and Torry, Malcolm (2000), *Managing Religious and Faith-based Organisations: A Guide to the Literature*, Birmingham: Aston Business School

Jeavons, Thomas H. (1998), 'Identifying Characteristics of "Religious" Organizations: An exploratory proposal', in Demerath III, N.J., Hall, Peter Dobkin, Schmitt, Jery and William, Rhys H. (eds.) *Sacred Companies: Organizational Aspects of Religion and Religious Aspects of Organizations*, New York and Oxford: Oxford University Press, pp. 79ff.

Johnson, Mark (1993), *Moral Imagination: Implications of Cognitive Science for Ethics*, Chicago: Chicago University Press

Kendall, Jeremy, and Knapp, Martin (1995), 'A loose and baggy monster: boundaries, definitions and typologies', in Davis Smith, Justin, Rochester, Colin and Hedley, Rodney (eds), *An Introduction to the Voluntary Sector*, London: Routledge, pp. 66ff.

Knoke, David (1990), *Organizing for Political Action: The Political Economies of Associations*, New York: Aldine de Gruyter

Lewis, Jane (1995), *The Voluntary Sector, the State and Social Work in Britain: The Charities Organisation Society/Family Welfare Association since 1869*, Cheltenham: Edward Elgar

Lohmann, R.A. (1992), 'The Commons: A Multidisciplinary Approach to Nonprofit Organisations, Voluntary Action, and Philanthropy', *Nonprofit and Voluntary Sector Quarterly*, **21** (3), 309–23

Marshall, T.F. (1996), 'Can we Define the Voluntary Sector?' in Billis, D. and Harris, M. (eds), *Voluntary Agencies*, Basingstoke: Macmillan, pp. 45ff.

Mason, David E. (1984), *Voluntary Nonprofit Enterprise Management*, New York and London: Plenum Press

National Council for Voluntary Organisations (2002), *Working Together: Annual Review and Impact Report 2001/2002*, London: National Council for Voluntary Organisations

Ostrander, S. (1989), 'Private Social Services: Obstacles to the Welfare State?', *Nonprofit and Voluntary Sector Quarterly*, **18** (1), 39–47

Paton, Rob (1991), 'The Social Economy: Value-based organizations in the wider society', in Batsleer, J., et al. (eds), *Issues in Voluntary and Non-profit Management*, Harlow: Addison-Wesley

Pickering, W.F.S. (1975), *Durkheim on Religion*, London and Boston: Routledge and Kegan Paul

Rosch, Eleanor (1999), 'Reclaiming Concepts', in Freeman, Walter J. and Núñez, Rafael (eds), *Reclaiming Cognition, Journal of Consciousness Studies*, **6** (11–12), 61–77

Rosch, Eleanor and Lloyd, Barbara B. (1978), *Cognition and Categorization*, Mahwah, New Jersey: Lawrence Erlbaum

Salamon, L. (1993), 'The Marketisation of Welfare: Changing Nonprofit and For-profit Roles in the American Welfare State', *Social Service Review*, **67** (1), 16–39

Salamon, Lester M., and Anheier, Helmut K. (1993), 'Measuring the non-profit sector cross-nationally: a comparative methodology', *Voluntas*, **4** (4), 530–54

Smith, David Horton (1983), 'Churches are Generally Ignored in Contemporary Voluntary Action Research: Causes and Consequences', *Review of Religious Research*, **24** (4), 295–303

Smith, David Horton (1984), 'Churches are Generally Ignored in Contemporary Voluntary Action Research: Causes and Consequences', *Journal of Voluntary Action Research*, **13** (4), October–December, 11–19

Smith, David Harton (1991), 'Four Sectors or Five? Retaining the Member-Benefit Sector', *Nonprofit and Voluntary Sector Quarterly*, **20** (2), 137–50

Stone, Melissa M. and Wood, Miriam M. (1997), 'Governance and the Small, Religiously Affiliated Social Service Provider', *Nonprofit and Voluntary Sector Quarterly*, **26** (s), s44–61

Swartz, David (1998), 'Secularization, Religion and Isomorphism: A Study of Large Nonprofit Hospital Trustees', in Demerath et al. (1998), pp. 323ff.

Torry, Malcolm N.A. (1990), 'The Practice and Theology of the South London Industrial Mission', unpublished PhD thesis, University of London

Van Til, Jon (2000), *Growing Civil Society*, Bloomington, Indiana: Indiana University Press

Weisbrod, Burton A. (1988), *The Nonprofit Economy*, Cambridge, Massachusetts: Harvard University Press

Wertheim, Edward G. (1976), 'Evolution of Structure and Process in Voluntary Organizations: A study of thirty-five consumer food co-operatives', *Journal of Voluntary Action Research*, **5** (1), 4–15

Wittgenstein, Ludwig (1967), *Philosophical Investigations*, trans. G.E.M. Anscombe, 2nd edn, Oxford: Oxford University Press

Yinger, J. Milton (1957), *Religion, Society and the Individual*, New York: Macmillan

CHAPTER 2

How Should We Study Religious and Faith-Based Organizations?

We have already decided that religious and faith-based organizations are voluntary organizations of particular types, so we shall first of all study them as organizations, secondly as voluntary organizations, and thirdly as organizations in categories of their own. In this short chapter we shall study one or two of the consequences of these decisions and then go on to decide what methods we should employ. We shall find ourselves using a variety of types of theory, and this is as we should expect. The study of religious and faith-based organizations and of their management is the study of a *field*: it is not itself a discipline; and the study of a field can, and should, employ the methods developed in a variety of disciplines. The social sciences in general and the study of organizations in particular will be the disciplines which will furnish the theory that we shall employ, and later on we shall create our own theories for use within our new field, theories which might be found to have wider usage in the social sciences and in the study of organizations.

What we shall not be doing is seeking theories and methods from within the religious traditions to which religious organizations relate. As we discussed in our introductory chapter, universities and theological colleges have tended not to study religious organizations as organizations. They might be studied as ideal organizations related to theological conceptual structures, but this is not to study them empirically as organizations (though to study the value-structures which help to inform how religious organizations function is an important element in any study of such organizations). There is no reason why connections shouldn't be made between a theology of organizations and empirical study of religious organizations which makes use of theories from other disciplines (and such connections would be particularly interesting in relation to Islam): but to my knowledge this has not been done in any systematic fashion, and it remains an item on the agenda for future work. Whilst Roberts (2002) and Chia (1996) raise questions about how terminology from other disciplines might be applied and about the practice of the study of management of organizations, neither they nor anyone else make positive suggestions as to whether particular methods might be suitable for the study of religious and faith-based organizations because they are religious or faith-based. This gives us another item for our agenda for future work.

But however long the agenda for future work, our task in this book is to study religious and faith-based organizations using the tools available to us, because that is the practical task which will enable people working for religious and faith-based organizations to manage them in ways appropriate to those organizations' characteristics.

Studying Religious and Faith-Based Organizations as Organizations

The study of organizations is a well-developed discipline, and when it comes to religious and faith-based organizations we shall discover and study many of the same characteristics as we find when we study other organizations: specialization, formalization, centralization, distribution of authority, and so on (Beckford 1973). By this means we shall be studying religion itself for, as we have realized, religion is its organizations just as much as it is beliefs, ideas and values (Beckford 1975b); and, as with the study of all organizations, we shall recognize that organizations are more than the sum of their individual members: they have structures and behaviours all their own – an insight which stems from Durkheim's work on suicide a hundred years ago in which he found that communities based on different religious principles exhibit different suicide rates (Durkheim 1952). Similarly, we shall explore the characteristics and behaviours of religious and faith-based organizations and shall seek explanations, as Durkheim did with the phenomena which he discovered. We shall find the many methods of Organizational Studies useful (Cameron 2004), and we shall find particularly helpful three pieces of research-based theory which apply to organizations in general: Weber's work on authority-types; Etzioni's more recent work on compliance structures; and DiMaggio and Powell's isomorphism theory.

Weber's Three Authority-types

Max Weber suggested that there are three different authority-types operating in organizations.

For Weber, 'authority' means 'that a specific command will be obeyed' (Weber 1922: 4), whether from custom or expediency, and within a legitimate power structure, of which there are three types:

1 'Classical', 'legal' or 'bureaucratic': 'Legal authority rests on enactment; its pure type is best represented by bureaucracy' (ibid.: 4). Obedience is owed to rules, not to people, and officials (including elected officials where they conform to rules) are trained specialists. States and industries are typical bureaucracies.
2 'Traditional': 'Traditional authority rests on the belief in the sacredness of the social order and its prerogatives as existing of yore. Patriarchal authority represents its pure type' (ibid.: 6). Office-holding is at the pleasure and discretion of the lord, and feudalism is a natural concomitant (ibid.: 8).

3 'Charismatic': Charismatic authority 'rests on the affectual and personal
   devotion of the followers to the lord and his gifts of grace (charisma)'
   (ibid.: 8). Prophets exercise this kind of authority, a type in which there
   are no rules, only devotion to the leader's mission. This type of authority
   tends to be authoritarian, can provoke revolutions (ibid.: 9), and leads
   eventually to 'routinization' as the charismatic leader's functions become
   the subject of rules as his (it is usually but not always 'his') authority
   wanes (ibid.: 10).

Compliance Structures

Amitai Etzioni has suggested that there are three types of compliance structure:

1 'Coercive': This is where force is used to ensure compliance with an
   organization's wishes, and to the extent that an organization's participants
   are involved they are involved negatively, 'alienatively'. Involvement tends
   to be high-intensity (Etzioni 1980: 88ff.).
2 'Normative': Here the norms which govern the organization have moral
   appeal, the participant is involved positively with a moral commitment, and
   rewards tend to be symbolic. Involvement tends to be high-intensity (ibid.:
   88ff.).
3 'Utilitarian' or 'remunerative': The organization has power over material
   resources and the participant conforms to the organization's wishes in
   order to gain a share of those resources. Involvement is 'calculative' and
   low-intensity (ibid.: 88ff.).

Participants at different levels experience the compliance structures differently
of course. The level of participation depends on the intensity and direction of
someone's involvement, the level of their subordination in the organization,
and their performance obligations. Someone who scores low on all three counts
is an 'outsider', such as a customer. Someone who scores high on all three is
thoroughly implicated in the compliance structures and their effects.

   There are, according to Etzioni, congruent states: coercive power and
alienative involvement; remunerative power and calculative involvement; and
normative power and moral involvement. Incongruent states are also possible,
such as normative and alienative, and this might occur when involvement is
related to another commitment, such as a religious one, which the participant
feels requires them to participate in an organization which alienates them.
Etzioni's hypothesis is that 'to the degree that the environment of the
organization allows, organizations tend to shift their compliance structures
from incongruent to congruent types and organizations which have congruent
compliance structures tend to resist factors pushing them toward incongruent
compliance structures' (ibid.: 93).

We shall not be employing this hypothesis to any great extent, largely because it applies less to religious organizations than it does to other types; but we shall find useful the three types of compliance structure.

Whilst they are not directly related, there are clearly connections between Weber's bureaucratic, charismatic and traditional authority types and Etzioni's utilitarian, coercive and normative compliance structures.

Isomorphism

DiMaggio and Powell's researches into organizations which relate to each other led them to conclude that 'the engine of rationalization and bureaucratization has moved from the competitive marketplace to the state and the professions. Once a set of organizations emerges as a field, a paradox arises: rational actors make their organizations increasingly similar as they try to change them' (DiMaggio and Powell 1983: 147). This is particularly true of organizations dependent on other organizations: organizations become like the organizations which fund them. But there are other links too: If the relationship between means and ends is uncertain, then organizations model themselves on organizations they perceive as successful (ambiguous goals have the same effect); organizations which recruit staff with similar academic or other backgrounds become like each other; and organizations which join umbrella organizations become like the other organizations belonging to them. A particularly strong predictor of isomorphism is involvement with the state, which causes organizations to become and to behave like state bureaucracies (ibid.: 154f.). An organization's formalization (Chapin and Tsouderos 1956) causes isomorphism (DiMaggio and Powell 1983: 156); and particularly important for our later study of the clergy is DiMaggio and Powell's conclusion that professionalization causes isomorphism (ibid.: 156).

Open Systems

Religious faith-based organizations, like most other organizations, are 'open systems': that is, they are affected by their environments and, in turn, cause their environments to change. The 'new institutionalism', which regards the openness of organizations to their environments as particularly important, has been a considerable help to the study of religious and faith-based organizations, as they are generally extremely open to the societies within which they operate and to other organizations to which they relate (whether they think they are or not); and so, when we study bureaucratization, professionalization, integration with civil society, and the secularization of religious organizations, we shall be regarding religious organizations as open systems, and faith-based organizations as even more so (Benson and Dorsett 1971).

Studying Religious and Faith-Based Organizations as Voluntary Organizations

Because we are studying religious and faith-based organizations as organizations, we shall find comparison with other types of organizations a fruitful means of studying them. In principle, comparison with *any* other organization might be useful, and Goldner draws attention to connections between beliefs and structures in the Roman Catholic Church and in commercial organizations (Goldner 1979); but we shall make most use of comparison with other voluntary organizations because religious and faith-based organizations are both very like other voluntary organizations and to some extent unlike them. They are like them because many voluntary organizations have purposes, goals, bureaucratic structures, professional leaderships, diverse decision-making processes, non-worship activity, work allocation mechanisms, and, above all, voluntary participants (Harris 1995b; 1998); and they are unlike them because religious and faith-based organizations are theological entities with authority-structures unlike those of other voluntary organizations.

Because congregations are somewhat like associations, and because they often evolve into more formal organizations, we shall find Chapin and Tsouderos's work on formalization helpful; and because they have characteristics which might locate them between the associational and bureaucratic spheres, we shall find ourselves referring to David Billis's theory on ambiguous voluntary organizations.

Formalization

As the number of members of a voluntary association rises, custom and practice develops, and eventually a set of rules (Chapin and Tsouderos 1956: 342). 'Associations with large memberships were found, in general, to tend towards impersonal criteria and an elaboration of a code of behaviour' (ibid.: 344). Their research leads them to two conclusions:

1 'The process of formalization is a general uniform process; as one component or variable part of the organization develops and differentiates, the other elements are likewise developed and differentiated'; and
2 'The process of formalization coincides with the growth of the membership' (ibid.: 344).

They found this 'formalization' process to be entirely independent of the goals of the organization.

David Billis's Theory of Ambiguous Voluntary Agencies

Important background to Billis's theory is Eliot Jaques' work on bureaucratic structures.

Jaques defines an 'association' as 'a group of individuals with a common goal who have come together and formed themselves into an institution with explicit rules and regulations governing membership' (Jaques 1976: 48) and 'bureaucracy' as 'a hierarchically stratified managerial employment system in which people are employed to work for a wage or salary; that is to say, a stratified employment hierarchy with at least one manager who in turn has a staff of employed subordinates' (ibid.: 49).

These are definitions which Billis employs, with the important difference that Billis includes the employing structure within the bureaucracy whilst Jaques regards the governing body of an organization as an association which establishes a bureaucracy – rather suggesting that in fact the governing body lies somewhere in an ambiguous zone between the association and the bureaucratic worlds. For Jaques, as well as for Billis, the important thing about a bureaucracy is that it is 'an accountability system' (ibid.: 64) and that employment in it is governed by a contract which establishes a means of accountability for the quality of work done (ibid.: 55).

Using Jaques' work, and on the basis of his study of a variety of organizations in the public and voluntary sectors, David Billis has developed a model which enables us to understand a number of aspects of governance in voluntary agencies. He describes the situation with a diagram (Figure 2.1) which enables us to locate different kinds of organization. 'Voluntary associations' are identifiable groups with names, purposes, membership criteria, and rudimentary rules about how to appoint office-holders and how to make decisions (Billis 1993: 160f.). The bureaucratic world is very different. Here there are paid staff organized into hierarchical roles, appointed by senior staff on the basis of their ability to do the job, and with clear lines of

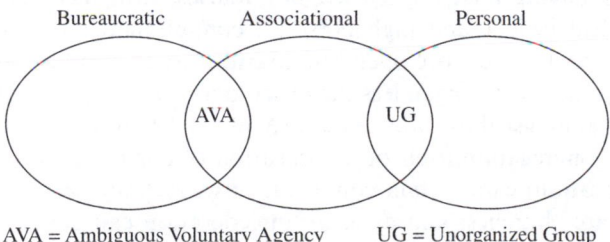

Figure 2.1   The personal, associational and bureaucratic worlds

Source: Billis, David (1993), *Organizing Public and Voluntary Agencies*, London and New York: Routledge, p. 163, figure 11.1. Reproduced with permission

accountability between them (ibid.: 161f.; Weber 1963). The personal sphere is that of personal relationships between family members and between groups of friends and neighbours (Billis 1993: 19f.). Then there are two ambiguous zones. Unorganized groups have no constitution or legal identity and generally no name, but they do have purposes (ibid.: 162f.). Ambiguous voluntary agencies fall between the associational and the bureaucratic worlds. If a voluntary association takes on paid staff to do the organization's work then it has entered this zone.

Billis's diagram and his explanations of various categories enable us to locate organizations and also to understand the ways in which they evolve, and they will enable us to locate religious organizations, particularly faith-based organizations, and to understand their behaviour.

Studying Religious and Faith-Based Organizations as Religious and Faith-Based Organizations

Whilst the similarities with other voluntary organizations are significant, the differences affect those similarities: for instance, the clergy are professionals, but not in the same way as other professionals are. We shall therefore need to take care not to apply research results relating to other voluntary organizations without first asking whether the particular characteristics of religious and faith-based organizations make those results only questionably applicable. We shall be on safer ground using the results of research carried out on religious and faith-based organizations – and throughout the book we shall make use of theories of categorization, and especially the ideas of Troeltsch and Niebuhr.

Church, Sect, and Denomination

Troeltsch distinguished between sects and churches (Troeltsch 1911; Gill 1996) – the former having relatively closed boundaries, firm membership criteria, firm theological beliefs, and high personal commitment amongst those who attend; the latter having more open boundaries, vague membership criteria (as everyone in principle belongs), less firm theological beliefs, and lower personal commitment amongst those who attend (Moberg 1970). It is not always clear whether the congregation itself or a federation of congregations is in view. A Church (federation) can contain congregations which are sects and congregations which are churches; and a sectarian federation can contain church-like congregations. I shall leave this issue somewhat unresolved, and the reader should assume that the congregations in church-federations are churches and that the congregations in sect-federations are sects unless the contrary is stated.

The issue is somewhat clearer when it comes to Richard Niebuhr's discussion of the 'denomination' (Niebuhr 1929): a bureaucratic form with some sectarian characteristics and some church characteristics. 'Denomination' always refers to the federation and its umbrella functions. Congregations of denominations generally share most of a particular set of characteristics (bureaucratic and democratic decision-making processes, relatively clear membership criteria, rather liberal theological views, and boundaries relatively open to the world), but some denominational congregations can have church-like characteristics and others can have sect-like characteristics.

A fourth category sometimes employed is that of the 'cult'. Stark and Bainbridge (1985: 25–30) suggest that cults arise spontaneously from new or imported ideas, whereas sects are formed through schism from larger institutions – though in practice it isn't always possible to tell precisely which are the most important factors in bringing about a new organization. Given the fact that terms such as 'sect' and 'cult' are often used interchangeably and with diverse meanings in public discourse, it might be better to be clear about the particular characteristics of the organizations in any particular categorization rather than use such terms as 'cult' and 'sect' without explanation.

Methods

As DiMaggio points out, study of organizations generally will be relevant to religious organizations, and the new open-systems approach has made this more possible, but every concept needs to be adapted so that it *does* apply to religious and faith-based organizations – and, similarly, discoveries in relation to religious and faith-based organizations will be of use when we study other kinds of organization, provided the necessary adjustments are made (DiMaggio, 1998). David Horton Smith believes such cross-fertilization to be essential. For too long, a sacred/secular divide, assumed in the social sciences since Durkheim (1915; 1919), has created a gulf between the study of secular organizations and the study of religious organizations (Smith 1983; 1984). Whilst they are different, these different kinds of organization have much to learn from each other.

So bodies of theory developed for the study of open systems, such as resource mobilization theory, will be useful to us (Kniss and Chaves, 1995), for all organizations employ resources obtained from their environments in order to fulfil their goals. For religious and faith-based organizations, those resources include values and ideas from the organization's past and from their religious tradition's past (which we shall count as environments), which is not true or not quite so true for other types of organization: but the theory is still applicable once this adaptation has been made. Similarly, contingency theory (like resource mobilization theory, but with more of an eye on organizational survival as the environment changes than on the meeting of goals) will be useful – but here, having to conform to a belief system will act as a constraint as religious and particularly faith-based organizations struggle to survive in a more secular society (Johnson and Chalfant 1993).

Methods employed by the social sciences will be as relevant for religious organizations as for other kinds. Amongst these, Narrative Analysis (Collins 2004), and even more Critical Discourse Analysis, which is a close reading of texts to uncover unstated organizational preferences, goals, and authority-structures, will be useful (Heather 2000; 2003); and study of society's attitudes to religious organizations and those attitudes' effects on organizations' behaviour (as in Jones's 1974 study of the Swedenborgians) might also be helpful. Social anthropology (Jenkins 2004), ethnography (Ward 2004; Collins 2004; McGrail 2004) and gender studies (Aune 2004) will all be found useful. There is a large sociological literature on religion (Homan 1986), much of which will be relevant to the study of religious and faith-based organizations.

Beckford suggests that we should seek sociological methods which are as little as possible contaminated by religious concepts (Beckford 1973). This might not be possible. Sociology began as the sociology of religion, and all of its concepts remain to some extent influenced by the discipline's history. The important thing is to recognize the connections between concepts and their religious roots and to subject every method to scrutiny to see what particular presuppositions it carries with it. No academic discipline or method is value-free.

Religious and faith-based organizations are social realities and they are organizations, so sociological methods and methods used in the study of organizations will be useful; but religious and faith-based organizations are also *theological* organizations, in the sense that their structures and practices are influenced by belief-systems and by religious behaviour-patterns. This is particularly true of the structures of congregations and of federations of congregations, which can only be studied properly if theological models are used as well as sociological ones (Dulles 1988). This is an issue to which we shall return.

Above all, thorough research is required. Presuppositionless research is of course impossible, especially in this field, as sociological, theological and other presuppositions will inform the questions asked and the patterns discovered in response to those questions. Again, the important thing is to recognize the presuppositions. One way of ensuring that this happens is for research into religious organizations to involve people at every level in the organization (Dudley 1991: for good examples see Becker 1999, Harris 1998 and Heskins 2001). Careful listening to responses should enable presuppositions to be recognized and new questions to be formulated which avoid the presuppositions discovered. If such careful listening does not occur, then what people say will be heard as confirming existing conceptual models.

A particularly interesting piece of research into a religious college's approach to crises shows how important it is to allow presuppositions to be questioned. By keeping their minds open to new possibilities, the researchers found that in a crisis commitment to the status quo rises, support for change drops, and change is *more* likely to occur; and when in the absence of crises new opportunities emerge, support for change rises, commitment to the status quo drops, and change is *less* likely to happen. This was something of a surprise (Dyck 1996). As far as I know this research has not been replicated in non-religious organizations, so it is not clear whether the conclusions apply only to religious organizations; but the important point is that careful listening to people at all levels in the organization led to some interesting counter-intuitive conclusions being established.

At the beginning of a new field of study it is instructive to study the development of research traditions in other fields – and, in our case, it will clearly be instructive to study the development of research traditions in the study of voluntary organizations.

Although Beveridge wrote his report *Voluntary Action* in 1948, it was not until 1978, when the Wolfenden Committee published *The Future of Voluntary Organizations*, that the 'voluntary sector' as a distinct category of organizations could be said to be an object of study. The Wolfenden Report gave to organizations a sense of shared identity, and also contributed to the 1979 Conservative government's understanding of the role which voluntary organizations could play in welfare provision, mainly as 'providers' providing services as contractors (Harris and Rochester 2001: 3). The first academic response was the Programme of Research and Training in Voluntary Action (PORTVAC) at Brunel University in 1978, which in 1987 moved to the School of Economics to become the Centre for Voluntary Organisation. The aim was to bridge the theory–practice divide by involving practitioners in research projects and testing research results against practitioners' practical experience. The only theory permitted was 'usable theory': theory generated by practical experience and for the purpose of enabling practitioners to understand their organizations and make appropriate responses to the opportunities and challenges they faced.

(It is not insignificant that early UK research was conducted in the context of the study of organizations in general, of bureaucratic commercial and public sector organizations, and of public service agencies in particular. Associations were thus often understood as the groups out of which such developed structures emerged, which led to associations being defined in relation to rules and to their being understood as institutions (Jaques 1976: 48) rather than as shifting networks or as fields of activity.)

During the 1980s and 1990s five areas of exploration emerged in the growing volume of research literature in the UK and the USA (where the Programme on Nonprofit Organizations was set up in 1976):

1   How do voluntary organizations differ from other organizations? (leading
    to research on the characteristics and problems of the sector, research
    which revealed how diverse the sector is)
2   What organizations comprise the sector? (with mapping exercises following
    from definitions)
3   How is the sector resourced? (involving careful study of the financial and
    voluntary and paid labour resources available to the sector)
4   Why do voluntary organizations exist? (the answer having to do with
    market failure: where neither commercial nor government provision meets
    social need, voluntary organizations emerge)
5   What is the voluntary sector's relationship with other sectors? (here study
    of voluntary organizations' relationships with local and national govern-
    ment has proved relevant).

Harris and Rochester summarize:

> Since 1978 ... researchers have built up an unprecedented body of
> knowledge about the characteristics of voluntary sector organizations, their
> numbers and the resources they deploy. They have suggested explanations
> for the existence of the sector and attempted to identify the features that
> differentiate voluntary organizations from for-profit companies and public
> sector bodies. They have also explored the relationship between voluntary
> agencies and the institutions of the other sectors (Harris and Rochester
> 2001: 14).
>   In order for this research to help the sector to face new opportunities and
> challenges, the authors set three questions:
>
> • 'How are different aspects of social policy playing out from a voluntary
>   sector viewpoint?
> • 'How are social policies affecting particular kinds of voluntary
>   organization?
> • 'How are social policies affecting key groupings within voluntary
>   organizations' (ibid.: 14).

And their book concludes by asking to what extent voluntary organizations
have changed in response to changes in their environment, whether change has
been forced or chosen, and whether voluntary organizations have played an
active role in forming social policy (ibid.: 16).

The present volume is intended as a contribution to a similar process, though
of course it won't be the same process. On the basis of the research literature
and of two case studies it will make tentative suggestions about one or two
pieces of what might be usable theory, but that theory will need to be tested on
a wider diversity of case studies; and reflection on practical experience will need
to generate more usable theory which in its turn will need to be tested and
refined. The result will be theory which practitioners can use to respond to the
challenges facing their own religious and faith-based organizations.

But already we can see what some of the questions which this new research tradition will be asking might be like:

1 How do religious and faith-based organizations differ from other organizations? (what are their characteristics, and how do they behave?)
2 What organizations comprise the category?
3 How is the sector resourced?
4 Why do religious and faith-based organizations exist? (and why do they carry on existing?)
5 What are the relationships between religious and faith-based organizations and other types of organization? (and between religious and faith-based organizations and civil society generally).

Whereas many of the issues facing voluntary organizations generally relate to social policy, this is not true to the same extent for religious and faith-based organizations (this is itself an interesting distinctive characteristic of such organizations). Whilst social action and welfare provision might be functions of religious and faith-based organizations, they are not the only functions, and they are often not given priority. Any religious or faith-based organization will have a number of stakeholders and a plethora of aims, and, as we shall see, it will have a somewhat indeterminate membership and also complex lines of accountability. This means that no simple threefold list of questions for study (Harris and Rochester 2001: 16) is likely to emerge. In a new field it is important not to be prescriptive. We shall simply have to use whatever combination of methods might prove fruitful (Ward 2004: 125) and wait and see what emerges from research, teaching and co-operative projects in this new field.

Above all, we must be explicit about the questions driving a research agenda, and what and whose the particular concerns are: Are they those of an academic community, group or individual trying to build a new discipline? Or those of organizations and of their workers seeking solutions to problems? Or those of elements of civil society wanting to make some use of the sector under discussion?

We cannot escape from making assumptions. The important thing is to try to recognize as such the assumptions which we and others are making.

A Particular Method

A particular research method which a number of scholars have found helpful is the study of financial data (and, in the case of faith-based organizations, details of contracts with local and central government agencies; Wolpert 1997). Such information can reveal how organizations change as their environments change (ibid.), and also ways in which religious and faith-based organizations might be different from other organizations (Grønbjerg and Nelson 1998).

Not only can funding information lead to other useful research (such as Benjamin's discovery of donors' and organizations' considerable misperceptions about each other; Benjamin 1977), but the figures themselves can be revealing. Engahl's discovery of donors' increasing interest in designated budgets and the consequent drive amongst denominations and congregations towards project-based activity reveals scepticism about congregational and denominational structures (Engahl 1991); Goldberg and Kosmin's study of the Jewish community's charitable giving reveals that more conservative religious beliefs lead to greater financial commitment and that increasing secularization and an ageing orthodox population might lead to a funding crisis for Jewish faith-based organizations (Goldberg and Kosmin 1998; Harris 1997; Halfpenny and Reid 2000); and study of giving amongst different Christian denominations tells us something (but perhaps not much) about levels of commitment (conservative Protestants give most, then liberal Protestants, then Roman Catholics; Hoge 1994).

Jeavons studies how *terms* are used in a financial context, and notices that 'stewardship' is now more likely to mean the careful use of resources than the more religious concept to do with generous giving in response to a sense that what we have is not our own, revealing secularization of religious organizations (Jeavons 1994a; 1994b); and Laughlin suggests that the nature of financial accountability between different levels of an organization tells us something about the organization: He finds that in the Church of England, the Diocese is accountable to the parishes; the Church Commissioners (who hold the historic resources and partly fund pensions) and the Central Board of Finance (now the Archbishops' Council: responsible for central expenditure) are less accountable; and that the parishes are accountable to the Diocese in theory but not much in practice. The Diocese's increasing accountability suggests that power is shifting to the parishes as today's money becomes more important than proceeds from historic assets (Laughlin 1990). More generally, Nitterhouse has worked out that as faith-based organizations grow they pass through predictable stages of financial accountability towards various stakeholders, which tells us about their relationships with those stakeholders at different stages of an organization's development (Nitterhouse 1997).

Conclusions

We have studied a variety of usable theories found helpful in the study of organizations generally, of voluntary organizations, and of religious organizations, and we shall apply these theories where they seem to be appropriate. But we shall also be somewhat suspicious of theory. As Robert Chia suggests, theories emerge out of a community's epistemological and ontological presuppositions, and even such concepts as 'organization' make assumptions about the nature of reality, about the ways in which we organize concepts, and about the ways in which our concepts and our ordering of them relate to some objective reality. The concept of 'management' is equally problematic, as we saw in our introductory chapter. We *do* attempt to order our worlds in order to make them understandable and controllable (Chia 1996: viii), so it might well be true that the theory we develop has as much to do with our needs and with the desire to create a new clearly demarcated discipline as it has to do with social or other reality.

What this suggests is that we should be suspicious of theory, not that we shouldn't use it or write it. It also suggests that when we study a group of organizations we should take great care to understand diversities within any category which we might choose to construct. Thus, if we find the sect/church categorization helpful, we must also ensure that we study organizations in their particularity. For, above all, it is important to see *what is there*, not to see only what our theories encourage us to seek. (An interesting example of this happening is to be found in the recent history of crystallography: It had been thought that it was impossible for crystals with five-way symmetry to exist, so when crystals with pentagonal sides emerged from cooling metal alloys, for some years nobody believed that they had seen them. They are still called 'quasi-crystals' rather than 'crystals', but they have now managed to revolutionize the science of crystallography.)

Thus, whilst the chapters ahead *do* employ existing and new categorizations and theories, I have tried to allow the research literature to lead the organization of the material. I have sought in the literature (and in my case studies) what appear to be the important issues, and have then gathered research results in order to discuss these issues. If this approach makes the material somewhat disorganized, then I can only plead that that reflects the organizations we are studying: for they are all different, and they can only be partially understood through categories and theories (and small faith-based organizations are particularly difficult to research because they are difficult to map and they are so different from each other; Cnaan and Milofsky 1997). No doubt, as the new field of the management of religious and faith-based organizations evolves, new categorizations and new theories will be tested and will give different orderings to the field and its material – but we should still remain suspicious.

For the time being, we shall understand religious and faith-based organizations as a complex field of organizations which share characteristics with other organizations, and particularly with voluntary organizations; and in ordering the research material on this field I shall make some initial decisions, and not least the decision to start with the congregation as the prototypical religious organization. I shall then treat denominations as federations of congregations. Both of these decisions make assumptions about what these organizations are, and both could be contentious. The only justification on offer is that this approach seems to explain how these organizations work. In relation to these decisions, and to others which I shall make as the work progresses, the important thing is to be specific about the decisions made and to justify them – and to keep our minds open so that we can be surprised.

We have surveyed a number of methods open to the student of religious and faith-based organizations, and Watkins makes the interesting suggestion that a combination of such methods should be termed the new discipline of 'organizational ecclesiology' (Watkins 1991). For the purposes of our study of religious and faith-based organizations we shall be relying on existing research-based literature and shall therefore benefit from the considerable variety of research methods which the authors of the books and papers have employed. One of the problems related to this approach is that most of the literature available is from the USA (including such excellent websites as http:// hirr.hartsem.edu/org/faith_congregations_research1.html) – and the UK's religious organizations are in many ways not like those in the USA; and another problem is that not much of the literature about the UK is recent (and much has changed during the past forty years) – so we shall have to take care how we apply the research literature available to us (and subsequently do all we can to generate up-to-date British research literature).

Equally problematic is the fact that most of the research literature is about Christian and Jewish organizations. There might be a reason for this. In Islam, the organization is not a separate issue, for Islam *is* the activity of the religious community, and it might therefore be difficult for the Moslem to be sufficiently 'outside' the mosque to be able to evaluate its activities objectively, even assuming that they might wish to do so. Some Christians and Jews will experience their own situations in a similar way, but at least in the West many Christians and Jews are relatively secularized and it is the secular Christian or Jew, or the secular aspect of a Christian's or a Jew's mind, which stands outside the Church or synagogue in order to evaluate its activity.

A 'religious organization' amongst other organizations, and a category of religious organizations amongst other categories of organizations, are some-what Western secular concepts.

So the related questions we need to answer are these: *Should* we be seeking research-based literature on religious organizations from a wide variety of religions? (I would answer 'yes', for mutual understanding will be increased at the same time as each religion's understanding of its own organizations will be enhanced.) Should we be seeking objective secular research into a wide variety of religious organizations? (Again 'yes', but only with the consent of the organizations concerned, which might be forthcoming if it looks as if a more objective knowledge of how the organization functions will lead to better management and thus increased effectiveness for the organization's members.) And should we be encouraging different religious traditions to undertake their own research and to disseminate the results? (Again 'yes', on the understanding that no research is without presuppositions, that research by the committed yields results not obtainable by the secular researcher, and that we shall be fairly clear what the researcher's biases might be and might thus end up with more usable research in some instances than we could obtain from a secular researcher with biases rather more difficult to determine.)

Basically, we need more research, and the more different kinds we get the better.

References

Aune, Kristin (2004), 'The Significance of Gender for Congregational Studies', in Guest et al. (2004), pp. 185ff.

Becker, Penny Edgell (1999), *Congregations in Conflict: Cultural Models of Local Religious Life*, Cambridge: Cambridge University Press

Beckford, James A. (1973), 'Religious Organization: A Trend Report', *Current Sociology*, **21** (2), 7–170

Beckford, James A. (1975a), 'Organization, Ideology and Recruitment: The Structure of the Watch Tower Movement', *Sociological Review*, **23** (4), 893–909

Beckford, James A. (1975b), 'Two Contrasting Types of Sectarian Organization', in Wallis, Roy (ed.), *Analyses of Religious and Non-Religious Sects*, London: Peter Owen, pp. 70ff.

Benjamin, Ellen J. (1977), 'Philanthropic Institutions and the Small Religious Nonprofit', *Nonprofit and Voluntary Sector Quarterly*, **26**, s29–43

Benson, J. Kenneth and Dorsett, James H. (1971), 'Toward a Theory of Religious Organizations', *Journal for the Scientific Study of Religion*, **10** (2), 139–51

Beveridge, W. (1948), *Voluntary Action*, London: Allen and Unwin

Billis, David (1993), *Organizing Public and Voluntary Agencies*, London and New York: Routledge

Cameron, Helen (2001), 'A perspective from the study of religious organizations', in Anheier, Helmut K. (ed.), *Organisational Theory and the Non-profit Form*, London School of Economics, report no. 2, London: Centre for Civil Society, pp. 52ff.

Cameron, Helen (2004), 'Are Congregations Associations? The Contribution of Organizational Studies to Congregational Studies', in Guest et al. (2004), pp. 139ff.

Chapin, F.S. and Tsouderos, J.E. (1956), 'The Formalisation Process in Voluntary Associations', *Social Forces*, **34** (4), May, 342–4

Chia, Robert (1996), *Organizational Analysis as Deconstructive Practice*, Berlin: Walter de Gruyter

Clark, David B. (1972), 'The Sociological Study of the Parish', in Mitton, C.L. (ed.), *The Social Sciences and the Churches*, Edinburgh: T. and T. Clark, pp. 198ff.

Cnaan, R. and Milofsky, Carl (1997), 'Small Religious Nonprofits: A Neglected Topic', *Nonprofit and Voluntary Sector Quarterly*, **26**, s3–13

Collins, Peter (2004), 'Congregations, Narratives, and Identity: A Quaker Case Study', in Guest et al. (2004), pp. 99ff.

DiMaggio, Paul (1998), 'The Relevance of Organisation Theory to the Study of Religion', in Demerath III, N.J., Hall, Peter Dobkin, Schmitt, Terry and Williams, Rhys H. (eds), *Sacred Companies: Organisational Aspects of Religion and Religious Aspects of Organisations*, New York and Oxford: Oxford University Press, pp. 7ff.

DiMaggio, Paul and Powell, W. (1983), 'The Iron Cage Revisited: Conformity and Diversity in Organisational Fields', *American Sociological Review*, **48**, 147–60

Dudley, Carl S. (1991), 'From Typical Church to Social Ministry: A Study of the Elements which Mobilize Congregations', *Review of Religious Research*, **32** (3), 195–212

Dulles, Avery (1988), *Models of the Church*, 2nd edn, Dublin: Gill and MacMillan

Durkheim, Emile (1915/1919), *The Elementary Forms of the Religious Life: A study in religious sociology*, London: Allen and Unwin

Durkheim, Emile (1952), *Suicide: A Study in Sociology*, London: Routledge and Kegan Paul.

Dyck, Bruno (1996), 'The Role of Crises and Opportunities in Organizational Change: A Look at a Nonprofit Religious College', *Nonprofit and Voluntary Sector Quarterly*, **25** (3), September, 321–46

Engahl, Richard L. (1991), 'Religious Fund-Raising: The Theology of Stewardship', *Nonprofit Management and Leadership*, **1** (4), Summer, 345–56

Etzioni, Amitai (1980), 'Compliance Structures', in Etzioni, Amitai and Lehman, E. (eds), *A Sociological Reader on Complex Organisations*, 3rd edn, Austin, Texas: Holt, Reinhart and Winston

Gill, Robin (ed.) (1996), *Theology and Sociology: A Reader*, new and enlarged edn, London: Cassell

Goldberg, Jacqueline and Kosmin, Barry A. (1998), *Patterns of Charitable Giving Among British Jews*, Report no. 2, July, London: Institute for Jewish Policy Research

Goldner, Fred H. (1979), 'Internal Belief Systems and Ideologies about the Organizational Structure of Church and Industry', in Lammers, C.J. and Hickson, D.J. (eds), *Organizations Alike and Unlike: International and Interinstitutional Studies in the Sociology of Organizations*, London and Boston: Routledge and Kegan Paul, pp. 124ff.

Grønbjerg, Kirsten A. and Nelson, Sheila (1998), 'Mapping Small Religious Nonprofit Organizations: An Illinois Profile', *Nonprofit and Voluntary Sector Quarterly*, **27** (1), March, 13–31

Guest, Mathew, Tusting, Karin and Woodhead, Linda (eds) (2004), *Congregational Studies in the UK: Christianity in a Post-Christian Context*, Aldershot: Ashgate

Halfpenny, Peter, and Reid, Margaret (2000), *The Financial Resources of the UK Jewish Voluntary Sector*, London: Institute for Jewish Policy Research

Harris, Margaret (1995b), 'The Organisation of Religious Congregations: Tackling the Issues', *Nonprofit Management and Leadership*, **5** (3), Spring , 261–74

Harris, Margaret (1997), *The Jewish Voluntary Sector in the United Kingdom: Its role and its future*, London: Institute for Jewish Policy Research

Harris, Margaret (1998a) *Organizing God's Work: Challenges for Churches and Synagogues*, London: Macmillan

Harris, Margaret and Rochester, Colin (eds) (2001), *Voluntary Organisations and Social Policy in Britain*, Basingstoke: Palgrave

Heather, Noel (2000), *Religious Language and Critical Discourse Analysis*, Bern: Peter Lang

Heather, Noel (2003), 'Discourse Ecumenism: Doin' It Long and Doin' It Large', *Theology*, **106** (830), March/April, 89–98

Heskins, Jeffrey (2001), *Unheard Voices*, London: Darton, Longman and Todd

Hill, Michael (1973c), *The Religious Order: A Study of Virtuoso Religion and its Legitimation in the Nineteenth Century Church of England*, London: Heinemann

Hoge, Dean R. (1994), 'Religious Giving in the United States', *Nonprofit Management and Leadership*, **5** (1), Fall, 53–66

Homan, Roger (1986), *The Sociology of Religion: A Bibliographical Survey*, New York: Greenwood Press

Jaques, Eliot (1976), *A General Theory of Bureaucracy*, London: Heinemann

Jeavons, Thomas H. (1994a), *When the Bottom Line is Faithfulness*, Bloomington and Indianapolis: Indiana University Press

Jeavons, Thomas H. (1994b), 'Stewardship Revisited: Secular and Sacred Views of Governance and Management', *Nonprofit and Voluntary Sector Quarterly*, **23** (2), Summer, 107–22

Jenkins, Timothy (2004), 'Congregational Cultures and the Boundaries of Identity', in Guest et al., pp. 113–24

Johnson, D. Paul, and Chalfant, H. Paul (1993), 'Contingency Theory Applied to Religious Organizations', *Social Compass*, **40** (1), 75–81

Jones, Robert K. (1974), 'The Swedenborgians: An Interactionist Analysis', in Hill, Michael (ed.), *A Sociological Yearbook of Religion in Britain*, vol. VII, London: Student Christian Movement, pp. 132ff.

Kniss, Fed and Chaves, Mark (1995), 'Analyzing Interdenominational Conflict: New Directions', *Journal for the Scientific Study of Religion*, **34** (2), 172–85

Laughlin, Richard C. (1990), 'A Model of Financial Accountability and the Church of England', *Financial Accountability and Management*, **6** (2), Summer, 93–114

Lukka, Priya and Locke, Michael (2000), 'Faith, voluntary action and social policy: a review of research', *Voluntary Action*, **3** (1), Winter, 25–42

McGrail, Peter (2004), 'Display and Division: Congregational Conflict among Roman Catholics', in Guest et al. (2004), pp. 85ff.

Moberg, David O. (1970), 'Theological Position and Institutional Characteristics of Protestant Congregations: An Exploratory Study', *Journal for the Scientific Study of Religion*, **9** (1), 53–8.

Niebuhr, H. Richard (1929), *The Social Sources of Denominationalism*, reprinted Gloucester, Massachusetts: Peter Smith, 1987

Nitterhouse, Denise (1997), 'Financial Management and Accountability in Small, Religiously Affiliated Nonprofit Organizations', *Nonprofit and Voluntary Sector Quarterly*, **26**, s101–121

Roberts, Richard H. (2002), *Religion, Theology and the Human Sciences*, Cambridge: Cambridge University Press

Smith, David Horton (1983), 'Churches are Generally Ignored in Contemporary Voluntary Action Research: Causes and Consequences', *Review of Religious Research*, **24** (4), 295–303

Smith, David Horton (1984), 'Churches are Generally Ignored in Contemporary Voluntary Action Research: Causes and Consequences', *Journal of Voluntary Action Research*, **13** (4), October–December, 11–19

Stark, Rodney and Bainbridge, William Sims (1985), *The Future of Religion: Secularization, Revival, and Cult Formation*, Berkeley: University of California Press

Troeltsch, Ernst (1911), *The Social Teaching of the Christian Churches*, vol. I, reprinted London: Allen and Unwin, 1931

Ward, Frances (2004), 'The Messiness of Studying Congregations Using Ethnographic Methods', in Guest et al. (2004), pp. 125–38

Watkins, Clare, (1991), 'Organizing the People of God,' *Journal of Theological Studies*, **52**, 693–711

Weber, Max (1922), 'The Three Types of Legitimate Rule', in Etzioni, Amitai and Lehman, E. (eds) (1980) *A Sociological Reader on Complex Organisations*, 3rd edn, Austin, Texas: Holt, Reinhart and Winston

Weber, Max (1963), *The Sociology of Religion*, Boston: Beacon Press

Wolfenden Committee (1978), *The Future of Voluntary Organisations*, London: Croom Helm

Wolpert, Julian (1997), 'The Role of Small Religious Nonprofits in Changing Urban Neighbourhoods,' *Nonprofit and Voluntary Sector Quarterly*, 26, s514–28

CHAPTER 3

Secularization

Now that we have begun to understand religious organizations, it is important to understand a process which is both changing their relationships with wider society and changing the organizations themselves: the process we call 'secularization'.

The term 'secularization' has been used in a variety of ways by those who research organizations. Benson and Dorsett (1971) use it to express a religious organization's positive involvement in the wider world; Norman (2002) and Brannon (1971) use it to refer to religious organizations abandoning their distinctive theological and ethical values in the face of a changing society; Callum Brown (2001) uses it to refer to a recent radical change in the way we see our lives, distancing us from Christian symbols; and there is a long history of the term's use as a description of a long-standing social process going back into the nineteenth century, a process which has distanced science's discourse and institutions from discourse within religious organizations (Bruce 1992; Martin 1969; 1978). It is in this last sense that I shall be using the term, for this is the sense which is about what is happening to religious organizations and to their relationships with the society in which they are set; but I shall also occasionally use it to refer to consequences for religious organizations of the wider social process.

It is important to study secularization because it is having far-reaching effects on religious and faith-based organizations and on Western society as a whole. Modernization has given us a diverse moral and cultural landscape, religious practice has declined (Bruce 1995), and a *diverse* secularization has occurred, distancing religious organizations, language and behaviours from all other organizations, language-uses and behaviour-patterns (ibid.) – something which seems not yet to have happened to the same extent in the USA (Davie 2002; Demerath and Williams 1992) but which is now beginning to happen there too (Gill 2003: 210). As Putnam has pointed out, lower membership of religious organizations and a more privatized religion is giving us 'the devoutly observant and the entirely unchurched' (Putnam 2000: 75), and neither group comprises the kind of people who contribute much to social capital:

> As the 21st century opens, Americans are going to church less often than we did three or four decades ago, and the churches we go to are less engaged with the wider community. Trends in religious life reinforce rather than counterbalance the ominous plunge in social connectedness in the secular community. (ibid.: 79; cf. McGrail 2004: 96f.)

So secularization isn't simply a matter for the churches.

There has been much debate as to whether secularization is mainly a change in prevailing ideas, mainly a collapse in religious practice, or mainly a change in relationships between institutions.

Hugh McLeod believes that the most important aspect of the secularization process is a religious change brought about by a flow of ideas common to Western Europe (McLeod 1974: 285), and Owen Chadwick has charted the change of attitudes caused by this process as it affected this country in the nineteenth century. By 1900, most people believed that miracles do not happen, people were honoured for sincerity rather than chided for lack of faith, no longer could religious facts escape historical study, Christians began to know that Jesus was a man, and God was distanced from the details of disaster (Chadwick 1975: 17, 37, 194, 225, 262; McLeod 1981: 93; MacIntyre 1967: 24ff.). According to Chadwick, there is no unitary phenomenon, but he still believes it right to use an 'umbrella term' ('The historian often has to use words to describe large processes') and that 'something happened to religious people which affected their attitude to the world ... We may have less sense of providence in our lives' (Chadwick 1975: 226, 258).

Peter Berger is less tentative. The presecularized society is one in which 'religion legitimates social institutions by bestowing upon them an ultimately valid ontological status, that is, by *locating* them within a sacred and cosmic frame of reference'. Pluralism creates subsocieties, each with its own plausibility structures, and 'secularization' follows: 'the process by which sectors of society and culture are removed from the domination of religious institutions and symbols' (Berger 1969: 33, 50; cf. Bell 1997: 199).

In his recent *The Death of Christian Britain*, Callum Brown writes: 'It took several centuries ... to convert Britain to Christianity, but it has taken less than forty [years] for the country to forsake it.' Whether and how the religious practices which Brown's book is about relate to Christian faith is a complex question, and whether Britain has ever been 'Christian Britain' is an equally complex one, but it is clear from his data that there was a turning-point in 1963, since when children have largely ceased to be baptized in Church, marriages have occurred less in Church, churchgoing has fallen (except amongst minority ethnic groups), and Sunday Schools have declined. Since 1963,

> a formerly religious people have entirely forsaken organized Christianity in a sudden plunge into a truly secular condition ... What emerges is a story not merely of Church decline, but of the end of Christianity as a means by which men and women, as individuals, construct their identities and their sense of 'self'. (Brown 2001: 1, 2)

What the book *in fact* relates is the collapse of a set of moral presuppositions and a set of practices – and, of course, an important religious practice is going to church. Voluntary activity has been in decline since the end of the Victorian era (Yeo 1976), and it is possible to regard a decline in church-going as one instance of this trend. Robin Gill offers another (or rather, an additional) explanation: that the Victorians built and rebuilt too many churches in rural Britain, that twentieth-century city centres became depopulated and lost their church-going middle classes, that the result was empty churches: and empty churches are not welcoming so they emptied even more (Gill 2003).

It looks as if there are several reasons for a decline in churchgoing – and there are reasons for pauses in that decline: African immigration has helped to halt the decline in South London, but this will clearly be a temporary phenomenon. But, whatever the causes, decline is what is happening, especially in rural areas. Congregations are their members, and congregations' member-ships are their only means of activity in their communities, so whilst for a while smaller numbers might be able to generate similar levels of engagement, ageing and smaller congregations in many communities mean that religious organizations will not relate so strongly to other social institutions.

So secularization is a change of attitude and belief and a decline in churchgoing – but it is also a change in the relationships between institutions, and we shall see later in this chapter that my own work on the history of the South London Industrial Mission (SLIM; see Torry 1990) has shown that important links between the Church and secular institutions disintegrated during the 1960s, and so to locate a process which we might call 'secularization' in the 1960s seems reasonable, provided we recognize that we are talking about a set of attitudes and institutional involvements which are not all there is to be said about 'Christianity'.

During the Second World War, which was when SLIM was born, religious institutions and symbols were frequently made welcome in industry and commerce, but by the mid-1960s the welcome was waning. As Bryan Wilson puts it more generally: 'The boards of large impersonally organized corporations find a place on their agenda for market research, but one may safely speculate that none of them accord time to the discussion of the religious implications of business activity' (Wilson 1982a: 39). Religion is of diminished relevance to the consciousness of individuals and to the activity of institutions, and these two parts of the process of secularization belong together and reinforce each other (ibid.: 54). There is still much religious belief, and some of those men and women sitting around the boardroom table may well be practising Christians attempting to put their faith into practice; but individually and corporately they are 'secularized' by a 'process by which religious institutions, actions and consciousness lose their social significance' (ibid.: 150). The 'social space' in which people operate renders their religious beliefs irrelevant (Wilson 1976: 6). Underlying the whole secularization process is 'the irreconcilability of the suppositions of faith in the supernatural and its arbitrary unexplained authority, and the suppositions that underlie all other activities and operations in which modern men engage in their everyday lives' (ibid.: 13).

Wilson suggests that institutions are of greater social significance than are private beliefs and that, for the sociologist, religion is primarily an institutional phenomenon (Wilson 1966: xviii). By making these choices, he renders 'common religion' irrelevant to the definition of 'secularization' (which is unnecessarily to restrict the debate) and concentrates our attention on institutions (which he is right to do). Organized religion is on the decline, the Churches are becoming service agencies alongside other autonomous agencies which have taken over many of the Church's former functions such as medicine, education and social welfare, clergy are no longer an important source of information or of ethical standards (industrial chaplains are no longer regarded as industrial relations experts, as they once were), and the Church reflects a moral consensus rather than defining it (Wilson 1966: 15, 18, 41, 65). (As we shall see, SLIM's history reflects the changing ethics of industry's management.) Secularization has now moved out from the economic sphere, where it began, and has gradually stripped the Church of its social influence, leaving us with a religion which is 'public rhetoric and private virtue' (Berger 1969: 133).

Callum Brown's view is that the Reformation, the Enlightenment and modern science have neither constituted nor caused the death of Christianity in this country; that people continue to believe in God, in the efficacy of prayer, and in life after death; and that the major change is that people now believe without belonging. This is true; but there seems also to have been a radical change in the way we think, not just in what we do, and Brown recognizes this when he writes: 'From the 1960s a suspicion of creeds arose that quickly took the form of a rejection of Christian tradition and all formulaic construction of the individual', and the result is that 'Britain is showing the world how religion as we have known it can die' (Brown 2001: 193, 198). Christian tradition and the way we think have simply parted company. No longer can religion provide an integrated set of definitions of reality which can serve as a common universe of meaning for society and its institutions; instead, it forms 'subworlds' and creates sectarian groups which compete for customers (Berger 1969: 133, 137). If industry is one such subworld, and religious organizations are another, then we should expect that denominations will find it difficult to justify paying for an industrial mission which does not serve the Church as an institution.

In 1969, David Martin questioned the notion of 'secularization' and initiated a widespread debate. He suggested that there are complex interrelations between the religious and the secular (Martin 1969: 4), that empirical methods are widespread only amongst intellectuals, that religious institutions thrive or decline for a variety of reasons, and that a variety of 'secularizations' occur and that the concept 'secularization' cannot be defined in a unitary manner (just as 'religion' cannot be). 'Secularization' includes 'a large number of discrete elements loosely put together in an intellectual hold-all' (ibid.: 4, 16, 57, 2).

On the basis of the discussion above, during which the notion of 'secularization' has included a loss of religious belief, the privatization of belief, a decline in churchgoing, and a loss of ecclesiastical influence in relation to other social institutions, I can sympathize with Martin's point. 'Secularization' is not 'a more or less unified syndrome of characteristics subject to an irreversible master-trend' (ibid.: 4).

But by 1978 Martin had thought again, and published *A General Theory of Secularization*, in which he makes a number of generalizations whilst at the same time detailing the wide variety of characteristics created by differing social contexts. He lists a number of factors which lead to secularization: urban concentration; heavy industry and predominantly proletarian populations (leading to decline in religious institutions); geographical and social mobility (which erode stable religious communities); differentiated societies (leading to pluralism in religion and to the Church becoming differentiated from other institutions such as those providing education and welfare); and a parallel differentiation between the religious and other aspects of the individual's life (leading to the disintegration of institutional religion). 'In the modern situation ... all organic solidarities, whether of nation or religion or class, are partly undermined', and the most general tendency is towards 'an apathy which retires from explicit institutional religion' (Martin 1978: 3, 83, 92).

Jeffrey Cox, in his detailed study of religious practice in Lambeth from 1870 to 1930 (Cox 1982), agrees with Martin's warnings about the concept of 'secularization', but chides him for developing a 'general theory' which he believes has become a substitute for enquiry about the causes of decline in religious institutions, the kind of enquiry which he conducted into Lambeth's churches. (Gill's similar enquiry into Victorian church-building led him to conclude that the Victorians built too many churches, that they were therefore half-empty, that therefore they weren't welcoming, and that secularization was the result; in Bruce 1992: 90–117.) A similar caveat is entered by Mary Douglas (Douglas 1970: 36, 40f.; cf. Bell 1997: 200) who points out that the Nuer and Dinka tribes have for centuries exhibited what we might call secular trends. Whilst agreeing with Martin and Cox that we must take care not to invent a unitary syndrome out of a diversity of tendencies, I believe that we can still link together the trends which Martin lists and that we can legitimately use the 'umbrella term' (Chadwick 1975: 266) 'secularization' to refer to them.

Grace Davie (2002) offers a different perspective: questioning the notion of secularization, pointing out that Europe is unusual, that other parts of the world are far from secular, and that there might be particular reasons for Europe turning its back on particular forms of religion – though not on religion in general, for people remain remarkably spiritual in outlook. But the most problematic areas are those of private religious beliefs and individual religious practice. Private 'common religion' is difficult to quantify and evaluate, and it is very difficult to know whether or not it has altered. Religious practice, as Cox suggests, is affected by a variety of historical circumstances, is difficult to quantify, and in the USA it is strong and still affects society at many points (Cox 1982: 12; cf. Bruce 1995: vii). This is a good reason for concentrating on the more visible institutional aspects of the diverse secularization phenomenon, particularly as institutional involvements are as likely to affect individual beliefs and behaviour as they are to affect organizational belonging. Accordingly, I take 'secularization' to mean: 'The drawing apart and declining integration of religious and secular institutions and their personnel', thus making 'secularization' part of the process of diversification and change rather than a process somehow separate from everything else which is going on in society. Catherine Bell offers a clear description of the consequences: 'Underlying many of the most nuanced discussions is the idea that secularism [a term which here means the result of the process of secularization] entails basic social processes in which major societal institutions are differentiated from each other and no longer represent the same values or work together to provide an overall coherence to social life' (Bell 1997: 198; cf. Martin 1995).

The South London Industrial Mission

All of the tendencies which David Martin lists under the heading 'secularization': urban concentration, heavy industry and predominantly proletarian populations (leading to decline in religious institutions); geographical and social mobility (which erode stable religious communities); differentiated societies (leading to pluralism in religion and to the Church becoming differentiated from other institutions such as those providing education and welfare); and a parallel differentiation between the religious and other aspects of the individual's life (leading to the disintegration of institutional religion) (Martin 1978: 83, 92) can be discovered in South London. South London was the most secular part of the country in 1851 when a church-attendance question was added to the national census, it has remained highly secular, and particularly from the 1960s onwards it has experienced a deep secularization (though here it was the *decline* of heavy industry which contributed to secularization, as we shall see). It is in this changing situation that the South London Industrial Mission (SLIM) operated.

During the 1950s SLIM's chaplains were more than welcome in the heavy industry along the South Bank of the Thames. This was largely because both industry's management and its shop-floor workers had been used to 'padres' in the army, and they saw SLIM's chaplains as padres in industry and referred to them as such. The perceived alienation between the church (in this case the

Church of England) and the working classes was seen by the chaplains as the major problem which needed to be tackled, and they regarded their visiting, their educational and welfare work, and their discussion groups and conferences, as a means of bridging the divide. Nothing specialist was intended, simply the reconnection of working people with the church's worship and other activity by the presence of the church's authorized personnel.

The chaplains were working in those corners of the social structure which were *not* yet secularized: hence their success, and the very full programme of lectures, discussion groups, conferences and religious services to which people came in large numbers.

As the 1950s drew to a close, SLIM began to understand that secularization was about a growing *institutional* alienation, and thus concentrated more effort on relationships with *firms* and not just with individuals and small groups within them; and during the 1960s SLIM began the long process of turning away from industry and its personnel, which were becoming difficult to relate to, and took up a mission to the denominations which funded its chaplains. This latter was clearly a displacement activity, as relationships with a more secular and more fragmented industrial scene were becoming difficult to maintain; and it was also a strategy for survival, for to educate the denominations and their people so that they could relate their faith to their work was to behave as a service organization for the denominations and thus to justify continuing financial support. But this transition also revealed that SLIM no longer saw itself as *belonging* to the denominations, but rather as a separate religious organization with relationships with both industry and the denominations: revealing a widespread belief, in SLIM as well as in the denominations, that the church itself was now unable to relate directly to a very secular industrial world.

In order to at least stay in touch with industry SLIM adapted to industry's structures and studied industrial relations techniques and economics; and in order to serve the denominations chaplains became industrial specialists, explaining industry to congregations and to denominational officers. The industry-directed approach and the denomination-directed approach became somewhat disconnected, and so being the representatives of the Christian tradition within industry took a back seat. As the 1970s progressed there is evidence that each chaplain faced a choice between apathy or domestication to the needs of industry.

But larger movements are made up of small changes, and it is possible to identify some of the changes which were leading to a decline in voluntary activity generally as well as to a decline in SLIM's events and in attendance at them – and to a decline in religious activity generally and thus to increasing secularization. The larger industries, with their stable large workforces, were closing, and social mobility (both geographically and in terms of income and culture) meant that long-term commitment to a voluntary organization such as to SLIM or to a congregation was becoming more difficult; flexitime was being introduced, thus reducing lunch hours to lunch half-hours, and making it more difficult for lunchtime voluntary activity to continue (and many of SLIM's 1950s discussion groups had been held during the compulsory one-hour lunch break); the newer industries had smaller workforces, often on more flexible shift-patterns, making any kind of corporate activity on industrial premises almost impossible to organize – and, as the 1980s arrived, companies in the financial and other sectors demanded greater commitment from their staff than the previously standard eight-hour day, so as people left the office when they'd finished their work mid-evening all they wanted to do was to go home. On the domestic scene, women were more likely to be employed outside the home, meaning that men were taking more domestic and child-care responsibilities, making it more difficult for men to attend evening and weekend events (and it *was* mainly men who attended SLIM's evening, day and weekend conferences during the 1950s and the early 1960s). These changes, when added together, were bound to increase a secularization already driven hard by the increasing relativization of all theological and moral ideas, and by the loss of a sense of a metanarrative holding it all together.

During the 1970s, as established chaplaincies ceased, it became more difficult to negotiate new ones with South London's newer industries, particularly as companies were now performing their own welfare and educational functions (in much the same way as the state had previously taken over healthcare and education from the denominations). The greater difficulty of relating organized religion to the institutions of industry led to a new stated aim: to relate the 'Christian faith' to industry. This could, of course, be done in highly theoretical ways, and by educating Christians at home – and the difficult task of visiting industry could be quietly sidelined. By the mid-1980s there was very little industrial visiting, whatever the lists published by SLIM might have suggested. By the end of the 1970s SLIM was calling itself an 'influence', and its task was to 'explore'.

But amidst all of this change, SLIM understood, possibly better than any other religious organization, the depth of what was happening, and during the 1970s it made a serious attempt to tackle secularization by opening its own boundaries by abandoning the concept of 'membership'. This was done from the best of motives, but unfortunately it meant that SLIM itself became even less of an organization, making it even more difficult for it to relate as one organization to others: for one issue which it didn't sufficiently understand was that secularization is a function of organizational realities, and that without religious organizations relating to secular organizations secularization will deepen. The process of secularization was by this stage so deep-seated that the consequence of opening the boundaries was in effect to define SLIM as the chaplains' team: an association with sectarian tendencies but with no corporate goals.

By the end of the 1970s there was no normative method for engagement with industry, there was a variety of activity with no clear focus, the chaplains were operating in an unwelcoming and very secular South London, and there is evidence of stress and depression amongst the chaplains. But SLIM was at least still trying to make connections, and none of the earlier practices was entirely abandoned: so industry was still visited, conferences were held, and newsletters were published – and, in spite of the difficulties, SLIM was probably more of a Troeltschian church than any other religious organization in London.

An important trend over the 50 years of SLIM's existence was from interest in the world to interest in itself, in its ideas, and in the denominations which funded it, and particularly towards seeing itself as being an organization over against the denominations – all signs that secularization was occurring *within* SLIM as well as in the world around it. The chaplains becoming a team of professionals was all part of this secularization as the religious organization became one service organization amongst others and began to behave like one (though rather unsuccessfully).

SLIM's history is thus a classic case study of secularization: of a religious organization being distanced from other organizations by strong social pressures, and of the religious organization's attempts to survive unintentionally making the gulf even wider – for SLIM's turning towards the denominations inevitably distanced it from industrial and commercial organizations (Torry 1990).

Conclusions

There is still much religious belief, but this is 'believing without belonging' (Davie 1994; 2000: 127), so religious organizations are in decline and institutional linkages are declining. So secularization is first of all a religious phenomenon (and not just a Christian one, for synagogues too are in decline, as are Sufi orders; Gilsenan 1967), but that's not all it is, for its effects will be felt well beyond religious organizations. To take two examples: much voluntary work is done by congregation members, so if congregations decline, voluntary work might do so too (Lukka and Locke 2000); but perhaps more importantly, now that religious authorities have less power and congregation members are bringing into congregations presuppositions from elsewhere, denominations are themselves becoming secularized, are becoming less distinctive, are losing touch with the historic Christian tradition (a process not quite so pronounced in the Roman Catholic Church, in orthodox Judaism, or in most Islamic organizations), and are thus ceasing to contribute to the diversity which civic society needs (Chaves 1993b; Bell 1997: 199). Similarly, faith-based organizations are becoming secular through their increasing contact with secular organizations (Cormode 1998), and thus not contributing to the voluntary sector the distinctive elements which they once did. A related trend is for sectarian religion to increase in both extent and influence, and for it to demand more commitment from its members: commitment which reduces the time and energy they can offer to other voluntary activity (Bell 1997: 201).

Voluntary activity is already in decline (and has been since the beginning of the twentieth century; Yeo 1976). The recent growth in highly focused voluntary activity, often undertaken as therapy or as a means to a better curriculum vitae, is not the large-scale movement of voluntary societies which used to be such an important part of our society; and so the loss of religiously-motivated voluntary activity might be serious. But the decline in voluntary activity is also one of the causes of secularization, and this poses a serious problem to the Christian tradition, *particularly* if we want to define that tradition in terms of organizations and their activity. Only revived religious organizations, closely connected both with their religious traditions and with wider society, will contribute distinctively to civil society. So the challenge facing the Church is to create constantly new and always changing connections between a changing tradition, changing religious and faith-based organizations, and other changing institutions. I would suggest that in this process the denominations will be greatly helped by those Christians who are actively involved in such bridge-building, and that active support of a revived industrial mission movement would be a significant contribution to this process.

We have discovered that secularization is a diverse process and that it affects everything, and particularly religious organizations' relationships with their traditions (making them more utilitarian) and religious organizations' social distance from other organizations. And it is when we put these institutional aspects of secularization together with the changes in ideas which the concept also connotes that we recognize that secularization is not a benign process. It might well correlate with a desirable positive tolerance of difference, but it also enfeebles tolerant religious organizations, encourages sectarian ones, is difficult for traditions such as Islam to handle, and causes the dissolution of public truth and rationality.

This situation calls for religious organizations' creative engagement in civil society and for a lot more faith-based organizations to bridge the widening gulf between the sacred and the secular. If this doesn't happen, both religious organizations and Western society, and every other society, will be the poorer.

References

Bell, Catherine (1997), *Ritual: Perspectives and Dimensions*, New York and Oxford: Oxford University Press

Benson, J. Kenneth and Dorsett, James H. (1971), 'Toward a Theory of Religious Organizations', *Journal for the Scientific Study of Religion*, **10** (2), 139–51

Berger, Peter (1969a), *The Social Reality of Religion*, London: Faber

Brannon, Robert C.L. (1971), 'Organizational Vulnerability in Modern Religious Organizations', *Journal for the Scientific Study of Religion*, **10** (1), Spring, 27–32

Brown, Callum G. (2001), *The Death of Christian Britain: Understanding Secularization 1800–2000*, London: Routledge

Bruce, Stephen (ed.) (1992), *Religion and Modernization: Sociologists and Historians Debate the Secularization Thesis*, Oxford: Clarendon Press

Bruce, Stephen (1995), *Religion in Modern Britain*, Oxford: Oxford University Press

Chadwick, Owen (1975), *The Secularisation of the European Mind in the Nineteenth Century*, Cambridge: Cambridge University Press

Chaves, Mark (1993b), 'Intraorganizational Power and Internal Secularization in Protestant Denominations', *American Journal of Sociology*, **99** (1), July, 1–48

Cormode, D. Scott (1998), 'Does Institutional Isomorphism Imply Secularization?: Churches and Secular Voluntary Associations in the Turn-of-the-Century City', in Demerath III, N.J., Hall, Peter Dobkin, Schmitt, Terry and Williams, Rhys H. (eds), *Sacred Companies: Organizational Aspects of Religion and Religious Aspects of Organizations*, New York and Oxford: Oxford University Press, pp. 116ff.

Cox, Jeffrey (1982), *The English Churches in a Secular Society: Lambeth 1870–1930*, Oxford: Oxford University Press

Davie, Grace (1994) *Religion in Britain since 1945: Believing without Belonging*, Oxford: Blackwell

Davie, Grace (2000), 'Religion in modern Britain: changing sociological assumptions', *Sociology*, **34** (1), February, 113–28

Davie, Grace (2002), *Europe: The Exceptional Case: Parameters of Faith in the Modern World*, London: Darton, Longman and Todd

Demerath III, N.J. and Williams, Rhys H. (1992), 'Secularization in a Community Context: Tension in a New England City', *Journal for the Scientific Study of Religion*, **31** (2), 189–206

Douglas, Mary (1970), *Natural Symbols: Explorations in Cosmology*, London: Barrie and Rockliff

Gill, Robin (2003), *The 'Empty' Church Revisited*, Aldershot: Ashgate

Gilsenan, M.D. (1967), 'Some Factors in the Decline of the Sufi Orders in Modern Egypt', *The Muslim World*, **57** (1), January, 11–18

Lukka, Priya and Locke, Michael (2000), 'Faith, voluntary action and social policy: a review of research', *Voluntary Action*, **3** (1), Winter, 25–42

McGrail, Peter (2004), 'Display and Division: Congregational Conflict among Roman Catholics', in Guest, Malcolm, Tusting, Karin and Woodhead, Linda (eds), *Congregational Studies in the UK: Christianity in a Post-Christian Context*, Aldershot: Ashgate, pp. 85ff.

MacIntyre, Alasdair (1967), *Secularization and Moral Change*, Oxford: Oxford University Press

McLeod, Hugh (1974), *Class and Religion in the Late Victorian City*, London: Croom Helm

McLeod, Hugh (1981), *Religion and the People of Western Europe, 1789–1970*, Oxford: Oxford University Press

Martin, David (1969), *The Religious and the Secular*, London: Routledge and Kegan Paul

Martin, David (1978), *A General Theory of Secularization*, Oxford: Blackwell

Martin, David (1995), 'Sociology, Religion and Secularization: An Orientation', *Religion*, **25** (4), October, 295–303

Norman, Edward (2002), *Secularisation*, London: Continuum

Putnam, Robert (2000), *Bowling Alone: The Collapse and Revival of American Community*, New York: Simon Schuster

Tomka, Miklós (1981), 'A Balance of Secularization in Hungary', *Social Compass*, **28** (1), 25–42

Torry, Malcolm (1990), 'The Practice and Theology of the South London Industrial Mission', unpublished PhD thesis, University of London

Wilson, Bryan (1966), *Religion in Secular Society*, London: C.A. Watts
Wilson, Bryan (1976), *Contemporary Transformations of Religion*, Oxford: Clarendon Press
Wilson, Bryan (1982a), *Religion in Sociological Perspective*, Oxford: Oxford University Press
Yeo, Stephen (1976), *Religion and Voluntary Organisations in Crisis*, London: Croom Helm

CHAPTER 4

Congregations: How They Work and How They Change

In order to understand how religious organizations should be managed, we need to understand what they are like. The archetypal religious organization is the congregation, so that is where we shall start.

The fundamental fact about any congregation is that it exists to worship God. This poses a difficulty. This book is not a theology book, and it is not about the faith commitments of any particular group. This means that we must take care not to stray into a discussion of the theological presuppositions underlying a congregation's worship. However, we cannot avoid the fact that a congregation's purpose is worship, so we shall have to discuss that fact.

We shall also discuss other important characteristics of congregations: their voluntary membership, their diversity, their cultures, their size, their subgroups, their relative autonomy, the ways in which they change as their environment changes, their leadership, the diversity of roles within them, and the conflict which they experience.

We shall conclude by asking how the fact that a congregation's purpose is worship relates to its other characteristics, and by summing up what we have discovered about how congregations work and how they change.

Worship

A for-profit company's purposes are to survive, to maximize profit, and to satisfy stakeholders: its activity is selling goods and services. A public sector organization's purpose is to provide the services society needs; its activities are making policy, delivering or purchasing services, and administration. A voluntary organization's purpose might be to improve the quality of life for a group of people; its activity will be service provision and maybe campaigning. A congregation's purpose is worship, and its primary activity is worship. Yes, there might be other purposes and other activities, but we know that they are secondary because if the congregation doesn't meet for worship then we know it's not a congregation. Organizations of all kinds sometimes discuss what their purpose might be, and this is particularly true of voluntary organizations in a changing world. A congregation might discuss *how* it ought to worship, but it won't discuss whether it should worship. It knows that it must. So more than any other type of organization a congregation's activity and purpose coincide.

As Harris puts it, a congregation's first goal is 'liturgical expression of religious commitment' (Harris 1998: 51).

But worship is not an isolated activity: it is always the activity of a particular congregation in a particular place, and it always relates to the congregation's other activities and to its own particular culture, i.e., to the story which it tells about itself (Hopewell 1987). As Mary Douglas concludes, all ritual forms are 'transmitters of culture, [and] are generated in social relations, and ... By their selections and emphases exercise a constraining effect on social behaviour' (Douglas 1970: 21). This suggests that we might be able to reason about relationships between a congregation's worship and its other characteristics. Pierre Bourdieu's research (Bourdieu 1990: 81–96) suggests that there is something *sui generis* about worship; but worship is nevertheless done by people in community, and those people are quite capable of discussing what they are doing in just the same way as they are capable of discussing art, music, intimate relationships or the meaning of life. Ritual is as much the construction of time as it is of eternity (Rappaport 1999: 27). Whilst there might be 'no clear and widely shared explanation of what constitutes ritual or how to understand it' (Bell 1997: x), it is possible to obtain 'consensus and common sense', as well as to experience 'the fluidity and confusion' which characterizes discussion of ritual (ibid.: x).

Bell defines 'ritual' as a medium for evoking relationships between people and between people and 'non-immediate sources of power, authority and value' (ibid.: xi). 'Definitions of these relationships in terms of ritual's vocabulary of gesture and word, in contrast to theological speculation or doctrinal formulation, suggest that the fundamental efficacy of ritual activity lies in its ability to have people embody assumptions about their place in a larger order of things' (ibid.: xi). Its characteristics are formality, tradition, disciplined invariance, rule-governance, sacral symbolism, and performance' (ibid.: 138), and this is certainly true of much of most congregations' worship (ibid.: 205f) and is particularly true of the manner of the presidency of worship and of the selection and training of those who preside (ibid.: 206) – though Bell also notes a distinction between 'church' worship (rule-governed and formal), 'sect' worship (custom-based and informal) and 'cult' worship (idiosyncratic, leader-focused and future-directed; ibid.: 207). ('Denominational' worship tends to be similar to Bell's 'church' worship. See Chapter 2 of this book on the distinctions between 'church', 'sect' and 'cult'.) Caplow et al. develop a similar framework by suggesting a category of 'holiness' rituals (with participants actively engaged, as in Pentecostal services) and 'solemn' rituals (such as a Solemn Mass), the former evoking a sense of common identity and the latter of sense of dependence on a powerful being (Caplow et al. 1983: 141). Caplow et al. found in their research in 'Middletown' that congregations lie at many points along a spectrum between 'holiness' and 'solemn' rituals rather than being located at the extremes (ibid.: 145). The more recent Kendal Project has discovered a different spectrum, running from congregations which bring people's lives as they are into some connection with the sacred to those where allegiance to some external authority is expected. Congregations at the former end are growing, and those at the latter are declining (Woodhead et al. 2004: 18).

There is thus a considerable diversity of worship practice, and, in general, context determines the character of ritual (Douglas 1970: 82), and a congregation's worship will express both 'the unifying vision of the congregation' and the differences within it (Ammerman et al. 1997: 55). The different styles of worship in neighbouring parishes will express the different socio-economic settings of their congregations (Gwilliams 2004), and each different congregation's worship will have a different importance relative to other activities (Becker 1999: 80).

For each individual and each congregation, the activity of worship will have a different meaning, but there will be continuities between those meanings; and for all of them the worship *matters*. Rejecting Habermas's prognosis that the rise of rational discourse will cause ritual to decline, Cheal finds that:

> [rituals] have a continuing importance in contemporary religious and social life, for three reasons ... 1. Rituals help to define alternative realities that are outside the totalising world views of modern elites and the institutions they control, 2. Where a range of possibly irreconcilable interests exist, rituals may be the most effective means for generating unity via feelings of identification that are detached from critical reasoning, 3. Rituals have not been completely displaced by discourse, because rituals themselves have evolved in response to changing social conditions. (Cheal 1992: 363)

The fact that the same congregation both worships and participates in other communal and individual activity means that worship's effects (and especially its ability to generate a sense of unity) will spill over into a congregation's other activities: so it is not just for theological reasons that worship and a congregation's mission activity cannot be separated from each other, and we should expect therefore that worship and a congregation's other characteristics will be closely related to each other.

Another important relationship is that between religious activity and the congregation as a body of people. The assembly itself will often be spoken of as holy (Ramshaw 1986: 93ff) as well as its being to 'produce the sacred' (Wuthnow 1994). This suggests that any management of a congregation which does not take seriously both its worship and the worship's relationship to the congregation as a body of people is not going to be appropriate management; that an understanding of how worship, culture and other congregational activities relate to each other will be important to any understanding of the congregation's management; and that, given the unique nature of worship (it is, after all, rather different from what other organizations do), we should expect the ways in which religious organizations function to be different from the ways in which other types of organization function – and we should expect their management to be significantly different from that of other kinds of organization.

Congregations' Voluntary Membership

So congregations are bodies of people who gather for worship. (I use the word 'congregation' because it can mean only that. The term 'parish' is ambiguous because it can mean either the congregation or the territory within which the congregation meets and from which – and from beyond which – it gathers its members.) And, unlike Wuthnow (1994: 44), I take a congregation to be any assembly of people gathered for worship. If two assemblies meet at different times in the same building, he calls that one congregation. I call it two.

After the fact that their purpose is worship, the most important thing about congregations is that their members are voluntary: they don't have to be there (unless they are paid ministers, and even then in many situations the minister has considerable control over when to attend). This means that congregation members can come frequently or rarely, they can alter the frequency with which they attend, they can choose whether and when to take on responsibilities (they might be elected to posts, but they still occupy them as volunteers), they can decide which events to attend and which not to attend, and they can decide when and whether to give up responsibilities. Tomorrow the most committed member of the congregation can decide never to come again.

Diversity of Membership

The next most important thing about congregations is their diversity. Some congregations are visibly diverse in terms of age profile, ethnicity, gender or relationship pattern; but even those which are not are doctrinally diverse. Stauffer finds that people gravitate towards people like themselves and therefore don't realize how different from other congregation members they might be in terms of belief and practice; and he finds that most people think that most people think like they do when in fact they don't (Stauffer 1973). The author's own experience of British congregations is that even people who are like each other and have known each other for a long time don't know how each other think about even the most basic issues, and that they are surprised when they find out. Not asking is here clearly a defence against discovering something you might not want to know, against having to reveal something personal, and against possible disruption of long-standing relationships. Guest similarly finds diverse narratives and little credal uniformity amongst the large evangelical congregations he studies (Guest 2004: 18).

The above rather suggests that a congregation might be an 'association': 'a group of individuals with a common goal who have come together and formed themselves into an institution with explicit rules and regulations governing membership' (Jaques 1976: 48). But *is* a congregation a 'group of individuals with a common goal'? Harris's researches suggest not. She notices that 'members of congregations are defined by social identification as those people who regard themselves as participants in a congregation and are regarded by others as such' (Harris 1995b: 262) and that the goals both of individuals and of the corporate body are difficult to clarify, particularly as some of the goals might be directed outwards and be somewhat ill-defined (ibid.: 263). Whilst worship might be the most important function of the congregation as a whole, other purposes are often less clear, and the goals of individual members might or might not include worship as an important component. Similarly, Cameron draws up a list of criteria against which to test whether congregations should be regarded as associations (Cameron 2004: 145), and concludes that, whilst no subscriptions are paid and paid staff (the clergy) undertake core work, congregations are groups of people within which work happens (for liturgy is work) and so can legitimately be regarded as associations.

As we shall see, the position of the clergy is unusual, to say the least, and it is difficult to see how a minister can be regarded simply as a member of an association; but neither is the minister simply a functionary within a bureaucracy. And the theological values on which congregations are to some extent based are yet another element which suggests that a congregation is difficult to define as a 'group of individuals with a common goal' (Harris 1995b: 267; Jaques 1976: 48), for an important element of the authority-structure lies outside the organization, which is not normally true for associations.

Congregations clearly have associational elements, and they are like other types of organizations in other respects, so we may well be able to employ such theories as Billis's (Billis 1993: 160; and see Chapter 2 above); but we shall need to take care that the ways in which we employ such theory does not conflict with the non-associational characteristics of congregations. As Harris suggests, congregations have their *own* characteristics (Harris 1995b: 270), and it is these which this chapter and this book are about.

Congregational Culture

The third important characteristic of congregations is that each one has its own culture, or, as Hopewell puts it, its own 'narrative': the story it tells about itself (Hopewell 1987; Heskins 2001). As the congregation relates its distinctive story to the world, people decide whether to join in that particular drama: that is, whether to join in, tell, and develop the narrative. As Wuthnow puts it:

> The congregation provides a crucible in which a new identity, a person undergoing change, can be moulded. This is why Church leaders know the importance of corporate identity, why congregations write their histories and commemorate their anniversaries, and why they also sometimes deliberately develop conceptions of themselves as mission churches, pilgrim churches, or churches oriented toward new beginnings, rebirth, and revival. (Wuthnow 1994: 61)

Hopewell assumes that a congregation's narrative changes little and slowly: Collins, on the other hand, finds that amongst the Quakers the meeting *is* a narrative, leading him to suggest that in any congregation there are three kinds of narrative: the canonic, or founding, narrative; vernacular, local narrative; and individual narratives (Collins 2004).

Having described some of the characteristics exhibited by all congregations, we now turn to areas where differences can be identified between them.

Congregational Size

An obvious difference is size: there are congregations of thousands of members and there are congregations of a handful. Two people meeting for worship counts as a congregation.

A particularly thorough piece of research on the determinants of size was conducted in South London by Rodney Bomford, once Vicar of St Giles, Camberwell (Bomford 1992). He used Diocesan statistics to show that congregational size correlates very closely with the average income of members. This means that in poorer areas we should expect congregations to be smaller – and there is now less pressure to close smaller congregations as it is recognized that all that that achieves is the unchurching of poorer communities. Similarly, there is no longer a policy in the Diocese of Southwark to amalgamate smaller congregations, as merging two small congregations simply creates one small congregation because each congregation has a 'natural size' related to the average income of its members, so adding new members results in pushing existing members out – unless, of course, the new members increase the average income. (The 'natural size' is the number in the congregation at the peak of the graph which plots the number of congregations which have a particular size against the size of the congregation. Pagden (1968) finds that in the suburbs congregations of 240 members or more are best at attracting new members, whereas in urban areas it is congregations of between 40 and 100 members; the latter figures support Bomford's findings.)

Wicker, in an American study, finds that in smaller congregations individual commitment in terms of time and money donated is higher than in larger ones – something probably equally true in the UK (Wicker 1969; Alston and Aguirre 1979); but Wilken shows that in terms of individual commitment age profile is more important than size, that older people participate less, and that younger people joining a congregation means that it is more likely to survive even if it is small – 'small' in American terms meaning hundreds rather than thousands (Wilken 1971).

If we divide members' activities between the 'expressive' (prayer, bible study, and so on) and the 'instrumental' (financial, educational, evangelistic, and other organization-related roles), then Ashbrook finds that instrumental activity is more important to smaller congregations – which is hardly surprising because if a congregation doesn't survive as an organization then it can't do the expressive things either (Ashbrook 1966).

As Bomford (1992) suggests, one way to avoid the capping effect of average income is for a congregation to develop subgroups. This enables the congregation's size to rise above the natural size, presumably because the natural size depends on the kinds and numbers of relationships normally formed in a group by people of different incomes and thus of different social classes and life experiences. By creating subgroups, people can relate to group members rather than to the congregation as a whole. Bomford calls such a congregation a 'raspberry', and finds this a more common pattern amongst congregations with higher average income (which is one of the means whereby such congregations grow beyond the numbers possible for congregations with lower socio-economic class members). Lower socio-economic groups probably form 'blackcurrant'-shaped congregations rather than the 'raspberry'-shaped congregations which higher socio-economic groups form because people with lower incomes are more likely to prefer simpler one-layer organizations to more complex organizations with multiple layers.

In the late 1950s the 'Church Growth Movement' found that by applying such rules as the 'Homogeneous Unit Principle' congregations could be made to grow (in this case because people prefer to be with people like themselves); and the current 'Church-health' movement similarly seeks methods which have been proved to increase numbers (Woodhead et al. 2004: 7). A further finding is that congregations can increase numbers by holding 'crowd' events, either regularly or occasionally: that is, events at which people are not *expected* to relate to each other (as at many Roman Catholic Sunday Masses, or at Christmas events in other denominations, or at Friday prayers in larger mosques). (And see Coleman (2004) on religious conferences as a particular form of congregation.) It is when the congregation or the subgroup is a 'club' rather than a 'crowd' (and many Roman Catholic congregations are now becoming clubs rather than crowds) that the natural size phenomenon emerges (Bomford 1992).

A particularly interesting finding is that, when numbers begin to drop, a congregation will soft-pedal its previous message and seek means to attract members (Guest 2004: 83).

Subgroups

There has been a good deal of study of subgroups within congregations. Cameron finds that they compete for resources and power (Cameron 2001; cf. Carrier 1965 on a Roman Catholic parish where this was happening); and Dhooghe finds that informal groups form around different attitudes towards authority-figures: active conformity, passive conformity, passive contestation and active contestation – and concludes that only if all four groups are taken into account when decisions are made will conflict be avoided, and that if the organizational efficiency of one group or attitude is maximized then it will be reduced for the other three (Dhooghe 1968). Herman also finds that networks of the reform-minded and networks of the more conservative both cross social network boundaries and that they inevitably struggle for supremacy (Herman 1984).

Local Control

But intracongregational conflict is not the only type which a congregation experiences. Another common type is conflict with denominational structures – though here we have to take particular care to draw conclusions from research related to actual behaviour because Luidens shows that local office-holders think they control denominational staff to some extent, that as their social class rises their perception of such local control rises, and that congregation members, on the other hand, think that denominational staff have a great deal of control over what happens locally (Luidens 1982).

Wuthnow suggests that denominational structures (which he calls 'hierarchies') suit the clergy and their professionalization and that they are therefore willing to give their own time to them and are more willing to agree to local resources being transferred to the denominational structures than the laity would be – for the laity would prefer local resources to be employed locally for the benefit of the congregation (Wuthnow 1994: 71–7). The laity might also sense more clearly than the clergy that bureaucratic structures are inimical to the production of the sacred (ibid.: 86f.). Bureaucracies are scared of anomaly and scandal, but 'some scandal may be necessary ... for the sacred to have a genuine role in public life' (ibid.: 87).

Hougland's and Wood's research leads to the conclusion that the size of the denomination as a whole determines the extent of local control (Hougland and

Wood, 1979a). Additional minor factors are the minister's attitude and tenure, the complexity and size of the congregation, and the average income (and following Bomford's work we now know that some of these variables are linked). One problem with this research, which Hougland and Wood recognize, is that people to some extent choose their denomination in relation to the issue of local as opposed to denominational control, meaning that existing tendencies will reinforce themselves, possibly making the observed differences between denominations greater that they might otherwise have been. A factor which is becoming more important is *denominational* accountability. With denominations being held responsible for child abuse committed by their clergy and other personnel, hierarchies are needing to exert greater control over congregations and clergy and, because of the seriousness of the issue, congregations and clergy are generally relinquishing local autonomy in this matter. McGrail shows how such shifts in control can affect the internal dynamics of a congregation as well as its relationship with its denominational authorities (McGrail 2004).

Whether or not there is local control is important in relation to a number of important issues. Relative autonomy from denominational structures (which in essence means the ability to allocate resources and to choose priorities) makes congregations more likely to behave ecumenically and to relate to secular organizations (Cantrell et al. 1983); and, as Ammerman et al. suggest, local control is essential for managing change in a challenging environment.

A Changing Environment

> It is one thing to acknowledge that religious organizations, like all organizations, must bend with the times or be broken by them; it is quite another to suggest that the leaders of religious organizations intentionally scheme to make their fiefdoms more successful, that power games are played in the halls of God, and that mechanisms are put in place to keep people out as well as to draw them in. Yet anyone who has ever served on a church committee or talked candidly with members of the clergy knows these are the harsh realities of religious life. (Wuthnow 1994: 34)

Whether it is a congregation of hundreds serving a wide area or a congregation of 20 on a local authority housing estate, every congregation has a changing social environment with which to contend, and for every congregation that environment is different. Ammerman's thorough study identifies a number of strategies which congregations employ in order to survive as their community changes around them: persistence, relocation, adaptation (of its structure or by adding new elements), and innovation (Ammerman et al. 1997), and recognizes that pressure for change is not all in one direction, for the decisions which the congregation makes will change its environment as well as itself. Because a congregation is an open system, renewal will inevitably be about renewal of the community from which the congregation draws resources (for example, new members, status, money) and to which it contributes; and Milofsky suggests, on the basis of research, that successful congregations occur where their communities are also being transformed and where the congregation is connecting with that community in new ways (Milofsky 1997).

Congregations need resources: time, money, and sometimes political resources (especially if a new building is needed). One way of attracting members and thus resources is by specializing, either in terms of social class (in the United States different denominations tend to attract different socio-economic groups: there is less of a tendency for this to occur in the UK) or in terms of congregational type. Wuthnow identifies four types: the small neighbourhood church; the small intentional church (either aiming to grow or aiming to remain small for its own reasons); the family church (or 'program' church) which attracts families with children – though there are also 'program' churches which attract different groups; and the megachurch (Wuthnow 1994: 50f). All of these congregations, whatever their specialization, will have diverse aims. As Wuthnow puts it, the small congregation's

> stated purpose may be to worship God, thereby giving public expression to the sacred, and yet its clergy and members would likely recognize other purposes as well: to help celebrate the good times experienced by the congregants, to bury and grieve their dead and comfort their survivors, to come together for fun and fellowship, to study new ideas and maintain their knowledge of basic scriptural teachings, perhaps to help a needy family, or to provide a clean basement to which people in the neighbourhood can come to hear a piano recital. (ibid.: 53)

But however diverse the congregation's activity, worship will be at its heart – and if it isn't then that congregation will die. We expect congregations to produce the sacred, and if they don't do that then people won't join them (ibid.: 56): 'In an otherwise secular society the Church must in fact be different. It must do strange things to provide a place where the voice of God can at least be imagined, if not actually heard' (ibid.: 58).

Leadership

I shall be dealing with leadership and with the clergy later, but it does need to be said here that the leadership exercised within a congregation is an important determinant of how the congregation changes in response to a changing environment.

Leadership can take many forms: it can be an individual leader of a Gospel Hall, the leadership of clergy in co-operation with a Church Council and office-holders, the leadership of office-holders in co-operation with a minister, or the leadership of a corporate body of elders; and the leadership can be collaborative or not. And there always is leadership, for, as Smith points out, if official leaders are not in control then unofficial leaders emerge to exercise authority and especially to manage change (Smith 1983).

Bubis's research into the leadership exercised by synagogue boards is instructive. In some, the rabbi and the board co-operate, with roles shared out regardless of status; in others, the board members manage the synagogue; in others, the rabbi manages the synagogue and the board; and in yet others a 'contingency model' operates in which the situation determines the roles exercised. What determines which model is followed seems to be the relative education-level and level of professionalization of the rabbi and the board (Bubis and Cohen 1998).

A particular paradox with which leaders of religious organizations have to grapple is this: members feel more satisfied if they control an organization than if they simply participate; leaders are only secure if members are contented to some extent; therefore the minister ought to promote participation in decision-making; and to that extent the leader will lose their status and control.

Roles

In Chapter 8 we turn to a discussion of members and volunteers and the difference between them, but here it is worth noting a characteristic of religious organizations related to that issue: If we categorize roles as we find them in voluntary organizations (say, trustee, staff, volunteer, member, user, funder) then in a religious organization we shall often find an individual fulfilling a variety of roles, and this is especially true of congregations in which someone might be a member, a volunteer, a trustee (for instance, a churchwarden), a user, a funder – and so on and so forth. The position of the clergy is particularly interesting, because they can be a member, a trustee, a volunteer, a staff member, a user, and a funder. User involvement in management and volunteering is drawing voluntary organizations into this world of multiple roles, a world in which boundaries are dissolved and in which management becomes complex because instead of categories of people to manage there is a diversity of individuals each with different complex relationships to the organization. This is a situation which religious organizations have always faced. A religious organization is thus a highly complex dynamic system, and we might find that complexity theory has something to offer to the emerging discipline of the study of the management of religious and faith-based organizations (Nicolis and Prigogine 1989).

Conflict

An organization is its action, and to every action there is a reaction:

> Whether they do so in the ... activity of prayer, the questions and answers of Talmud study, the dispensing of kibbudim [honours], or the exchange of gossip and jokes, members sustain a vital system of ebb-and-flow which turns the shul [synagogue] into a living and changing community. While efforts are made toward achieving interactional equilibrium, each action stimulates reaction, which in turn brings on counteraction, and so on ...
> (Heilman 1976: 263)

Leadership's role is to handle change in a changing environment (for example, Heskins 2001), and an important part of this task (and not a different task) is to handle conflict in the organization, conflict which matters because lack of conflict means institutional failure (Ammerman et al. 1997) and because conflict avoidance can lead to poor decision-making because decision-makers are ignoring important issues (Baum 1994).

Becker's research points her to the conclusion that there are different kinds of congregation (the house of worship, the family congregation, the community congregation, the 'leader' congregation, and the mixed or transitional type; Becker 1999) and that conflict is the result of competition between different types within the one congregation, or sometimes the consequence of competition between instrumental and expressive elites, of the boundary between the organization and the exterior world not being clear (ibid.; Sharot 1977), of existing members trying to maintain the status quo whilst others feel that this needs to change, or of theological differences – though here there are generally other local reasons too (Warner 1988). The minister will normally feel the conflict acutely, as the congregation's conflict will often relate to the minister's internally conflictual understanding that both the tradition and new approaches are essential. In most congregations, of course, there is accommodation as well as conflict, with often low-key permanent conflict as clergy and laity (or groups of laity) try to control the organization's direction.

Ultimately, if conflict goes out of control, schism results as some members of the congregation leave to form a new congregation or to join another one. A different kind of schism is that in which a congregation and/or its leadership decide to take the congregation into an alternative denomination, and Borchhardt lists the warning signs of this being about to happen (Borchhardt 1983).

Conclusion

As the field of religious organizations and of their management evolves, we shall, I am sure, see studies of how a congregation's worship relates to the congregation's membership, authority-structure, subgroups, and other activity, but currently we have far too little research literature on the subject to enable us to draw robust conclusions. The studies by Hopewell (1987), Ammerman et al. (1997) and Becker (1999) deal with worship, but only obliquely, and never as the congregation's main function, which is what it is (even if for many of a congregation's members that isn't what they're there for). There are, of course, anthropological, historical and sociological studies of worship, and a growing literature on the study of ritual (see above, and for example Stringer 1999), and these will provide a mine of information when scholars set about the necessary task of relating the congregation's worshipping activity to the other functions and characteristics of the congregation, and we shall expect to find that worship articulates a congregation's values (Cameron 2001) and relates to the characteristics of a congregation which we have discussed above.

In the absence of robust research, all I can do here is make suggestions about possible relationships between the different characteristics of a congregation.

The very fact that in worship a congregation relates to an authority beyond the congregation itself (beyond its institutional and social boundaries), and the fact that every member relates individually to that external authority, is bound to mean that congregations expect their memberships to be voluntary and that members will expect to determine whether or not they are members. Hence the difficulty in determining membership criteria (see Chapter 8) and the wide variety of roles which an individual can fill.

The indeterminacy of the external authority's prescriptions means that diversity of viewpoint is bound to be endemic (and the author's experience of the Jehovah's Witnesses suggests that even in apparently rigidly controlled sects there is considerable diversity of viewpoint, though the outside world will rarely see it). A related consequence will be the existence of subgroups, and another the inevitability of conflict.

The fact that each individual and each congregation involved in worship experiences an authority structure beyond the boundaries of their own institution, and certainly beyond the boundary of any denominational structures, means that local autonomy will be both assumed and experienced, that we shall expect the culture of each congregation to be determined both by its religious tradition and by its social environment, and that we shall expect size to be a matter determined by a variety of factors. The fact that individuals involved in denominational structures (and this might include a congregation's authority-figures and office-holders) recognize an authority beyond their congregation's boundaries means that they will experience conflict between their denomination's authority and their congregation's authority, as neither of those two authorities can ever be totally determinative of the other.

For the purposes of this study it is of no consequence whether there is some objective authority to which worship relates the congregation and its members. What matters is that worship occurs and, whether from within or without, it 'produces the sacred' (Wuthnow 1994): an authority-structure outside the congregation which results in the characteristics which we have discovered.

No amount of research into worship will ever take us beyond the activity of worship, though further research might reveal interesting connections between that activity and the various characteristics of congregations. We should therefore encourage such research for it will give us a better understanding of the nature of religious organizations and thus insight into how they should be managed.

References

Alston, Jon P. and Aguirre, B.E. (1979), 'Congregational Size and the Decline of Sectarian Commitment: The Case of the Jehovah's Witness in South and North America', *Sociological Analysis*, **40** (1), Spring, 63–70

Ammerman, Nancy Tatom, Farnsley II, Arthur E. et al. (1997), *Congregation and Community*, New Brunswick, New Jersey: Rutgers University Press

Ashbrook, James B. (1966), 'The Relationship of Church Members to Church Organization', *Journal for the Scientific Study of Religion*, **5** (3), 397–419

Baum, Howell (1994) 'Community and Consensus: Reality and Fantasy in Planning', *Journal of Planning Education and Research*, **13**, 251–62

Becker, Penny Edgell (1999), *Congregations in Conflict: Cultural Models of Local Religious Life*, Cambridge: Cambridge University Press

Bell, Catherine (1997), *Ritual: Perspectives and Dimensions*, New York and Oxford: Oxford University Press

Billis, David (1993), *Organizing Public and Voluntary Agencies*, London and New York: Routledge

Bomford, Rodney (1992), 'Are you a groupie, crowdie, or clubbie ?' *Church Times*, 10 April

Borchhardt, Henry C. (1983), 'Before we Lose Them: Causes, Warning Signals and Intervention Strategies for Church Disassociation', *Review of Religious Research*, **25** (2), 63–75

Bourdieu, Pierre (1990), *The Logic of Practice*, trans. Richard Nice, Cambridge: Polity Press

Bubis, Gerald B. and Cohen, Steven M. (1998), *American Jewish Leaders View Board-staff Relations*, Jerusalem: Jerusalem Center for Public Affairs

Cameron, Helen, (2001), 'A perspective from the study of religious organisations', in Anheier, Helmut K. (ed.), *Organisational Theory and the Non-profit Form*, report no. 2, London: Centre for Civil Society, London School of Economics

Cameron, Helen, (2004), 'Are Congregations Associations? The Contribution of Organizational Studies to Congregational Studies', in Guest et al. (2004), pp. 138ff.

Cantrell, Randolph L., Krile, James F. and Donohue, George A. (1983), 'Parish Autonomy: Measuring Denominational Differences', *Journal for the Scientific Study of Religion*, **22** (3), 276–87

Caplow, Theodore, Bahr, Howard, Chadwick, M. and Bruce, A. (1983), *All Faithful People: change and continuity in Middletown's religion*, Minneapolis: University of Minnesota Press

Carrier, Hervé, (1965), *The Sociology of Religious Belonging*, New York: Herder and Herder

Cheal, David (1992), 'Ritual: Communication in Action', *Sociological Analysis*, **53** (4), 363–74

Coleman, Simon (2004), ' "Conference People": Congregational Studies in a Globalizing World', in Guest et al. (2004), pp. 39ff.

Collins, Peter (2004), 'Congregations, Narratives and Identity: A Quaker Case Study', in Guest et al. (2004), pp. 99ff.

Dhooghe, Jos, (1968), 'Organizational Problems Regarding Different Types of Membership in the Church', *Social Compass*, **15** (2), 93–9

Douglas, Mary (1970), *Natural Symbols: Explorations in Cosmology*, London: Barrie and Rockliff

Douglass, Truman B., (1967), 'Ecological Change and the Church', in Knudten, Richard D. (ed.), *The Sociology of Religion*, Appleton-Century-Crofts, New York, pp.147ff.

Guest, Mathew, Tusting, Karin and Woodhead, Linda (eds) (2004), *Congregational Studies in the UK: Christianity in a Post-Christian Context*, Aldershot: Ashgate

Guest, Mathew (2004), '"Friendship, Fellowship and Acceptance": The Public Discourse of a Thriving Evangelical Congregation', in Guest et al. (2004), pp. 71ff.

Gwilliams, Dianna (2004), 'What we do in church', in Torry, Malcolm (ed.), *The Parish*, Norwich: Canterbury Press

Harris, Margaret (1995b), 'The Organisation of Religious Congregations: Tackling the Issues', *Nonprofit Management and Leadership*, **5** (3), Spring, 261–74

Harris, Margaret (1998a), *Organizing God's Work: Challenges for Churches and Synagogues*, London: Macmillan

Heilman, Samuel C. (1976), *Synagogue Life: A study in symbolic interaction*, Chicago and London: University of Chicago Press

Herman, Nancy J. (1984), 'Conflict in the Church: A Social Network Analysis of an Anglican Congregation', *Journal for the Scientific Study of Religion*, **23** (1), 60–74

Heskins, Jeffrey (2001), *Unheard Voices*, London: Darton, Longman and Todd

Hopewell, James F. (1987), *Congregation: Stories and Structures*, London: SCM Press

Hougland, James G. and Wood, James R. (1979a), 'Determinants of Organizational Control in Local Churches', *Journal for the Scientific Study of Religion*, **18** (2), 132–45

Hougland, James G. and Wood, James R. (1979b), '"Inner Circles" in Local Churches: An Application of Thompson's Theory', *Sociological Analysis*, **40** (3), 226–39

Hougland, James G. and Wood, James R. (1982), 'Participation in Local Churches: An Exploration of its Impact on Satisfaction, Growth and Social Action', *Journal for the Scientific Study of Religion*, **21** (4), 338–52

Jaques, Eliot (1976), *A General Theory of Bureaucracy*, London: Heinemann

Luidens, Donald A. (1982), 'Bureaucratic Control in a Protestant Denomination', *Journal for the Scientific Study of Religions*, **21** (2), 163–75

Milofsky, Carl, (1997), 'Organization from Community: A Case Study of Congregational Renewal', *Nonprofit and Voluntary Sector Quarterly*, **26** (s), s139–60

McGrail, Peter (2004), 'Display and Division: Congregational Conflict among Roman Catholics', in Guest et al. (2004), pp. 85–98.

Nicolis, Grégoire and Prigogine, Ilya (1989), *Exploring Complexity: an introduction*, New York: W.H. Freeman

Pagden, Frank, (1968), 'An Analysis of the Effectiveness of Methodist Churches of Varying Sizes and Types in the Liverpool District', in Martin, David (ed.), *A Sociological Yearbook of Religion*, vol. I, London: Student Christian Movement, pp. 125 ff.

Ramshaw, Gail (1986), *Christ in Sacred Speech: The meaning of liturgical language*, Philadelphia: Fortress Press

Rappaport, Roy A. (1999), *Ritual and Religion in the Making of Humanity*, Cambridge: Cambridge University Press

Sharot, Stephen, (1977), 'Instrumental and Expressive Élites in a Religious Organization', *Archives des Sciences Sociales des Religions*, **43** (1), 141–55

Smith, David Horton (1983), 'Churches are Generally Ignored in Contemporary Voluntary Action Research: Causes and Consequences', *Review of Religious Research*, **24** (4), 295–303

Smith, David Horton (1984), 'Churches are Generally Ignored in Contemporary Voluntary Action Research: Causes and Consequences', *Journal of Voluntary Action Research*, **13** (4), October–December, 11–19

Stauffer, Robert E., (1973), 'Church Members' Ignorance of Doctrinal Pluralism: A Probable Source of Church Cohesion', *Journal for the Scientific Study of Religion*, **12** (3), 345–8

Stringer, M.D. (1999), *On the Perception of Worship*, Birmingham: University of Birmingham Press

Warner, R. Stephen (1988), *New Wine in Old Wineskins: Evangelicals and Liberals in a Small-Town Church*, Berkeley: University of California Press

Wicker, Allan W. (1969), 'Size of Church Membership and Members' Support of Church Behaviour Settings', *Journal of Personality and Social Psychology*, **13** (3), 278–88

Wilken, Paul H. (1971), 'Size of Organizations and Member Participation in Church Congregations', *Administrative Science Quarterly*, **16** (2), June, 173–9

Wind, James P. and Lewis, James W. (eds) (1994), *American Congregations*, Chicago and London: University of Chicago Press

Woodhead, Linda, Guest, Mathew and Tusting, Karin (2004), 'Congregational Studies: Taking Stock', in Guest et al. (2004), pp. 1ff.

Wuthnow, Robert (1994), *Producing the Sacred: an essay on public religion*, Urbana and Chicago: University of Illinois Press

CHAPTER 5

Federations of Congregations: Sects, Denominations, Churches and More...

The fundamental religious organization is the congregation, for that is the body of people which gathers for worship, for other religious activities, for mission, and for education in the religious tradition. But ever since Jews, Moslems, Christians, Hindus, Sikhs, Buddhists, or adherents of any other religious tradition have travelled from place to place, there have been connections between different congregations within the same religious tradition. The theory has often been that it is the larger unit, made up of several congregations, which is the basic unit: the Diocese, the district, the Church of England, Reform Judaism and so on. But it is not so. Without the Diocese of Southwark and without a Bishop of Southwark there would still be congregations; but without congregations there would be no Diocese and no Bishop (Moore et al. 1986).

This is not to say that the larger group is not real in some way: it is. But it *is* to say that the larger grouping is a federation of congregations with accompanying umbrella organizations to fulfil functions which it is useful to the congregations to have carried out centrally. Different voluntary organizations have different structures: the corporate, where the local group is a local branch of a national organization, and reliant upon it – as local Scout groups are (they have a certain amount of autonomy, but rules are set nationally); the 'trade association', which provides services centrally in a manner more efficiently than could be achieved by each local organization doing it separately; and the indeterminate, where different people have different perceptions of the situation and leadership can only be by persuasion. Similarly, different structures relate to different religious organizations: in the Salvation Army and the Jehovah's Witnesses, the local group is clearly a local branch of a national organization; the Evangelical Alliance is more like a 'trade association', as each Evangelical Free Church manages its own affairs entirely; and the Church of England is of a rather 'indeterminate' structure, and different people have different perceptions of the situation, Archdeacons sometimes regarding congregations as local branches of a national organization and subject to its commands (I once heard an Archdeacon tell a group of priests to tell the members of their congregations to pay more), and congregations and parochial clergy often regarding the congregation as constituting the Church of England in their parish with the Diocesan office acting rather like a trade association and providing useful services. To take an example: the liturgy in a parish church on a Sunday morning is created out of an authorized liturgical text (or not), but in every place the way it is done is different. And over appointments, the care of church buildings, and much else, there is a mixture of the national, the Diocesan, and the local. What clergy, churchwardens and congregations are managing are congregations, so to them the Church of England appears as a federation of congregations. What Bishops and Archdeacons are managing are the Diocesan aspects of appointments, changes to buildings, and so on – so to them the organization can appear to be a Diocesan one with local branches.

For the purposes of this study, the congregation is the centre of attention; but this isn't to say that this is the only way of organizing the study of religious organizations.

And, of course, none of this discussion of federations of congregations and of congregations as the basic religious organization is to deny the pastoral importance of Bishops and the like, or the importance of the theological rationales offered for the larger groupings and their authority-figures. Federations matter, whatever sort they are.

One of the problems with categorizing the federations of congregations is that scholars have not always been careful to distinguish between federations and the congregations which constitute them. Thus Troeltsch distinguished between sects and churches (Troeltsch 1911; Gill 1996) – the former having relatively closed boundaries, firm membership criteria, firm theological beliefs, and high personal commitment amongst those who attend; the latter having more open boundaries, vague membership criteria (as everyone in principle belongs), less firm theological beliefs, and lower personal commitment amongst those who attend (Moberg 1970). (Stanley (1967) describes the difference between sect and church as the difference between 'involuted' and 'involved' organizations); but Troeltsch doesn't make it very clear whether the congregation or the federation is in view. If all of the congregations in any federation were similar, this would not matter: but they aren't. A church (federation) can contain congregations which are sects and congregations which are churches.

I shall leave this issue somewhat unresolved, and the reader should assume that the congregations in church-federations are churches and that the congregations in sect-federations are sects unless the contrary is stated.

The issue is somewhat clearer when it comes to Richard Niebuhr's discussion of the 'denomination' (Niebuhr 1929): a bureaucratic form with some sectarian characteristics and some church characteristics. 'Denomination' always refers to the federation and its umbrella functions. Congregations of denominations generally share most of a particular set of characteristics (bureaucratic and democratic decision-making processes, relatively clear membership criteria, rather liberal theological views, and boundaries relatively open to the world), but some denominational congregations can have church-like characteristics and others can have sect-like characteristics.

There are, of course, characteristics which the church, the denomination and the sect all share: they all have cultural, social and organizational aspects to study (Beckford 1973), but within this generality we find differences: for instance, we find that higher social classes tend to relate to churches (but not necessarily attend them very often), that the middle classes and aspiring working classes gravitate towards denominations (and to churches which are taking on denominational characteristics), and that lower socio-economic classes tend to belong to sects (Cameron 2001); though the larger sect-like congregations of churches and denominations attract the middle classes in considerable numbers. Similarly, in Hinduism, we find higher-caste Hindus belonging to church-like organizations and lower-caste Hindus belonging to sect-like organizations (Hertel 1977). In all three types we find both associational and bureaucratic structures, but with different balances for each: so the sect is predominantly associational, the denomination bureau-cratic, and the church an unusual sort of open-boundaried association.

Once we have discussed sects, churches and denominations and the ways in which they behave, we shall briefly mention cults (which allow individual belief-systems at the same time as demanding commitment to the group until a charismatic prophet turns up to demand adherence to an orthodoxy), 'market' religious organizations, established sects, and church movements.

Bruce (1995) offers a categorization to aid our understanding of the four major categories. He distinguishes between those religious organizations in which members recognize only their own organization as legitimate ('uniquely legitimate') and those in which they recognize other organizations as legitimate ('pluralistically legitimate'). The outside world will regard a religious organization as either 'respectable' or 'deviant'. He characterizes a 'church' as respectable and uniquely legitimate, a denomination as respectable and pluralistically legitimate, a sect as deviant and uniquely legitimate, and a cult as deviant and pluralistically legitimate.

This set of characterizations is useful provided we recognize that cults and sects often seek respectability, that churches and denominations can be temporarily deviant, that churches and sects can legitimize themselves pluralistically, and that denominations and cults can regard themselves as uniquely legitimate (as some black-led, highly bureaucratized Pentecostal federations do).

Sects

'Sects' can be defined using the 'prototype', the 'classical', or the 'family resemblance' method. Using the classical method, we can define a sect as a congregation or a federation of congregations the boundaries of which are clear – that is, there are clear criteria for membership, firm beliefs are held, and there are usually clear distinctions between the group's way of life and that of the world around it. Using the prototype method, we might choose a body such as the Amish or the Jehovah's Witnesses (see below) as the typical sect and then compare other groups to these. Using the family resemblances method, we might collect a larger number of possible characteristics and ask how many of them a group exhibits: for instance, sects demand substantial personal commitment, sects tend to anathematize or isolate deviant members or those who leave, sects often have a nucleus of members who maintain long-term control over the group (Calley 1965), and sects tend to draw their members from lower socio-economic classes (though the direction of the causal link might not be clear here, as belonging to a sect makes considerable demands on someone's financial and time resources and therefore might help to determine someone's socio-economic class (Yinger 1967a) and/or a third factor might mean that someone both joins a sect and is in a lower socio-economic class). An organization which exhibits a number of these characteristics is likely to be a sect.

Sects are extremely diverse, and a number of scholars have attempted to categorize them. They can be conversionist (encouraging individual conversion experiences and regarding such an experience as a gateway to membership); they can be adventist (looking for Christ's second coming and often predicting its date); they can be gnostic (regarding themselves as possessors of secret knowledge about God and the future, knowledge believed to give members a privileged position in heaven); and they can be introversionist (seeking God within themselves, and thus having little need to relate to the wider world) (Wilson 1959; Young 1967).

There is considerable diversity amongst sects, and in fact considerable diversity *within* them: for instance, the 'Jesus Movement', strong during the 1960s and 1970s, whilst clearly sectarian in relation to its characteristics, had a fairly loose structure and was internally diverse (Leming and Smith 1974). Social reactions to sects are equally diverse (ibid.).

Amongst particular sects the Jehovah's Witnesses are unique in that the movement originated with a publishing house and *The Watchtower* is still the chief means of the organization's unity (Beckford 1972; 1977). The organization keeps its distance from the world around it through such policies as refusing blood transfusions and not celebrating festivals such as Christmas; its theology is distinctive (not in relation to its views on what will happen as the end of the world approaches, which other groups share, but in relation to the combination of these views with a denial of Jesus' divinity); and it has a distinctive and successful evangelistic method. Whilst Beckford is correct to suggest that 'certainty' is *the* characteristic of the Jehovah's Witnesses (for this is what they wish the world to believe about themselves; Beckford 1978), I have found a fair level of open debate and internal disagreement amongst Jehovah's Witnesses I have known. This is an area in need of research – but research which will, of course, be difficult to conduct, because the Jehovah's Witnesses, like other sects, likes to show a united front to the world.

An important sect is the Amish, part of a longstanding sectarian tradition which includes the Huttites and the Moravians, and which forms its own society (Cavan 1977) and resists modern developments as being at best a distraction from spiritual growth and from the life of the Christian community and at worst the work of the devil. The Amish have developed strategies to perpetuate themselves as the world around them changes. For instance: some groups encourage their young people to go out into the world so that they can decide whether to commit themselves to the Amish way of life: many of them do. And the group will sometimes divide, enabling new processes of evolution to occur and thus new and strengthened communities to develop (Casanova 1994), a process which Whitworth has observed passing from stagnation to 'conservative' and 'adaptor' groups parting company and then forming a new alliance in order to recommend the Amish way of life to the world, a way of life strengthened by reconnection with the tradition and by new contact with the outside world (Whitworth 1975). In this way the Amish both retain their spiritual roots and change in relation to a changing environment.

An important group of sects in the UK is those which formed post-1950 as large numbers of people arrived from the Caribbean. People newly arrived in a strange country were often frozen out or worse by congregations of the denominations to which they had belonged back home, so they either joined or formed their own associations which then became black-led congregations, often with links to federations of similar congregations in the United States. These organizations are still quite sectarian, their members tend to be relatively deprived (though this is not true of more recent African congregations in the UK, which have become sects of the upwardly-mobile and which explicitly run career development programmes for their members). The pastors of black-led congregations, and thus the congregations themselves, have played an important role in integrating black people into British society, mainly through the relationships which ministers have formed with ministers of other sects, churches and denominations and with the secular authorities (Williams 1984).

(It is *not* true, as Lee (1967) suggests, that different types of organization suit different ethnic groups. Many people from the Caribbean were happily Roman Catholic, Methodist or Anglican before being rejected by congregations of these and other established denominations in the UK. Sectarian religion has been an important element in the survival of black culture and an important means to a sense of belonging in a hostile culture. If that culture becomes less hostile, traditional sectarian religion will become less attractive, as it already has for younger black people, for whom assimilation into a secular society or the more exotic Rastafarian sectarian religion appear to be more attractive options.)

A new category of religious organization is that of the 'New Religious Movement'. These tend to be sectarian, but they form a subcategory of their own because of their active (and sometimes manipulative) recruitment of young people, and particularly of students. They have thus caused considerable concern, and their relationships with wider society have sometimes been tense (Barker 1982). (Barker, whilst not minimizing causes for concern, sees New Religious Movements as belonging to a long history of dissent and sees society's reactions as consistent with reactions to previous examples of the phenomenon; Barker 1983.) Lofland and Richardson find considerable diversity amongst these movements, categorizing the types as clinic, congregation, collective, corps, and colony. Some organizations pass through these stages in order, some in a less orderly fashion, and all of the organizations continue to exhibit some characteristics of each type (Lofland and Richardson 1984).

Particularly important to a study of New Religious Movements is an understanding of members' motivations, and Saliba uses a functional approach to ask how members *experience* the organization's explanatory, emotional, social, validatory and adaptive functions (Saliba 1995).

Like all organizations, New Religious Movements evolve: they routinize charismatic authorities as Weber (1963) suggests they will, and they formalize themselves as they grow, as Chapin and Tsouderos (1956) suggest they will, so that they can function in a consistent manner and relate to the society from which they need to draw new members, and also so that they can avoid the authority vacuum which would emerge as charismatic authority subsided and there was no traditional authority to enable the organizations to formulate goals and to achieve them (Wilson 1982). The author's own experience of a particular New Religious Movement, the International Churches of Christ, suggests that as young people become older and start to ask questions and to expect a say in the organization's direction, the organization adapts to enable this to happen.

New Religious Movements are clearly normally sectarian, but is the New Religious Movement Scientology a sect? It isn't eschatological, and it isn't very theological either, but it has many of the characteristics of a sect, and Wallis thinks it should be included in the category (Wallis 1973). And are religious orders sects? To some extent, yes, as they have closed boundaries and they have firm rules on practice; but reform is generally by recourse to traditional authority and the beliefs of members are often a matter for themselves. Religious orders are therefore 'quasi-sects' (Hill 1973c).

We have seen that sects are diverse both between and within themselves and that they change – and a particular point at which many of them change is when they start to employ paid ministers, for the ministers often form relationships with ministers of other religious organizations and thus draw their organization into relationships with other organizations which in turn makes the organization's boundaries more porous (Young 1967). The problem which sects face when they evolve in this way is that they can become distanced from their 'charter goals' (Beckford 1975b). When charter goals are less rigid than the practice of community life, as for the Children of God during the 1970s, feedback and decision mechanisms can occur more freely, making it possible to preserve recruitment and financial stability in a changing environment (Davis and Richardson 1976; Wallis 1976); but where charter goals are a strong element in the organization's understanding of itself then schism can occur (see below).

However the organization changes, tensions occur, mainly because a sect needs to retain its isolation from the world in order to maintain its ideological or other purity, but it also needs to be *in* the world in order to attract recruits. This balancing act is often achieved by *partial* bureaucratization, the recruitment process becoming routinized but the ideological purity being preserved and developed through a preaching tradition through which a traditional authority based on the founders' utterances can emerge. (It is sometimes important for a sect not to socialize all of its converts so that a few can become the new charismatic leaders which the sect will need for its survival; Jacobson 1973).

Just as sects often contain two different authority-structures in tension, so they often exhibit two apparently opposed organizational tendencies: schism and networking.

As tensions mount within a sect, the ideological distance between 'conservatives' and 'adaptors' can become too much for the organization to bear and a group leaves to form a new organization, often with an ideological purity which its members could no longer find in the organization which they have just left. (Schism is precipitated by intentional and unintentional pushes – from the original organization which is finding its more radical elements difficult to handle within the formalizing and bureaucratizing organization (Chapin and Tsouderos 1956); and pulls – from the radical group's ideology). But whilst this is the normal pattern, it can sometimes be a more liberal group with 'church' tendencies which decides to leave what they see as an organization increasingly out of touch with their own emotional maturity (Templeton and Demerath 1998). Whichever process occurs, there are usually predictable stages: structural conduciveness, structural strain, a precipitating factor, a mobilizing agent, and forces of social control to enable the new sect to coalesce (Wilson 1971). (Jones (1972) tests these steps on the Catholic Apostolic Church, Wright (1972) tests them on the Order of Ethiopia, a breakaway from the Methodist Church in South Africa which later joined the Anglican Church, and Zuckerman (1999) discusses a synagogue which split, though not in quite the same terms.)

At the same time as experiencing potential schism, sects might participate in networks (Percy 1996), sometimes because the minister of the sect feels in need of support from other ministers as he or she handles a difficult situation. Such relationships, often within local fraternities of ministers who share similar theological positions, can involve the sect in joint activities with other sects (this can be either evangelical or social activity). This joint activity can draw sect members into relationships with members of other sects, making the boundaries of the sect more porous to new ideas, and relativizing the sect's beliefs and practices – thus giving the more radical members even more reason to leave.

Whilst many members of a sect might think that the sect's main aim is the pursuit and communication of a particular apocalyptic vision, a conversion experience, or secret knowledge, the sect's aim is in fact to survive, and it will adapt in order to do so, developing new organizational forms whilst at the same time preserving as much ideological connection with the past as possible (Beckford 1975b); and in order to survive, some sects will turn into sect-like churches or into denominations.

Churches

By 'church' I mean a church as opposed to a denomination or a sect: that is, a congregation or a federation of congregations open to the world with (almost) non-existent boundaries and with considerable latitude allowed to members (or, perhaps better, 'attendees') as to what they believe and to what extent they are actively committed. The typical church is the parish church of the Church of England of which everyone in the geographical parish is regarded as a member unless they decide otherwise, and the aim of which is the spiritual well-being of the whole community (Ecclestone 1988). Thus events will be organized for the wider community, and these will be regarded as the church's work; and Christmas cards will be delivered to inform people of service times rather than evangelistic literature being delivered. If a special Christmas event is held to which lots of people come who will not be seen again until the next Christmas then this is felt to be the natural thing for the parish church to be doing and little attempt will be made to use the event to recruit active members – which may be why they come.

At the level of the federation, a church will allocate paid clergy on the basis of the population of the geographical parish rather than on the basis of the financial contribution the congregation makes to the Diocese or on the basis of congregational numbers (especially since Bomford's research on the connection between low average income and low congregational numbers; Bomford 1992); though one mark of increasing secularization, which creates a boundary between the church and society both in the mind of society and in the mind of the church, is an increasing tendency to allocate paid clergy on the basis of the congregation's financial contribution to the Diocese and on the basis of congregational numbers. To this extent the Church of England is becoming less of a church. The restriction of church school places to congregation members' children is another sign of the increasing secularization of a church.

The Roman Catholic Church is a church if its community is regarded as all those with a Roman Catholic heritage. The church will try to make them into active members, but even if they don't become regular communicants they will still be treated as members, they will be welcome at the social club, their children will be admitted to church schools, and they will be buried by the parish priest.

Pinto and Crow have found that small congregations of churches tend to have sect-like characteristics (Pinto and Crow 1982). This is because the majority of the congregation must be active members if the congregation is to survive, so demands are made on new members, and this can look sectarian – which doesn't mean that it is. It is possible for large church congregations to be sect-like (as many larger evangelical Anglican congregations are) and it is possible for small congregations to run open and welcoming policies and events. Churches of any size can be 'selective and dispersed' (that is, associational and sect-like) or 'neighbourhood' (that is, parish churches; Shippey 1967). Shippey thinks that the mixed sect-church nature of some congregations is inherently unstable: but it needn't be, for, as Bomford (1992) has shown, congregations can contain subgroups which operate relatively autonomously, and even though there might be tensions between them, the relative freedom which a church gives people in terms of behaviour and beliefs means that, unless the congregation becomes too sect-like, individuals might leave but schism won't occur.

What *might* happen is that the federal church might become a denomination.

Denominations

Niebuhr noticed that Troeltsch's distinction between church and sect did not capture the reality of most American religion, and he posited the 'denomination' as a separate category (Niebuhr 1929).

Denominations are bureaucratized federations of relatively bureaucratic congregations within which membership is defined (but everyone is welcome to attend) and within which a fair amount of latitude over religious belief is offered. Denominational congregations are associational and they are therefore not as open to the world as a church congregation might be, but they are more open than sect congregations.

Denominations tend to relate to wider society by setting up separate organizations to do so (and many of the faith-based organizations discussed below came about in this way); and, because these organizations relate to other organizations and because the denomination's clergy are often involved in them, the culture of the clergy can become even more distant from that of the congregation than mere professionalization of the clergy would suggest that it should (Martin 1972). During the 1970s and 1980s denominational church congregations involved in unemployment projects experienced considerable conflict between ministers and congregations, especially when the congregation's building was involved in the project.

As Niebuhr noticed, denominational congregations tend to be made up of middle-class or aspiring working-class people (Niebuhr 1929); and as Martin has noticed, denominations are a distinctively British and American phenomenon, with their combination of liberalism, individualism, pragmatism, and disunity within consensus being characteristics both of themselves and of British and American society (Martin 1962). The denomination also relies on social stability, and this it has had in recent British and American history. Rapid change is more likely to favour the church or the sect.

Like sects, denominations construct survival strategies. In the USA they have left poor urban areas and migrated to the suburbs (unlike sects and churches; Winter 1961) largely in order to survive financially; and their bureaucratic structures, which can sometimes become an end in themselves, aid survival in the more secular, more mobile suburban world – though, as Demerath and Hammond note, this might be survival as professionalized and bureaucratized organizations with little to do with religion (Demerath and Hammond 1969). Whilst denominations are national or international bodies, their congregations are still voluntary organizations (Scherer 1980) with considerable local control, and they can and sometimes do leave the denomination, thus seeking their own survival in a sectarian form (Knudten 1967: 121ff.). But a more common transition is for sects to become denominations (Warburton 1967), often at the expense of their core values (Wilson 1959) – though they often retain a fairly fundamentalist theology in a context of few behavioural tests for membership, more democratic and bureaucratic decision-making processes, and a more professionalized leadership. Conversionist sects are the most likely to become denominations, and Adventist, gnostic and introversionist ones less likely (ibid.). The Quakers, once fairly sectarian, are now clearly a denomination (Isichei 1967); and Methodism, which started as a sectarian movement within the Church of England, is perhaps the largest denomination, but because it started within a church it has always exhibited a variety of sect-like characteristics (Hill 1973b). Its original transition to denominational structures was messy, as some parts of the movement made the transition long before other parts did, but reunification of the movement during the 1930s was relatively successful, probably because the single founder of the movement could still be regarded as a focus for unity. (Sometimes denominational and sectarian characteristics can exist over long periods in an organization unsure of what it is. This appears to have happened to the Plymouth Brethren; Embley 1967.)

Churches, too, become denominations, and even though the Church of England remains doctrinally diverse and has a traditional leadership structure (Thompson 1970), progressively bureaucratizing central structures (The Archbishops' Commission 1995) and more associational congregations are moving the Church of England in a denominational direction. Recent plans to restrict the franchise for electing churchwardens to members of the parish's electoral roll (rather than it being everyone living in the parish, as it is now), the abandonment of the calling of banns before the marriage of parishioners, and the progressive restriction of church school places to the children of regular churchgoers, are taking the Church of England in a denominational and possibly even a sectarian direction. The process will have significant consequences: it will enable the secular authorities to disengage from the Church of England, and it will make it easier (eventually) for organic unity to occur between the Church of England and other denominations. Because organizations which relate to each other become more like each other (DiMaggio and Powell 1983: 147), denominations involved in ecumenical conversations become more like each other (Richter 2004) and over time the case for merger becomes compelling.

Other Types of Religious Organization

Nelson suggests that there are correlations between Weber's three authority types (charismatic, traditional and bureaucratic) and different kinds of religious organization (Nelson 1993): the sectarian, the church, and the denominational. This appears to be the case. It is also possible to fit other types of religious organization into this structure.

The Salvation Army retains sect-like qualities at the same time as becoming denominational in structure. Robertson calls it an 'established sect' (Robertson 1967; cf. Johnson 1967). The Army experiences high levels of public support for its substantial social work programme, it has a distinctive military style and various prohibitions (to maintain boundaries against wider society), and it contains a diversity of views: the conservative, the pragmatic, and the 'modernist'. Its leadership is highly bureaucratic.

Steinberg calls Reform Judaism a 'Church movement' (Steinberg 1973). It is neither a sect nor a church (as orthodox Judaism aims to be). It emerged because orthodox Judaism didn't relate well to wider society and some Jews wanted to do so at the same time as remaining in touch with their culture and tradition. Reform Judaism looks rather like a loosely structured denomination with a mixture of authority-types.

Warner suggests a new category: 'market' religious organizations. This is how he terms large American organizations designed to thrive in an open market. They are pluralistic and adaptable, they encourage both individualism and financial commitment to the organization, and they employ the latest multimedia wizardry (Warner 1993). To the extent that they are religious organizations at all, they are sects, with the individual's prosperity as the stated aim, the leadership's prosperity as the actual aim, and a charismatic leadership style highly vulnerable to adverse public opinion when things go morally askew.

A more established category is the cult. This is a grouping, and often a community, of people who get together around some kind of religious focus, for mutual support or in order to overcome a variety of deprivations (Glock 1973: 277ff.); or the cult is put together by a group or individual in order to sell a 'philosophy'. Cults are generally self-generated, and are not sects, which are usually formed by schisms from churches or denominations (Stark and Bainbridge 1985: 25–30; cf. Chapter 2 above). The cult sets out to attract adherents and starts to grow (Campbell 1972), and sometimes a cult becomes a sect when a charismatic prophet emerges – the process which scientology has gone through (Wallis 1975a).

Is an umbrella body, such as a national Council of Churches, a religious organization? If so, of what type? In the USA, the National Council of Churches was established nearly a hundred years ago. Strong denominations ignored it, but when they became weaker they found it useful, and even conservative denominations remained members as they experienced status benefits from membership (and they were able to remain members because denominational leaders tend to be more liberal than congregation members; Pratt 1974). This, other such national and regional bodies, and the World Council of Churches, have religion as their purpose, their members are religious organizations (though often in practice the active members are self-selected members of élites or of governing bodies of denominations), they are bureaucratic, and their belief-requirements tend to be minimal. They are therefore quasi-denominations.

A most interesting set of organizations is that of religionless churches. These have similar organizational characteristics to congregations and denominations (Demerath 1969) and they disintegrate faster. An important example is the Findhorn community: a community with characteristics like those of a religious order but without an explicit agreed belief-system (Rigby and Turner 1972). No: these are not religious organizations, but they can be very like them.

Labels?

Are these categories useful? Are the assignment of category labels in fact a means of stereotyping and criticizing organizations we have problems with –

for have not different religious organizations always labelled and stereotyped each other in order to establish their own identities and boundaries over against other organizations? And might not this practice be an important root of conflict between religious organizations and within and between societies (Cavan 1977)? And maybe there is no justification for drawing boundaries anyway?

Jackson and Jobling think that there is no clear line between churches, sects and cults because behaviour connected to each category can be found in organizations we might locate in the others (Jackson and Jobling 1968); and whilst we recognize that the church/sect, open/closed distinction resonates with the extrinsic/intrinsic distinction found helpful by psychologists, and with our own experience of other groups and communities, Dittes can find few practical uses for the distinctions (Dittes 1971) as each organization is so different from other organizations (just as each person is so different from every other) that such simple distinctions might do little to reflect the reality and might blind us to more important characteristics of the organizations in question. Similarly, the whole categorization exercise is questioned by Lurkings, who suggests that congregations are not homogeneous and that any church, denomination or sect contains a variety of kinds of congregation and that categorizing as church, sect and denomination suggests that organizations are homogeneous, which they are not (Lurkings 1972). Moberg and McCann make a different but connected point about American religion: American religion is superficially diverse, but actually it all behaves in similar ways: as theologically-driven federal voluntary organizations (McCann 1993); and it also all behaves similarly in relation to clergy roles, social functions, social norms, and members' psychology (Moberg 1962), suggesting that for American religion at least a single denominational category is indeed sufficient, as Richard Niebuhr suggested (Niebuhr 1929).

But an interesting piece of research by Iannaccone on how the members of congregations allocate resources in order to maximize utility has found that two distinct patterns emerge and thus two distinct categories of organization are indicated (he calls them 'church' and 'sect', but he probably means 'denomination-church' and 'sect'). These categories are not ad hoc, but reflect organizational and membership realities (Iannaccone 1994). Iannaccone's theory, based on this research, is that the greater strictness of sectarian religion reduces free-riding and thus results in a very different kind of organization (Iannaccone 1998). There seem to be few organizations in the statistical field between the sect and the denomination-church, suggesting that anything between the two is unstable and likely to become either a sect or a denomination-church.

Scholars are rarely short of alternative categorizations to offer, and in this field there have been plenty of suggestions.

Dudley (1991) offers survivor, crusader, pillar, pilgrim and servant churches (by which he means congregations and their federations); Gustafson (1967) categorizes congregations as having particularistic or universalistic attitudes and as regarding the means of grace as objective or subjective, thus giving four categories; Davidson et al. (1969) suggest that congregations and federations are hierarchical or democratic, have a variety of perceptions of where authority lies, give to the laity differing amounts of control, and perceive the relationship between clergy and laity differently, resulting in a large number of potential categories; McCann (1993) suggests hierarchy (fief and bureaucracy), clan (familia and guild), collegium (team and professional organization) and arena (coalition and market), making four categories and eight sub-categories; and Woodhead et al. (2004) offer a survey of typologies containing some of the above and some others too.

Scalf et al. (1973) suggests 'formal'/'communal'; Spruit (1983) lists Volkskirche, church as service institution, and church as grassroots church; Snook (1974) offers a multidimensional system about symbolism, structure, intensity of commitment, and pervasiveness of the ideology in people's lives – a categorization he thinks more cross-cultural; Becker (1999) suggests house of worship, family congregation, community congregation, 'leader' congregation, and a mixed or transitional type; and Dulles (1988) lists theological categories: institution, mystical communion, sacrament, herald, servant, and community of disciples.

Just as Troeltsch's and Niebuhr's categorizations have been questioned and modified, so has Weber's categorization of authority types as traditional, charismatic and classical (bureaucratic; see Weber 1963; Hill 1973a). Rudge suggests that 'group' should be added in order to incorporate an associational authority, and that 'systemic' would recognize a type of authority which adjusts to changing environment (Rudge 1968, 1972). Sommerfield prefers familial (Roman Catholic), democratic (most denominations) and dominical (Lutheran and Calvinist) to Weber's categories (Sommerfield 1968).

Categories have their uses, provided we recognize their limitations, for every organization *is* different from every other. The important thing in each case is to examine the organization's behaviours and structures and to examine how authority works within it, and then to ask whether Troeltsch's, Niebuhr's, Weber's, or anyone else's categories might be of some use, and whether the evidence suggests yet another new categorization; but David Martin's ability to express the church, denomination and sect categories as carol, hymn and chorus has always seemed to me a strong recommendation for the traditional Troeltsch/Niebuhr pattern, and unless compelling evidence to the contrary is forthcoming this will probably remain an important means of categorizing religious organizations.

What *is* clear is the *diversity* of the religious organizations we have encountered: among them congregations, federations, religious orders, agencies, associations (Cameron 2001) – and that's only in Britain and

America. What is equally clear is that secularization and other changes in society are causing considerable changes in religious organizations – and that we are going to need all the tools and all the research we can muster in order to understand what's going on so that we shall be in a position to plan for the future.

References

Alston, Jon P. and Aguirre, B.E. (1979), 'Congregational Size and the Decline of Sectarian Commitment: The Case of the Jehovah's Witness in South and North America', *Sociological Analysis*, **40** (1), Spring, 63–70

Ammerman, Nancy Tatom, Farnsley II, Arthur E., et al. (1997), *Congregation and Community*, New Brunswick, New Jersey: Rutgers University Press

Archbishops' Commission (1995), *Working as One Body: The Report of the Archbishops' Commission on the Organisation of the Church of England* [The Turnbull Report], London: Church House Publishing

Barker, Eileen (ed.) (1982), *New Religious Movements: A Perspective for Understanding Society*, New York and Toronto: Edwin Meller Press

Barker, Eileen (1983), 'New Religious Movements in Britain: The Context and the Membership', *Social Compass*, **30** (1), 33–48

Baum, Howell (1994), 'Community and Consensus: Reality and Fantasy in Planning', *Journal of Planning Education and Research*, **13**, 251–62

Becker, Penny Edgell (1999), *Congregations in Conflict: Cultural Models of Local Religious Life*, Cambridge: Cambridge University Press

Beckford, James A. (1972), 'The Embryonic Stage of a Religious Sect's Development: The Jehovah's Witnesses', in Hill, Michael (ed.), *A Sociological Yearbook of Religion in Britain*, vol. V, London: Student Christian Movement, pp. 11ff.

Beckford, James A., (1973), 'Religious Organization: A Trend Report', *Current Sociology*, **21** (2), 7–170

Beckford, James A. (1975a), 'Organization, Ideology and Recruitment: The Structure of the Watch Tower Movement', *Sociological Review*, **23** (4), 893–909

Beckford, James A. (1975b), 'Two Contrasting Types of Sectarian Organization', in Wallis, Roy (ed.), *Analyses of Religious and Non-Religious Sects*, London: Peter Owen

Beckford, James A. (1977b), 'The Watchtower Movement Worldwide', *Social Compass*, **24** (1), 5–31

Beckford, James A. (1978), 'Sociological Stereotypes of the Religious Sect', *Sociological Review*, **26** (1), 109–23

Benson, J. Kenneth and Dorsett, James H. (1971), 'Toward a Theory of Religious Organizations', *Journal for the Scientific Study of Religion*, **10** (2), 139–51

Biddle, Jeff E. (1992), 'Religious Organizations', in Clotfelter, Charles T. (ed.), *Who Benefits from the Nonprofit Sector?*, Chicago and London: University of Chicago Press

Bomford, Rodney (1992), 'Are you a groupie, crowdie, or clubbie?', *Church Times*, 10 April

Bruce, Stephen (1995), *Religion in Modern Britain*, Oxford: Oxford University Press

Calley, Malcolm J.C. (1965), *God's People: West Indian Pentecostal Sects in England*, London and New York: Oxford University Press

Cameron, Helen (2001), 'A perspective from the study of religious organisations', in Anheier, Helmut K. (ed.), *Organisational Theory and the Non-profit Form*, London: Centre for Civil Society, London School of Economics, report no. 2

Campbell, Colin (1972), 'The Cult, the Cultic Milieu and Secularization', in Hill, Michael (ed.), *A Sociological Yearbook of Religion in Britain*, vol. V, London: Student Christian Movement, pp. 119ff.

Casanova, José (1994), *Public Religions in the Modern World*, Chicago: University of Chicago Press

Cavan, Ruth (1977), 'From Social Movement to Organized Society: The Case of the Anabaptists', *Journal of Voluntary Action Research*, **6** (3 and 4), July–October, 105–11

Chapin, F.S. and Tsouderos, J.E. (1956), 'The Formalisation Process in Voluntary Associations', *Social Forces*, **34** (4), May, 342–4

Coleman, John A. (1968), 'Church-Sect Typology and Organizational Precariousness', *Sociological Analysis*, **29** (2), Summer, 55–66

Davidson, James D., Schlanger, Joseph A. and D'Antonio, William V. (1969), 'Protestant and Catholic Perceptions of Church Structure', *Social Forces*, **47** (3), 314–22

Davis, Rex and Richardson, James T. (1976), 'The Organization and Functioning of the Children of God', *Sociological Analysis*, **37** (4), Winter, 321–39

Demerath III, N.J. (1969), 'Irreligion, A-Religion and the Rise of the Religionless Church: Two Case Studies in Organizational Convergence', *Sociological Analysis*, **30** (4), Winter, 191–201

Demerath III, N.J. and Hammond, Phillip E. (1969), *Religion in Social Context*, New York: Random House

DiMaggio, Paul and Powell, W. (1983), 'The Iron Cage Revisited: Conformity and Diversity in Organisational Fields', *American Sociological Review*, **48**, 147–60

Dittes, James E. (1971), 'Typing the Typologies: Some Parallels in the Career of Church-Sect and Extrinsic-Intrinsic', *Journal for the Scientific Study of Religion*, **10** (4), Winter, 375–83

Dudley, Carl S. (1991), 'From Typical Church to Social Ministry: A Study of the Elements which Mobilize Congregations', *Review of Religious Research*, **32** (3), 195–212

Dulles, Avery (1988), *Models of the Church*, 2nd edn, Dublin: Gill and MacMillan

Ecclestone, Giles (ed.) (1988), *The Parish Church? Explorations in the Relationship of the Church and the World*, London and Oxford: Mowbray

Embley, Peter L. (1967), 'The Early Development of the Plymouth Brethren', in Wilson, Bryan (ed.), *Patterns of Sectarianism: Organization and Ideology in Social and Religious Movements*, Heinemann, London, pp. 213ff.

Gill, Robin (1996), *Theology and Sociology: A Reader*, new and enlarged edn, London: Cassell

Glock, Charles Y. (1973), 'Religion and the Integration of Society', in Knudten (1967), pp. 72ff.

Guest, Mathew, Tusting, Karin and Woodhead, Linda (eds) (2004), *Congregational Studies in the UK: Christianity in a Post-Christian Context*, Aldershot: Ashgate

Gustafson, Paul (1967), 'UO-US-PS-PO: A Restatement of Troeltsch's Church-Sect Typology', *Journal for the Scientific Study of Religion*, **6** (1), Spring, 64–8

Hertel, Bradley R. (1977), 'Church, Sect and Congregation in Hinduism: An Examination of Social Structure and Religious Authority', *Journal for the Scientific Study of Religion*, **16** (1), 15–26

Hill, Clifford (1971), 'From Church to Sect: West Indian Religious Sect Development in Britain', *Journal for the Scientific Study of Religion*, **10** (2), 114–23

Hill, Michael (1973a), *A Sociology of Religion*, London: Heinemann

Hill, Michael (1973b), 'Methodism as a Religious Order: A Question of Categories', in Hill, Michael (ed.), *A Sociological Yearbook of Religion in Britain*, vol. VI, London: Student Christian Movement, pp. 91ff.

Hill, Michael (1973c), *The Religious Order: A Study of Virtuoso Religion and its Legitimation in the Nineteenth Century Church of England*, London: Heinemann

Iannaccone, Laurence R. (1994), 'A Formal Model of Church and Sect', *American Journal of Sociology*, **94** (s), s241–69

Iannaccone, Laurence R. (1998), 'Why Strict Churches Are Strong', in Demerath III, N.J., Hall, Peter Dobkin, Schmitt, Terry and Williams, Rhys H. (eds), *Sacred Companies: Organizational*

Aspects of Religion and Religious Aspects of Organizations, New York and Oxford: Oxford University Press, pp. 269ff.

Isichei, Elizabeth (1967), 'From Sect to Denomination among English Quakers' and 'Organization and Power in the Society of Friends, 1952–59', in Wilson, Bryan (ed.), *Patterns of Sectarianism: Organization and Ideology in Social and Religious Movements*, London: Heinemann, pp. 161ff. and 182ff.

Jackson, John and Jobling, Ray (1968), 'Towards an Analysis of Contemporary Cults', in Martin, David (ed.), *A Sociological Yearbook of Religion*, vol. I, London: Student Christian Movement, pp. 94ff.

Jacobson, Cardell K. and Pilarzyk, Thomas J. (1973), *The Growth, Development, and Demise of a Conversionist Sect: The Milwaukee Jesus People*, Milwaukee: University of Wisconsin

Jeavons, Thomas H. (1998), 'Identifying Characteristics of "Religious" Organizations: An Exploratory Proposal', in Demerath III, N.J., Hall, Peter Dobkin, Schmitt, Terry and Williams, Rhys H. (eds), *Sacred Companies: Organizational Aspects of Religion and Religious Aspects of Organizations*, New York and Oxford: Oxford University Press, pp. 79ff.

Johnson, Benton (1967), 'On Church and Sect', in Knudten (1967), pp. 123ff.

Jones, Robert K. (1972), 'The Catholic Apostolic Church: A Study in Diffused Commitment', in Hill, Michael (ed.), *A Sociological Yearbook of Religion in Britain*, vol. V, Student Christian Movement, London, pp. 137ff.

Knudten, Richard D. (ed.) (1967), *The Sociology of Religion*, New York: Appleton-Century-Crofts

Lee, J. Oscar (1967), 'Religion among Ethnic and Racial Minorities', in Knudten (1967), pp. 357ff.

Leming, Michael R. and Smith, Ted C. (1974), 'The Children of God as a Social Movement', *Journal of Voluntary Action Research*, **3** (3 and 4), July–October, 77–83

Lofland, John and Richardson, James T. (1984), 'Religious Movement Organizations: Elemental Forms and Dynamics', *Research in Social Movement Conflicts and Change*, **7**, 29–51

Lurkings, E.H. (1972), 'Types of Christian Organisation', in Mitton, C.L. (ed.), *The Social Sciences and the Churches*, Edinburgh: T. and T. Clark, pp. 221ff.

McCann, Joseph F. (1993), *Church and Organization: A Sociological and Theological Enquiry*, Scranton, Pennsylvania: University of Scranton Press

Martin, David (1962), 'The Denomination', *British Journal of Sociology*, **13** (1), 1–14

Martin, David (1967), *A Sociology of English Religion*, London: SCM Press

Martin, David (1972), 'Church, Denomination and Society', in Hill, Michael (ed.), *A Sociological Yearbook of Religion in Britain*, vol. V, London: Student Christian Movement, pp. 85ff.

Moberg, David O. (1962), *The Church as a Social Institution*, Englewood Cliffs, New Jersey: Prentice-Hall

Moberg, David O. (1970), 'Theological Position and Institutional Characteristics of Protestant Congregations: An Exploratory Study', *Journal for the Scientific Study of Religion*, **9** (1), 53–8

Moore, Charles, Wilson, A.N. and Stamp, Gavin (1986), *The Church in Crisis*, London: Hodder and Stoughton

Nelson, Reed E. (1993), 'Authority, Organization and Social Context in Multinational Churches', *Administration Science Quarterly*, **38** (4), December, 653–82

Niebuhr, H. Richard (1929), *The Social Sources of Denominationalism*, reprinted Gloucester, Massachusetts: Peter Smith, 1987

Percy, Martyn (1996), *Words, Wonders and Power: Understanding Contemporary Christian Fundamentalism and Revivalism*, London: Society for Promoting Christian Knowledge

Pinto, Leonard J. and Crow, Kenneth E. (1982), 'The Effects of Size on other Structural Attributes of Congregations within the same Denomination', *Journal for the Scientific Study of Religion*, **21** (4), 304–16

Pratt, Henry J. (1974), 'Organizational Stress and Adaptation to Changing Political Status', *American Behavioural Scientist*, **17** (6), 865–83

Richter, Philip (2004), 'Denominational Cultures: The Cinderella of Congregational Studies?', in Guest et al. (2004), pp. 169ff.

Rigby, Andrew and Turner, Bryan S. (1972), 'Findhorn Community, Centre of Light: A Sociological Study of New Forms of Religion', in Hill, Michael (ed.), *A Sociological Yearbook of Religion in Britain*, vol. V, London: Student Christian Movement, pp. 72ff.

Robertson, Roland (1967), 'The Salvation Army: The Persistence of Sectarianism', in Wilson, Bryan (ed.), *Patterns of Sectarianism: Organization and Ideology in Social and Religious Movements*, London: Heinemann, pp. 49ff.

Rudge, Peter F. (1968), *Ministry and Management*, London: Tavistock Publications

Rudge, Peter F. (1972), 'Styles of Administration in Churches and their Theological Presuppositions', in Mitton, C.L. (ed.), *The Social Sciences and the Churches*, Edinburgh: T. and T. Clark, pp. 172ff.

Saliba, John A. (1995), *Perspectives on New Religious Movements*, London: Geoffrey Chapman

Scalf, John H., Miller, Michael J. and Thomas, Charles W. (1973), 'Goal Specificity, Organizational Structure and Participant Commitment in Churches', *Sociological Analysis*, **34** (3), Fall, 169–84

Scherer, Ross P. (ed.) (1980), *American Denominational Organization: A Sociological View*, Pasadena: William Carey Library

Scherer, Ross P. (1988), 'A New Typology for Organizations: Market, Bureaucracy, Clan and Mission, with Application to American Denominations', *Journal for the Scientific Study of Religion*, **27** (4), 475–98

Shippey, Frederick A. (1967), 'The Variety of City Churches', in Knudten (1967), pp. 157ff.

Snook, John B. (1974), 'An Alternative to Church-Sect', *Journal for the Scientific Study of Religion*, **13** (2), 191–204

Sommerfeld, Richard (1968), 'Conceptions of the Ultimate and the Social Organization of Religious Bodies', *Journal for the Scientific Study of Religion*, **7** (2), Fall, 178–96

Spruit, Léo (1983), 'Conceptions Ecclésiales et Modèles Pastoraux', *Social Compass*, **30** (4), 441–56

Stark, Rodney and Bainbridge, William Sims (1985), *The Future of Religion: Secularization, Revival, and Cult Formation*, Berkeley: University of California Press

Stark, Werner (1967), *The Sociology of Religion*, London: Routledge and Kegan Paul

Steinberg, Stephen (1973), 'Reform Judaism: The Origin and Evolution of a Church Movement', in Glock, Charles Y. (ed.), *Religion in Sociological Perspective*, Belmont: Wadsworth, pp. 221ff.

Templeton, Mark N. and Demerath III, N.J. (1998), 'The Presbyterian Re-Formation: Pushes and Pulls in an American Mainline Schism', in Demerath III, N.J., Hall, Peter Dobkin, Schmitt, Terry and Williams, Rhys H. (eds), *Sacred Companies: Organizational Aspects of Religion and Religious Aspects of Organizations*, New York and Oxford: Oxford University Press, pp. 195ff.

Thompson, Kenneth A. (1970), *Bureaucracy and Church Reform: The Organizational Response of the Church of England to Social Change, 1800–1965*, Oxford: Clarendon Press

Troeltsch, Ernst (1911), *The Social Teaching of the Christian Churches*, vol. I, reprinted London: Allen and Unwin, 1931

Wallis, Roy (1973), 'The Sectarianism of Scientology', in Hill, Michael (ed.), *A Sociological Yearbook of Religion in Britain*, vol. VI, London: Student Christian Movement, pp. 136ff.

Wallis, Roy (1975a), 'Scientology: Therapeutic Cult to Religious Sect', *Sociology*, **9** (1), 89–100

Wallis, Roy (1976), 'Observations on the Children of God', *Sociological Review*, **24** (4), 807–29

Warburton, T. Rennie (1967), 'Organization and Change in a British Holiness Movement', in Wilson, Bryan (ed.), *Patterns of Sectarianism: Organization and Ideology in Social and Religious Movements*, London: Heinemann, pp. 106ff.

Warner, R. Stephen (1993), 'Work in Progress Towards a New Paradigm for the Sociological Study of Religion in the United States', *American Journal of Sociology*, **98** (5), March 1044–93

Weber, Max (1922), 'The Three Types of Legitimate Rule', in Etzioni, Amitai and Lehman, E. (eds) (1980), *A Sociological Reader on Complex Organisations*, 3rd edition: Austin, Texas: Holt, Reinhart and Winston

Weber, Max (1963), *The Sociology of Religion*, Boston: Beacon Press

Whitworth, John M. (1975), 'The Shakers – Ideological Change and Organizational Persistence', in Hill, Michael (ed.), *A Sociological Yearbook of Religion in Britain*, vol. VIII, London: Student Christian Movement, pp. 78ff.

Williams, Jr, Charles (1984), 'Contemporary Voluntary Associations in the Urban Black Church: The Development and Growth of Mutual Aid Societies', *Journal of Voluntary Action Research*, **13** (4), October–December, 19–30

Wilson, Bryan R. (1959), 'An Analysis of Sect Development', *American Sociological Review*, **24** (1), 3–15

Wilson, Bryan R. (1982b), 'New Religious Movements: Preliminary Considerations', in Barker, Eileen (ed.), *New Religious Movements: A Perspective for Understanding Society*, New York and Toronto: Edwin Mellor Press

Wilson, John (1971), 'The Sociology of Schism', in Martin, David (ed.), *A Sociological Yearbook of Religion in Britain*, vol. IV, London: Student Christian Movement, pp. 1ff.

Winter, Gibson (1961), *The Suburban Captivity of the Churches: An Analysis of Protestant Responsibility in the Expanding Metropolis*, New York: Doubleday

Woodhead, Linda, Guest, Mathew and Tusting Karin (2004), 'Congregational Studies: Taking Stock', in Guest et al. (2004), pp. 1ff.

Wright, Beryl (1972), 'The Sect that Became an Order: The Order of Ethiopia', in Hill, Michael (ed.), *A Sociological Yearbook of Religion in Britain*, vol. V, London: Student Christian Movement, pp. 60ff.

Yinger, J. Milton (1967a), 'Religion and Social Change: Functions and Dysfunctions of Sects and Cults among the Disprivileged', in Knudten (1967), pp. 482ff.

Young, Frank W. (1967), 'Adaptation and Pattern Integration of a California Sect', in Knudten (1967), pp. 136ff.

Zuckerman, Phil (1999), *Strife in the Sanctuary: Religious Schism in a Jewish Community*, Walnut Creek, California: Altamira Press

CHAPTER 6

The Governance of Religious Organizations

'To govern is to accept responsibility for *the whole life* of the institution ...
Governance takes account of all the interests that affect the viability,
competence, and moral character of an enterprise' (Selznick 1992: 290). It is
thus prior both in time and in importance to management narrowly
understood, and its strategies will be political: the accommodation of interests,
the informing of opinion, the determining of ends, and the deciding on
methods of achieving them. 'Therefore governance cannot take obedience for
granted. Rather, governance comes into play at the margins of harmony and in
the shadow of dissensus' (ibid.: 290), and it starts where people become
interested in an organization. It is a complicated business.

This chapter is not a survey of the governance structures of religious
organizations. There are so many types, and within each type each structure is
so different, that the task would be impossible within the space available.
Rather, this chapter is about the issues faced by anyone involved in the
governance of religious organizations. We shall survey the literature for useful
research-based theory, and we shall apply the theory we discover to the issues
faced in a variety of contexts, and particularly the governance of denominations and governance issues raised by ecumenical relationships. In order to
begin to raise the issues we shall first of all introduce two particular
organizations to which we shall return later in the chapter: the South London
Industrial Mission and the Church of England.

The South London Industrial Mission

In 1943, Cuthbert Bardsley, Rector of St Mary's, Woolwich, began to visit the
deep air raid shelters of Siemens Brothers, a large engineering company on the
South Bank of the Thames. Colin Cuttell, a member of staff at Southwark
Cathedral, took over from him, and also visited other factories and offices in
the London Bridge area. Other South Bank clergy began to visit the industries
in their parishes. A network thus evolved. Few corporate decisions were
required, and all that was needed was an occasional meeting to share
experience.

In 1952, the Bishop of Southwark's Industrial Advisory Council was
appointed by the Bishop to support the chaplains' activity, and in 1956 this
turned into the South London Industrial Mission (SLIM) which had a

constitution which gave subscription-paying members (mainly shop stewards and managers) the responsibility for electing part of the Council. A voluntary organization had clearly been born, with a governing body (the Council), a Senior Chaplain (Colin Cuttell), and chaplains. But Colin Cuttell was a member of staff at Southwark Cathedral, and the other chaplains were incumbents of parishes and thus independent of any attempt to control them by the Council – except that the Council's General Purposes Committee began to raise money and to pay small honoraria to the chaplains, thus giving itself some slight influence. In 1956, Robert Gibson's honorarium was raised from £50 to £100 p.a. (a large increase then) 'in view of the excellent work he was doing'. This wording suggests that the honorarium was more an incentive bonus than working expenses, and he certainly saw honoraria as a recognition that industrial mission involved work additional to the parish ministry. Amongst the dozen or so chaplains in the team during the 1950s, most were paid by their denominations, but one, Charles Birtles, was paid by the Industrial Christian Fellowship (an independent charity) and another, Roy Beattie, was paid half by the Methodist Church and half by SLIM itself.

During the 1960s, the period in which Robert Gibson and then Peter Challen were Senior Chaplains, a full-time team developed. Few of the chaplains retained parish responsibilities, but they were still paid by their denominations. This situation continued until the end of the 1980s, at which point the denominations became unwilling to pay chaplains and the full-time team again became a team of part-time chaplains, disappearing altogether in 2002.

During the period when SLIM had a large team of full-time chaplains the team met weekly to study together, to discuss their work, and to plan events. When Peter Challen was appointed in 1967, the post of Rector of Christ Church Southwark was combined with the post of Senior Chaplain, and Christ Church became the Mission's base: so the Senior Chaplain was at the physical as well as the organizational hub of the Mission's work. He also had a personal vision for the organization's work, and was clearly the organization's leader. Honoraria soon died out, and the Council and its Executive Committee no longer had much control over the Mission's activity; and the denominations, which paid the chaplains, found that they had little control over the team's activity either. Thus the chaplains' team *became* the South London Industrial Mission, and it is arguable that, whilst SLIM had a structure which made it look like a bureaucratized voluntary organization, in fact it was an association, or perhaps even just a network, of individual clergy who met once a week – though there was a certain amount of formalization, evidenced by regular meetings (Chapin and Tsouderos 1956). A complicating factor throughout the 1960s, '70s and '80s was that the industries which chaplains visited made donations to SLIM's funds. Whilst these were not large in relation to the chaplains' salaries, they provided the Mission with funds of its own, and there was therefore pressure on the chaplains not to be too critical of the industries to which they ministered.

Any genuine governance there was (in relation to corporate events, publications, and so on) was by the chaplains' team; there was leadership (Cuttell's largely by example; Gibson's by team-building; Challen's by a rather personal ideology – a leadership sometimes challenged by team members); and there was professionalization (for the chaplains were mainly clergy, who regarded themselves, and were regarded by others, as being trained in a particular expertise).

In 1996, John Paxton became Senior Chaplain. Since his appointment the task has been survival, but the team of chaplains has not survived and, although SLIM's Board of Directors still exists, and still holds an Annual General Meeting, it is doubtful whether any meaningful activity can now be achieved. Throughout its history SLIM *was* its chaplains and their activity (with much help from people who ought to have been called 'friends' rather than 'associates' or 'members'), and so, without the chaplains, SLIM has in fact ceased to exist as an association or perhaps just a network – which is all it ever was (Torry 1990).

The Church of England

A relatively new development is that the telephone at Church House, Westminster, is now answered with the words 'The Church of England'. This is a lie. But since the publication of the report *Working as One Body* (Archbishops' Commission 1995) and the implementation of its recommendations, in particular the establishment of the Archbishops' Council with its Divisions, Church House has seen itself as the corporate headquarters of a national organization rather than as the home of General Synod: a national co-ordinating body elected by and accountable to the Church's Dioceses and parishes. It is difficult to disagree with Richard Roberts' diagnosis that the Church of England is suffering from a serious bout of 'managerialism': 'The "body", at the various levels of the individual physical body, the corporate organizational body – and the mystical "Body of Christ" – is committed to the appropriate deployment of instruments of co-ordination and integration of what is, for members of the body … a systematically irresistible power' (Roberts 2002: 162). He suggests that the Church's crisis of identity has encouraged the application of management techniques which are believed to have revived other types of organization (techniques suggested by Gill and Burke in their 1996 *Strategic Church Leadership*). *Working as One Body* assumes that the Church's goals are 'given' (Archbishops' Commission 1995: 3), which is not the case; they are permanently contested and negotiated. Part of the problem, of course, is that Bishops' peers are often the managers of public, commercial and industrial organizations in which aims are clearer and in which an administrative management model is at least partially relevant. The result is that a managerial ideology, and not just a collection of management methods, has invaded the Church (Roberts 2002: 172) and has become an end in itself, and that the clergy have become operatives who are rewarded for delivering management objectives. 'It is easy and profitable for all institutional operatives simply to follow directives and relapse into rule-governed behaviour rather than engage in demanding, critically reflective action for which they may well be penalized' (ibid.: 177).

The problem with *this* kind of management is that it treats the Church as something it isn't. The Church of England is its parishes, which each have considerable autonomy. The people of the parish elect Churchwardens, people on the electoral roll elect Parochial Church Councils, and patrons (often not the Bishop) appoint clergy who still frequently have the 'freehold' and can remain in post until the age of 70 if they wish to. The Diocese relies for its funds on the 'quota' or 'parish share' paid by the parishes – in fact, voluntary contributions – and out of the funds raised the stipends of the clergy are paid. Because the Diocesan authorities have little control over the number of clergy in post, budgeting can be problematic. Bishops and clergy are expected to conform to Measures and Acts agreed in General Synod, but what actually happens is that change evolves on the ground and Diocesan Synods and then General Synod eventually catch up (the clearest recent examples being modern-language liturgy, admission of children to communion before confirmation, and the remarriage of divorcees in church).

There is governance at many levels in the Church of England, and it is probably better to see the Church of England as a federation of parishes with Dioceses and then the national bodies as umbrella organizations, than to see it as a headquarters with local branches (hence my complaint about the way the telephone is answered at Church House). Each parish is its own voluntary organization, with some parishes operating more like associations and some behaving more like bureaucratized voluntary agencies. But these are not ordinary voluntary organizations, for the incumbent is Chair of the Parochial Church Council and is paid by the Diocese and not by the parish. He or she is also a professional, with acknowledged training and expertise. It is true that the Parochial Church Council elects a secretary and a treasurer, and there are certain decisions which can only be made by a majority vote of the Council, but given the fact that the incumbent is both the only paid staff member (usually) *and* the Chair of the Council, it is no surprise that the clergyperson is the leader in the parish (unless he or she decides to relinquish authority either generally or over particular issues).

Research-Based Theory

These case studies raise issues which we shall explore further on the basis of a body of research-based theory. Some of this theory we have already encountered, and where we have I shall merely summarize; but some of it we have not dealt with before, and here I shall go into greater detail.

Weber's Three Authority Types

We have encountered Max Weber's authority types: the charismatic (which here means the forceful and gifted personality's ability to control a community); the traditional (a body of tradition to which a community looks when decisions need to be made, with tradition-interpreting authority-figures generally being hereditary or appointed by existing post-holders); and the classical or bureaucratic, within which a body of law evolves, post-holders are appointed by rational methods and on the basis of ability, decision-making processes are formalized, and there are rational means (whether democratic or otherwise) for changing the body of law. In a bureaucratic authority-structure, the structure which makes major policy decisions is normally separate from that which manages the organization's work, the latter being accountable to the former; and post-holders in the operational part of the organization are hierarchically organized and generally paid to carry out the organization's work.

Weber (1922) suggested that communities with charismatic authority-figures tend eventually to 'routinize' decision-making (that is, to create routines for doing what had previously been done by the charismatic leader and by those who regarded the leader as an authority), and so become more bureaucratic. It is also normal for traditional authority-structures to become more bureaucratic as the organization's environment changes and the body of tradition can no longer respond adequately on its own. And, as Chapin and Tsouderos (1956) have shown, it is normal for any association to formalize as it grows.

Miller's interesting historical research suggests that today's bureaucratic structures (and Weber's insights) can be traced back to the bureaucracy which Rome developed in order to control its empire (Miller 1983). As the empire collapsed, the Church in the West preserved similar bureaucratic structures which, with their accompanying administrative techniques, it then passed on to emerging nation states – so that the rational organization of geographical units, the training of personnel for particular functions, appointments on the basis of ability, structures for passing information and instructions back and forth between the local and the centre, the subsidiarity necessary for the system to be responsive to local needs and for the centre not to become overloaded, and so on, are now normal elements in many organizations and we rarely comment on their existence because such structures and techniques have been such a normal part of life for so long. We only notice when they are absent or compromised, as they sometimes are in religious organizations.

An issue of which we shall need to be aware as we study governance-related issues in religious organizations is that Weber's are *ideal* types, and that in most religious organizations combinations of the charismatic, the traditional and the bureaucratic will be found, and that this is what makes these organizations so complex and so interesting.

Billis's Theory of Ambiguous Voluntary Agencies

We have already decided that religious organizations are voluntary organizations, and we shall therefore expect to find helpful any theory which has been developed to aid understanding of the governance of voluntary organizations.

On the basis of his study of a variety of organizations in the public and voluntary sectors, David Billis has developed a model which enables us to understand a number of aspects of governance in voluntary agencies. He describes the situation with a diagram (Figure 6.1) which enables us to locate different kinds of organization. 'Voluntary associations' are identifiable groups with names, purposes, membership criteria, and rudimentary rules about how to appoint office-holders and how to make decisions. A group of people who get together to organize amateur musicals might be an association (Billis 1993: 160f.).

The bureaucratic world is very different. Here there are paid staff organized into hierarchical roles, appointed by senior staff on the basis of their ability to do the job, and with clear lines of accountability between them. The civil service, local government and most commercial enterprises are organized on the basis of this 'classical' structure (ibid.: 161f.; Weber 1922).

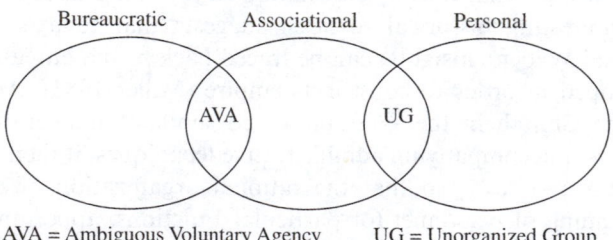

AVA = Ambiguous Voluntary Agency   UG = Unorganized Group

**Figure 6.1   The personal, associational and bureaucratic worlds
           [Second quotation]**

Source: Billis, David (1993), *Organizing Public and Voluntary Agencies*, London and New York: Routledge, p. 163, figure 11.1. Reproduced with permission

The personal sphere is that of personal relationships between family members and between groups of friends and neighbours. Whilst particular individuals might normally perform certain functions, there are no labelled posts, and decision-making is ad hoc, even if in any particular family or group it normally falls into predictable patterns (Billis 1993: 19f.).

Then there are two ambiguous zones. Unorganized groups have no constitution or legal identity and generally no name, but they have purposes. A group which regularly meets to play jazz on Friday evenings might fall into this category (ibid.: 162f.). Ambiguous voluntary agencies fall between the associational and the bureaucratic worlds. If a voluntary association takes on paid staff to do the organization's work then it has entered this world. To take an example: In 1996, the Greenwich, Blackheath and East Greenwich Trust for the Arts was formed with the purpose of running community drama events and particularly a large-scale passion play during the year 2000. It was governed by a trust deed and was a registered charity, and was run by volunteer trustees and other volunteers as necessary. It sometimes paid a fee to a director for a particular piece of work, and sometimes paid musicians, but all management functions remained with the trustees. It was therefore just into the ambiguous zone. In 1998, the organization appointed a director for the passion play and he took on a variety of management functions such as the appointment of additional staff who, with the agreement of the trustees, answered to him rather than to the trustees. Some management functions remained with the trustees, and other volunteers continued to carry out a variety of aspects of the Trust's work. The organization had clearly become an ambiguous voluntary agency with strong bureaucratic and associational characteristics. (The organization was still small. Size is not an issue here; it is the structure which determines which zone the organization is in.) After the passion play project was successfully completed the director and other staff members ceased to work for the Trust, which then reverted to being an entirely voluntary association.

Thus Billis's diagram and his explanations of various categories enable us to locate organizations and also to understand the ways in which they evolve. We shall find this theory useful when we study the governance of religious organizations.

O'Dea's Five Dilemmas

Thomas O'Dea's 'five dilemmas' form an important piece of theory because they have been worked out on the basis of research on religious organizations.

O'Dea's research led him to suggest that religious organizations go through processes of incipient organization, organization and efficiency, formalization, and finally disorganization, and that throughout its evolution any such organization needs to cope with five dilemmas:

1 Mixed motivation (goal displacement, as the organization becomes a focus of attention and thus displaces the original religious goals with its own need to survive);

2 Symbolism (the necessary objectification of religious symbols so that those symbols can relate to the organization's structure; but this objectification means that the symbols' religious power is reduced and religiously-motivated members are alienated from them);

3 Administration (which can become an end in itself and transfer the member's commitment from expressive activity to instrumental activity);

4 Delimitation (as the religious message needs to be applied to particular situations and the application then becomes the message); and

5 Power (as the organization takes on the values of surrounding organizations and seeks power amongst them).

O'Dea's general point is that, if religion is to be available, then it needs to be institutionalized, and that that compromises the religion thus institutionalized. His subsequent prognosis is that, if a religious organization enters a disorganized phase, then the five dilemmas will hasten its demise (O'Dea 1967).

This theory has been questioned. Mathisen's study of the Moody Bible Institute shows that the five dilemmas have little explanatory power in relation to that organization's evolution (Mathisen 1987), and Takayama (1975) has suggested that there is a difference between organizations as seen through such theories and their complex organizational realities, with the implication that in the interstices between the complex realities the dilemmas are not as acute as O'Dea's theory makes out. On the other side of the argument, Desmond Brown employs the theory in relation to deinstitutionalization in the Roman Catholic Church to some useful effect (Brown 1977) and Poloma successfully uses both O'Dea's theory and Weber's authority-types to study the routinization of the Toronto blessing (a Pentecostalist phenomenon): a routinization which has left sufficient social space for new charismatic figures to emerge (Poloma 1997). This suggests that the theory, whilst being based on research into religious organizations, might not be equally applicable to all religious organizations (for they are, after all, very different from each other), and that the theory should be regarded as a useful tool rather than as a sufficient explanatory scheme.

Compliance Structures

Etzioni's research has led him to posit three types of compliance structure in organizations: the normative (in which values and norms are at the root of compliance with an organization's goals); the utilitarian (a constantly negotiated social contract model); and the coercive (in which sanctions enforce compliance; Etzioni 1980). Harris tests the theory on a Welsh Diocese and finds a normative structure, but one within which change occurs, including changes in normative beliefs on the basis of normative beliefs, suggesting that in fact a utilitarian compliance structure is operating (Harris 1969). Similarly, Nelson and Hiller find utilitarian compliance structures at work, and suggest that as social class rises so normative compliance structures atrophy as people who are used to utilitarian compliance structures in other areas of their lives apply them to religious organizations in which they have governance responsibilities (Nelson and Hiller 1980).

This raises the issue of the place of values in decision-making in religious organizations, for the resources available in them are like those in non-religious organizations (staff and voluntary labour, skills, finance, goodwill, and so on), but they also include cultural symbols, rituals, ethical and theological values, and other religious assets (Williams and Demerath 1998): that is, resources which make normative compliance structures possible. According to Kavagy, what happens is that some areas of the organization's life, such as social action and ecumenical relationships, are controlled by negotiation with a changing environment (for which utilitarian compliance structures are useful), but that some functions, such as evangelism and worship, continue to be controlled by theological values and thus by a normative compliance structure. Kavagy's research backs up this hypothesis (Kavagy 1992). Thus, in Weber's terms, the organization operates with traditional authority-structures in some areas and with bureaucratic authority-structures in others.

We shall be dealing with the clergy in a separate chapter, but here the link needs to be made: if the above is anything like correct, then the clergy will be more likely than congregation members to carry out leadership roles because they hold positions within both traditional and bureaucratic authority structures (and sometimes exercise charismatic authority as well); and it also follows that the clergy will be good leaders if they operate normative and utilitarian compliance structures in the areas to which they are appropriate.

Applying the Theory

Just as the clergy and leadership are issues which I shall deal with elsewhere, so the difference between volunteers and members and how they fit into religious organizations and their governance structures will be pursued in a separate chapter. Here I shall tackle two particular governance structures, the denominational and the ecumenical, before returning to SLIM and the Church of England.

The Governance of Denominational Structures

Not only are denominations bureaucratic structures but they experience pressure to bureaucratize further (Benson and Dorsett 1971) because traditional authority is problematic in the context of most denominations' liberal theological traditions. As bureaucratic structures, denominations assume that they have members who are served by a hierarchically organized, professional staff; so they have to assume that people belong to the denomination rather than to the congregation (Anderson 1971). Members' own experience is ambiguous. Some congregation members, when away from home, will not attend a congregation at all; some will attend a nearby congregation, whatever its denomination; and some will seek out a congregation of the same denomination as their congregation at home. This suggests that, whilst membership is always of a congregation, it is variably of a denomination. (Congregational belonging is regarded as the theoretical norm in some more congregational denominations; in Methodism the theory of belonging does not even refer to the congregation but to the class, a smaller group which is supposed to meet regularly.)

Berger has discovered that whether a denomination is secure or insecure determines to some extent what its structures will be, but what does *not* affect structures is precisely *which* denomination it is – and, indeed, the same bureaucratic structures can be found in the company of opposing theological positions (Berger 1969b: 139ff.). The suggestion that structures are not denomination-specific is backed up by the finding that all of the bureaucratic structures in American denominations mirror those found in commercial enterprises, and that all of the structures of European denominations mirror state structures (ibid.; Hinings 1979). Richard Brown (1973) charts the development of American denominations from associational congregations (which met psychological needs as well as pursuing charter goals) to local and then nonlocal associations (made possible by a professionalizing clergy with nonlocal connections) which continued to satisfy the need for a sense of identity (as, for example, 'Baptist', 'Methodist') and which were useful to ministers as they could use both local and nonlocal bureaucratic structures to bypass ideological conflict (Thompson 1968). It is this common history which has given birth to similar structures. Most British denominations were originally dissenting groups which either left the Church of England or were ejected from it, and a common history which began within an established church has given them all structures which reflect that origin.

Bureaucratic structures are a means of exercising power, usually through a hierarchically-ordered paid staff. Denominations and their office-holders sometimes find it hard to exercise the power they think is theirs because they experience resistance at the level of the congregation and the minister. There is a particular problem for the denomination: if it is the congregation which chooses a new minister (and now that many Church of England posts are advertised that church is moving in this direction), the only powers which the denomination retains are the power to ordain, the power to license to new posts (thus giving it a veto over appointments), and the power to abolish paid posts when they fall vacant, because such powers are normally constitutionally safeguarded to the Diocesan structures. There is very little scope here for strategic planning: hence the frequent frustration felt by Diocesan and other denominational authorities.

In order to understand the ways in which denominations behave, Chaves has suggested that they are 'dual structures', containing 'religious' and 'agency' structures. He employs this theory to understand conflict within denominations and also to explain why denominations have become so internally secularized: it is because their agency structures relate to the bureaucratic agency structures of secular organizations (Chaves 1993a, 1993b) and a process of isomorphism occurs as it always does when different organizations relate to each other. (Chaves also thinks that religious uncertainties are more stable than institutional ones, which is why denominations pay more attention to agency functions (Chaves 1998a). I disagree. Religious uncertainties are now highly *un*stable, and in many situations have collapsed into conceptual structures with few relationships with any other conceptual structures, thus secularizing the religious organization.) Just as Chaves has found agency and religious functions in denominations (that is, in their congregations and in the umbrella organizations), so Sharot has found both instrumental and expressive élites in synagogues, and that it is the instrumental élites which hold the power because instrumental goals are necessary to survival whereas expressive goals are not. Similarly, van Billoen finds that the pronouncements of the Roman Catholic curia are designed to keep the institution afloat rather than to propound uncomfortable truth, leading to a devaluing of truth-seeking and a crisis of authority which is making the institution more fragile, not less (van Billoen 1973).

What we see happening here is a complex mixture of normative and utilitarian compliance structures (and in some cases a coercive compliance structure too) applied to different aspects of the organization's work; we see both associational and bureaucratic structures side by side, along with everything in-between, including the ambiguous voluntary agency structure; and we see both traditional and bureaucratic authority-structures and sometimes the charismatic as well. It is these mixtures which make governing religious organizations so complex.

A particularly complex issue is the ordination of women. Some denominations ordain women as ministers, some do not. Chaves has discovered that the degree of centralization is what determines whether women are ordained, suggesting that the decision has little to do with a shortage of male clergy or with theological factors. Where women are not ordained it is because congregations have more power and a continuing traditional authority resists change, whereas in a more centralized denomination denominational leaders have more power and they are often more liberal-minded than congregation members are, which is probably why such denominations tend to ordain women (Chaves 1998b). (Where women ministers are not appointed to posts it is generally because a view has been taken that a woman would not enable the congregation to thrive. According to Lehman (1981), there is little or no theological element in the decision in most cases.)

More generally, the issue of whether power lies with the congregation or with denominational authorities is a complex one. Congregations which belong to the American Baptist Convention theoretically have power to control the umbrella body, but not in practice because leaders of the Convention, having no explicit power, exercise power through informal channels and thus in less accountable ways and in ways difficult for congregations to control (Harrison 1959). Generally, where a bureaucracy does not exist, professional clergy will develop one and exercise power through it; and, whilst the compliance structure is meant to be normative, it is in fact rather utilitarian.

Perhaps the most important connection between our bodies of theory is that denominations and their congregations employ different associational and bureaucratic structures to deal with different areas of the organization's life (they are dual structures), thus locating denominations and their congregations firmly within the ambiguous voluntary agency zone in Billis's diagram (see Figure 6.1).

Ecumenism

We have already discussed councils of churches as a type of religious organization. We now turn to what ecumenical relationships tell us about the governance of religious organizations.

'Ecumenism' is a broad term, meaning everything from congregations of different denominations talking to each other to two denominations merging into a single denomination. As costs rise and memberships drop, congregations and federations of congregations look towards ecumenism – that is, co-operation and sometimes merger – in order to solve their problems (Bolden 1985). They are thus doing what resource mobilization theory would lead us to believe they are likely to do. But whilst theological considerations will generally take second place to resource issues, they are still important, for we are, after all, discussing *religious* organizations. This suggests that, if co-operation and merger are theologically-driven issues for a stronger denomination in dialogue with a weaker one, then resource issues might be uppermost for the weaker partner (in fact if not in theory), whilst theological constraints might outweigh resource factors for the stronger party, particularly as resource reasons are rarely explicitly stated and theological reasons for and against merger usually are. This seems to be what has happened over a period of 30 years in relation to dialogue between the Methodist Church and the Church of England.

Heather employs Critical Discourse Analysis (a method which studies what is actually said and written in order to uncover presuppositions) to discuss denominations' and congregations' real ecumenical interests, and finds that people like to be with people like themselves, that employing a 'technology' of instruments to achieve the amalgamation of denominations tends to standardize religious discourse and thus to reduce its diversity, and therefore that denominational mergers are likely to cause fewer active members in total (Heather 2003). But one important element missing from Heather's language-based study is any sense that there can be at least as much diversity within a denomination as between denominations, so that to combine denominations would not necessarily reduce diversity – though it might do so as congregations near to each other were merged following a denominational merger. Neither is there any recognition that different types of congregation (including those within the same denomination) behave very differently. Over this issue, as over many issues we have tackled, the diversity between congregations matters.

Bolden (1988) finds that hierarchical denominations are more ecumenically active than less hierarchical ones. There might be reasons of congregational structure and attitude for this, as the less hierarchical denomination is likely to have more sectarian congregations than the more hierarchical ones – but the totally unecumenical, very hierarchical character of the Jehovah's Witnesses rather suggests that the level of hierarchical organization and the attitude to ecumenism are not directly related. It might simply be that the more associational, less bureaucratic congregations of less bureaucratic denominations are less likely to seek merger with other congregations, and there will therefore be no pressure from below to encourage denominational structures to pursue negotiations with other denominations. It is only those organizations firmly in the ambiguous voluntary agency category which are likely to behave bureaucratically about resources. More associational congregations are less likely to do so.

Clark finds that, at a congregational level, more 'cosmopolitan' people pursue ecumenical relationships and that more locally-oriented people don't, which means that a congregation will pursue ecumenical relationships only if cosmopolitan people are in control (Clark 1971) – and since more sectarian congregations are likely to contain more locally-oriented members, and more bureaucratic and liberal congregations are likely to contain more cosmopolitan people, this might be another reason why more hierarchical denominations are more likely to pursue ecumenical relationships. We thus have a link between rational decision-making, bureaucratic authority-structures and ecumenism: bureaucratic decision-making as opposed to the traditional authority-structures preferred by more locally-oriented people who are generally of a lower socio-economic class, who will be less likely to exercise bureaucratic power in other areas of their lives, and who will be less likely to have had their religious views relativized by contacts with a wide variety of alternative and explicitly-stated religious views. (The unecumenical approach of larger middle-class sectarian congregations does not conflict with this: if cosmopolitan people are fundamentalist in their belief-system and sectarian in their religious belonging then it is because they feel a need to build a defensive wall against the relativism which the secular world they know so well is trying to impose on them.)

Yinger suggests that, in the USA, Protestant denominations' activities are as much determined by the American way of life as by a religious tradition, that they therefore feel that they belong together, and that co-operation and merger thus seem natural. This is not true of Jews and Roman Catholics, who are less influenced by the prevailing culture (Yinger 1967b). The reason that Protestant congregations *are* influenced so heavily by the culture in which they are situated is their internal secularization: they have taken on secular values (largely through their 'agency' elements) and their religious distinctiveness, not being an agency matter, has failed to counteract the secularizing tendency. Thus, in this context, ecumenism is a result of secularization and both ecumenism and secularization have roots in the denomination's structures.

When ecumenical co-operation happens, clergy find themselves relating closely to clergy of other denominations, which changes their role sets and thus changes their organizations' options. Thus ecumenism becomes a self-reinforcing cycle (Koch and Johnson 1997). (There have been occasions when denominations have removed their clergy from ecumenical partnerships because they feared that they were becoming too like the clergy of other denominations and endangering their own denomination's distinctiveness.) The fact that some denominations consistently fail to build new ecumenical links does not contradict this notion of a self-reinforcing ecumenism. The Church of England is looking several ways ecumenically, with those clergy and congregations with relationships with Roman Catholic clergy and congregations being changed in that direction and those clergy and congregations with relationships with more Protestant or evangelical churches being changed in a rather different direction. Isomorphism thus occurs in opposed directions in different fairly autonomous parts of the same church-denomination and the result is an unecumenical isolation.

A fundamental element of our body of theory is that religious organizations are organizations and will to some extent behave like other organizations. During the 1970s there were two civil service trades unions. For several years running their national conferences voted for merger, but each time their executive committees failed to agree a plan – and so at the next national conferences decisions were once more taken to merge. The reason for this regular failure to merge appears to have been unwillingness on the part of some office-holders to contemplate losing their jobs. Eventually, severe resource constraints as civil service numbers dropped, and a long history of poaching of each others' members, led to merger as Unison, an aptly named new union. The same might be happening with denominations. Whatever the resource factors, and whatever the theological reasons *for* merger, organizational constraints might be preventing progress (Martin 1977: ch. 9).

But religious organizations are also *religious* organizations, and however secular they become there are still core values at stake, values which can come to seem particularly important elements of congregations' and individuals' self-identities when the organization is facing co-operation or a merger with an organization with values not quite the same. This can be a problem when it comes to joint social action, as different theological and ethical values might encourage or prevent different courses of action (Tamney and Johnson 1990); and a subsequent problem which involvement in joint action can bring for the denomination is that disquiet can affect the members of the denomination's congregations, thus causing the number attending to drop and financial difficulties to ensue (Wood 1972a). Such ethical and theological values can be a problem when it comes to mergers of churches, as for those doing the negotiating they can seem less of a problem than the theological and resource reasons for merger seem advantageous; but bodies making final decisions, if representative of members of the denomination's congregations, are often less liberal than those conducting the negotiations, and their traditional values can halt the process, surprising the negotiators (Turner 1972).

In 1960, Lee surveyed the ecumenical scene and thought that there was going to be rapid and far-reaching church unity (Lee 1960). He was wrong, and we can now begin to see why. In this particular field of the governance of religious organizations there is a plethora of factors at work, and we find ourselves referring to a variety of theoretical frameworks in order to understand what is going on. This suggests that there will be no one trend, and that we shall continue to see a rather chaotic scene, the direction of which it will be impossible to predict.

The Management of Change

Much of the research literature on the management of change in religious organizations is about religious orders. Coghlan has found that many religious orders formulate strategy and mission statements, that they study their resources and the needs which they might meet, that they watch their environments for possible changes to which they will need to react, and that they create, carry out and review strategies, in pursuit of which they communicate with, reward and motivate the order's members (Coghlan 1987). Here are organizations which can behave like tightly governed bureaucracies, because that is what they are. But they are not all the same. Campbell-Jones has discovered that in one religious order, in which offices are regularly rotated, change is constant and appropriate, but that in another a new charismatic leader was needed to provoke radical and necessary change (Campbell-Jones 1979). The reason is probably that one order was behaving like a bureaucracy, asking who was the most appropriate person for each task at any given time, whereas the other was operating within a traditional authority-structure – and in such a structure change is difficult until a charismatic leader effectively forms a new organization but with most of the same people as the old one. Fay (1978) has found that when such change occurs in the context of authoritarian, traditional and nonrational structures, members of the order can experience severe disorientation unless they are committed to the reformed practices or have a high degree of moral autonomy. Those who remain disorientated are those whose organization has been taken from them but who have not in practice joined the new one; those who support the new practices have joined the new organization and are members of it; and the morally autonomous have each become their own organization, even if they live in the same building as the religious order.

Looking at change more generally, Crittenden has shown that religious organizations don't need complete strategic planning packages in order to create appropriate change: individual elements will often do the job (Crittenden et al. 1988). This is probably because the bureaucratic structures are already largely in place, and there is already a fairly utilitarian compliance structure; it's just that some traditional authority-structures and normative compliance structures are preventing change. New bureaucratic structures which bypass the remaining traditional and normative structures can unblock the process. Just as religious orders are both community (*Gemeinschaft*) and bureaucracy (*Gesellschaft*) (with the Jesuits at the most bureaucratic end of the spectrum), and just as the bureaucratic and associational elements can reinforce each other, particularly in the context of a religious tradition (O'Connell 1971), so other religious organizations are always in fact mixtures of the two, with elements of governance structures relating to both the community and the bureaucratic aspects and to the related charismatic/traditional and bureaucratic authority structures. This means that change must be brought about openly, in relation to the organization's charter goals, and in relation to clear and agreed goals related to a changing environment if all parts of the organization are to be involved in the process of change and the different structures are to remain coherent (as has recently happened in the Mothers' Union; see Grant 2001). This co-ordinating task is at the heart of the successful governance of religious organizations.

The Church of England

Returning to the Church of England: one issue where change has been highly unsuccessful is in the establishment of team ministries. These were a creation of the 1960s and were intended to replace the incumbent with the freehold by teams of clergy serving groups of congregations in larger parishes. The largest one ever attempted was in Sunderland, and covered the whole city.

But it hasn't worked. Most teams operate as groups of separate parishes (as the team ministry I serve in East Greenwich does), fall apart in acrimony, or suffer long-term, low-level conflict. The reason is that traditional and quasi-bureaucratic structures are operating in the same parts of the organization and because the church's core theological values have been ignored.

One member of the clergy team is called a Team Rector and the others are Team Vicars, and they all have fixed-term contracts, giving a quasi-bureaucratic structure: but it is *quasi*-bureaucratic because there are no specified roles attached to the posts, because there is no specified accountability of the Team Vicars to the Team Rector, and because all of the post-holders are told that they are of incumbent status, thus preserving to each of them their traditional authority and giving the team and its environment a statement of the priests' equality with each other – that is, *Gemeinschaft* (community) rather than *Gesellschaft* (bureaucracy). The Team Rector might feel that by virtue of their job title they are expected to manage the Team Vicars. The Team Vicars might think that they are of equal status with the Rector. Conflict is inevitable unless the Rector chooses not to behave as a line manager in a bureaucracy.

The Church of England is a church (though one becoming a denomination). Thus, the parish's population is the basic reality to which it addresses itself; the congregation represents that wider community, often in fact regarding itself as the active spiritual aspect of the parish as a whole; and the incumbent serves as pastor to both community and congregation. The team ministry structure turns this theological reality upside down by starting with the team of clergy, organizing the congregations around the clergy (often with the Rector imposing a pattern of worship which *doesn't* ensure that all church buildings are open on Sundays and major festivals), and losing the link between the congregation and the geographical parish because the parish boundaries are abolished. Beveridge is partly right to say that the team ministry model has been imported from secular structures (Beveridge 1971): only partly right because some traditional elements remain. The motive for the legislation establishing team ministries seems to have been to give to senior clergy a career structure and to make the best use of the clergy's differing talents, the idea being that each priest would use their particular gifts across the whole team parish. These were laudable aims. But the Church of England is not only a religious organization with traditional as well as bureaucratic authority structures, it is also a church: an open-boundaried organization, community as well as bureaucracy, the spiritual aspect of the wider community as well as a congregation, and within which normative and utilitarian compliance structures operate – which is why Team Rectors who attempt to operate coercive compliance structures experience fierce and public resistance. But such internal problems are not the major issue. Benson has found that bureaucratizing a church is likely to prevent it from integrating with the world around it (Benson and Dorsett 1971). Team ministries make the team of clergy the centre of attention (for with team ministries the parish ceases to be 'the parish of x' and becomes 'the Team Ministry of x') and thus draw the church's focus away from where it belongs, with the geographical parish and its people, to concentrate instead on its clergy – who are now chaplains to congregations rather than pastors to communities. Thus team ministries have become a seriously secularizing influence in the church.

Another longer-standing problem, to which we have already referred and which stems from the same root, is that in a Church of England parish the priest is both a paid staff member and the chair of the Parochial Church Council (PCC). In their role as priest, the priests exercise traditional authority; in their role as paid servant of the Diocese they exercise bureaucratic control; and in their role as chair of the PCC they exercise a second bureaucratic role. Thus, most of the power in the parish ends up in the priest's hands, and at the same time the benefits of bureaucracy are lost because the bureaucratic structure is mixed up with the traditional authority-structure rather than the two authority types being able to operate effectively in different areas of the organization's life: traditional authority in the religious sphere and bureaucratic authority in the agency sphere. To remove the priest from the chair of the PCC would do no end of good for both the congregation's expressive activity and its instrumental activity; and the same would go for removing the Bishop from the chair of the Diocesan Synod (and from appointments processes) and for removing the Archbishops from the chair of General Synod.

A third problem, and perhaps one more important than all the others put together, is the need to protect children from paedophiles working as clergy or church youth leaders or in similar positions of trust. For the first time it is becoming clear that here is an issue over which the clergy *must* be made to conform to a set of norms in relation to behaviour – so a coercive compliance structure is needed for the first time, and this can only be provided with a bureaucratic structure within which the priest has a line manager who can demand compliance under threat of dismissal. This is not the role for the pastoral figure, nor for traditional authority-structures, nor for normative compliance structures, so denominations, sects and churches are going to have to construct bureaucratic structures, preferably related to this issue alone (though maybe to one or two other important behavioural issues). What must *not* be allowed to happen is the wholesale reshaping of authority-structures in a bureaucratic direction, and in this respect the denominations are right to resist attempts to turn their clergy into bureaucratically-controlled employees. The argument of this chapter suggests that that would be the end of religious organizations.

The South London Industrial Mission

SLIM offers us another example of multiple roles (cf. Cameron 1999 on multiple roles in religious organizations), with the Senior Chaplain being one chaplain amongst others, the Rector of the parish in which the mission has its physical base, and the 'senior chaplain' (with the meaning of this undefined) – but at least in this case he is not the chair of the board of directors as well. There is similar confusion, as we have seen, over the members' roles: whilst they *are* now members in the legal sense (as the organization is now a company limited by guarantee and paid-up members vote for the board), they are not usually members in any other sense. It is the chaplains who have wielded traditional and professional authority (of which more later), and it is the chaplains' team which has been the normal forum for decision-making in relation to the issues faced by SLIM and its work. It will be interesting to watch what happens now that there is no chaplains' team. Either the Mission will die, or it will become a member-led organization with organizational substance rather than merely organizational forms.

Conclusions

Beyer and Nutzinger (1993) have uncovered a distinct contrast between religious organizations' staff's experience of hierarchical management styles and the expressed ideal of a co-operative style. This should be no surprise, for religious organizations are both *Gemeinschaft* (community) and *Gesellschaft* (bureaucracy). At local level they are more community than bureaucracy, but at regional or national level they might be more bureaucracy than community: so at local level a 'principled eclecticism' is required. Roberts suggests that this approach is needed throughout the Church of England, rather than what he calls 'the Tupperware Party solution to the threat of secularization' (Roberts 2002: 186), and given that the heart of the Church is its parishes, it would certainly be better to err on the side of regarding the Church as a whole as community than to err on the side of regarding it as a bureaucracy, however many bureaucratic characteristics it might have collected during the past forty years or so. To recognize the different structures at work in an organization, and to aim at best practice in *all* of them (Zaleski and Zech 1997) would go a long way towards righting many of the wrongs done by religious organizations. What is essential is that methods believed to be appropriate at one level of an organization should not be assumed to be appropriate at another. What is also essential is that we recognize that governance of complex religious organizations is never going to be easy, for what constitutions exist are generally implied rather than explicit, there are different authority and compliance structures at work at the same time, change is threatening (because managing change in a complex organization is complex), and denial and avoidance set in; and in such a situation absence of communication is inevitable and subgroups emerge and compete for resources. At the same time, the needs of neither the members nor the organization are met, and the clergy's multiple roles become a source of conflict (Cameron 2001; Harris 1998a: 174).

Organizations of all religious traditions (Davis 1982) suffer from both internal and external conflict. To some extent this is a sign of health, as without it we would know that the organization was dead (Ammerman et al. 1997); but handling conflict is a necessary task for governance structures, because if it is not handled well then the organization will damage its members, it will not fulfil its purposes, and it might break up (though this last result of conflict, if it results in the formation of new organizations, should not necessarily be regarded as a disaster). Handling conflict is challenging because it requires the exploration of all of the structures at work in the organization.

Williams' research on a theological college (Williams 1984; 1998) explores the normative and utilitarian compliance structures at work, the differences between staff and student expectations, the dilemmas the management faces as it negotiates a changing resource base, the college's multiple constituencies, and organizational precariousness (as the college is being used as a pawn in others' conflicts) – and this is a fairly simple organization. Congregations, and their relationships with their federations, communities, and other congregations, are extremely complex organizations, as are their federations, and as are agencies such as SLIM, related as they are to religious traditions, to federations of congregations and to secular institutions. An interesting question on which some future research effort ought to be expended is whether the similarities and differences between governance structures are more to do with the similarities and differences of their religious traditions or more to do with presuppositions about governance structures to be found in the social contexts in which they are set. Knoke's study of collective action organizations in the USA suggests that it is the latter (Knoke 1990: 160), but he does not include religious and faith-based organizations in his study. It would be interesting to know whether religious organizations are different from other types of organizations in this respect.

The management of change and of conflict in these organizations (not to mention the management of failure such as that which the Jehovah's Witnesses faced and successfully negotiated when the world didn't end in 1975; Zygmunt 1977) is a complex business which is going to employ a wide range of theories if it is to stand any chance of success. We have outlined and employed a variety of theories, and there are more (Zech (1998) lists rational choice theory;

bounded rationality theory; the new institutionalism, (the 'open systems' theory which we have employed); and organized anarchy theory). As religious organizations adapt to new circumstances at the same time as remaining true to their charter goals (Harris 1998a), the theories we need will change and the issues to which we need to apply them will also change; and at all times we shall need good governance: 'The objective is not harmony based on [the] powerlessness [of the managed]. It is the creation of a civic order, guided by the ideals of community, within which the terms of co-operation can be negotiated and decisions can be monitored, criticized, and changed' (Selznick 1992: 318).

References

Ammerman, Nancy Tatom, Farnsley II, Arthur E. et al. (1997), *Congregation and Community*, New Brunswick, New Jersey: Rutgers University Press

Anderson, William H. (1971), 'The Local Congregation as a Subculture', *Social Compass*, **18** (2), 287–91

Archbishops' Commission (1995), *Working as One Body: The Report of the Archbishops' Commission on the Organisation of the Church of England* [The Turnbull Report], London: Church House Publishing

Beckford, James A. (1973), 'Religious Organization: A Trend Report', *Current Sociology*, **21** (2), 7–170

Benson, J. Kenneth and Dorsett, James H. (1971), 'Toward a Theory of Religious Organizations', *Journal for the Scientific Study of Religion*, **10** (2), 139–51

Berger, Peter (1969b), *The Sacred Canopy*, New York: Doubleday

Beveridge, W.E. (1971), *Managing the Church*, London: SCM Press

Beyer, Heinrich and Nutzinger, Hans G. (1993), 'Hierarchy or Co-operation: Labour–Management Relations in Church Institutions', *Voluntas*, **14** (1), 55–72

Billis, David (1993), *Organizing Public and Voluntary Agencies*, London and New York: Routledge

Bolden, Dean A. (1985), 'Organizational Characteristics of Ecumenically Active Denominations', *Sociological Analysis*, **46** (3), 261–74

Bolden, Dean A. (1988), 'Formal Church Polity and Ecumenical Activity', *Sociological Analysis*, **49** (3), 293–303

Brown, Desmond (1977), 'Dilemmas of Deinstitutionalization', *Sociological Analysis*, **38** (2), 140–44

Brown, Richard (1973), 'The Emergence of Voluntary Associations in Massachusetts, 1760 to 1830', *Journal of Voluntary Action Research*, **2** (2), April, 64–73

Cameron, Helen (1999), 'Are members volunteers? An exploration of the concept of membership drawing upon studies of the local church', *Voluntary Action*, **1** (2), Spring, 53–66

Cameron, Helen (2001), 'A perspective from the study of religious organisations', in Anheier, Helmut K. (ed.), *Organisational Theory and the Non-profit Form*, London: Centre for Civil Society, London School of Economics, report no. 2

Campbell-Jones, Suzanne (1979), *In Habit: An anthropological study of working nuns*, London and Boston: Faber and Faber

Cantrell, Randolph L., Krile, James F. and Donohue, George A. (1983), 'Parish Autonomy: Measuring Denominational Differences', *Journal for the Scientific Study of Religion*, **22** (3), 276–87

Chapin, F.S. and Tsouderos, J.E. (1956), 'The Formalisation Process in Voluntary Associations', *Social Forces*, **34** (4), May, 342–4

Chaves, Mark (1993a), 'Denominations as Dual Structures: An Organizational Analysis', *Sociology of Religion*, **54** (2), 147–69

Chaves, Mark (1993b), 'Intraorganizational Power and Internal Secularization in Protestant Denominations', *American Journal of Sociology*, **99** (1), July, 1–48

Chaves, Mark (1998a), 'Denominations as Dual Structures: An Organizational Analysis', in Demerath III, N.J., Hall, Peter Dobkin, Schmitt, Terry and Williams, Rhys H. (eds), *Sacred Companies: Organizational Aspects of Religion and Religious Aspects of Organizations*, New York and Oxford: Oxford University Press, pp. 175ff.

Chaves, Mark (1998b), *Ordaining Women: Culture and Conflict in Religious Organizations*, Cambridge, Massachusetts: Harvard University Press

Clark, David B. (1971), 'Local and Cosmopolitan Aspects of Religious Activity in a Northern Suburb: Processes of Change', in Martin, David (ed.), *A Sociological Yearbook of Religion in Britain*, vol. IV, London: Student Christian Movement, pp. 141ff.

Coghlan, David (1987), 'Corporate Strategy in Catholic Religious Orders', *Long Range Planning*, **20** (1), 1987, 44–51

Conrad, Charles (1988), 'Identity, Structure and Communicative Action in Church Decision-Making', *Journal for the Scientific Study of Religion*, **27** (3), 345–61

Crittenden, William E., Crittenden, Vicky L. and Hunt, Tammy G. (1988), 'Planning and Stakeholder Satisfaction in Religious Organizations', *Journal of Voluntary Action Research*, **17** (2), April–June, 60–73

Davis, J. (ed.) (1982), *Religious Organization and Religious Experience*, London: Academic Press

Etzioni, Amitai (1980), 'Compliance Structures', in Etzioni, Amitai and Lehman, E. (eds) (1980), *A Sociological Reader on Complex Organisations*, 3rd edn: Austin, Texas: Holt, Reinhart and Winston, pp. 87ff.

Fay, Leo F. (1978), 'Differential Anomic Responses in a Religious Community', *Sociological Analysis*, **39** (1), Spring, 62–76

Gill, Robin and Burke, Derek (1996), *Strategic Church Leadership*, London: SPCK

Grant, Jane W. (2001), 'Governance, Continuity and Change in the Organised Women's Movement', unpublished PhD thesis, University of Kent

Harris, C.C. (1969), 'Reform in a Normative Organization', *Sociological Review*, **17** (2), July, 167–85.

Harris, Margaret (1998a), *Organizing God's Work: Challenges for Churches and Synagogues*, London: Macmillan

Harrison, Paul M. (1959), *Authority and Power in the Free Church Tradition: A Social Case Study of the American Baptist Convention*, London and Amsterdam: Feffer and Simons

Heather, Noel (2003), 'Discourse Ecumenism: Doin' It Long and Doin' It Large', *Theology*, **106** (830), March/April, 89–98

Hinings, C. (1979), 'Continuities in the Study of Organizations: Churches and Local Government', in Lammers, C.J. and Hickson, D.J. (eds.), *Organizations Alike and Unlike: International and Interinstitutional Studies in the Sociology of Organizations*, London and Boston: Routledge and Kegan Paul

Hinings, C. Robin and Foster, Bruce D. (1973), 'The Organization Structure of Churches: A Preliminary Model', *Sociology*, **7** (1), 93–106

Kavagy, Conrad L. (1992), 'Social Action, Evangelism, and Ecumenism: The Impact of Community, Theological and Structural Variables', *Review of Religious Research*, **34** (1), 34–50

Kniss, Fed and Chaves, Mark (1995), 'Analyzing Interdenominational Conflict: New Directions', *Journal for the Scientific Study of Religion*, **34** (2), 172–85

Knoke, David (1990), *Organizing for Political Action: The Political Economies of Associations*, New York: Aldine de Gruyter

Koch, Jerome R. and Johnson, D. Paul (1997), 'The Ecumenical Outreach Coalition: A Case Study of Converging Interests and Network Formation for Church and Community Co-operation', *Nonprofit and Voluntary Sector Quarterly*, **26** (3), September, 343–58

Lee, Robert (1960), *The Social Sources of Church Unity: An Interpretation of Unitive Movements in American Protestantism*, New York: Abingdon Press

Lehman Jr., Edward C. (1981), 'Organisational Resistance to Women in Ministry', *Sociological Analysis*, **42** (2), 101–18

Martin, David (1977), *Reflections on Sociology and Theology*, Oxford: Clarendon Press

Mathisen, James A. (1987), 'Thomas O'Dea's Dilemmas of Institutionalization: A Case Study and Re-evaluation after Twenty-five Years', *Sociological Analysis*, **47** (4), 302–18

Miller, Maureen (1983), 'From Ancient to Modern Organization', *Administration and Society*, **15** (3), November, 275–93

Nelson, John J. and Hiller, Harry H. (1980), 'Norms of Verbalization and the Decision Making Process of Religious Organizations', *Journal for the Scientific Study of Religion*, **20** (2), 173–80

O'Connell, John J. (1971), 'The Integration and Alienation of Religious to Religious Orders', *Social Compass*, **18** (1), 65–84

O'Dea, Thomas F. (1967), 'Five Dilemmas in the Institutionalization of Religion', in Knudten, Richard D. (ed.), *The Sociology of Religion*, New York: Appleton-Century-Crofts, pp. 285ff.

Poloma, Margaret M. (1997), 'The "Toronto Blessing": Charisma, Institutionalization and Revival', *Journal for the Scientific Study of Religion*, **36** (2), 257–71

Roberts, Richard H. (2002), *Religion, Theology and the Human Sciences*, Cambridge: Cambridge University Press

Selznick, Philip (1992), *The Moral Commonwealth: Social Theory and the Promise of Community*, Berkeley: University of California Press

Sharot, Stephen, (1977), 'Instrumental and Expressive Élites in a Religious Organization', *Archives des Sciences Sociales des Religions*, **43** (1), 141–55

Takayama, K. Peter (1975), 'Formal Polity and Change of Structure: Denominational Assemblies', *Sociological Analysis*, **36** (1), Spring, 17–28

Tamney, Joseph B. and Johnson, D. (1990), 'Religious Diversity and Ecumenical Social Action', *Review of Religious Research*, **32** (1), 16–26

Thompson, Kenneth (1968), 'Bureaucracy and the Church', in Martin, David (ed.), *A Sociological Yearbook of Religion in Britain*, vol. I, London: Student Christian Movement, pp. 32ff.

Torry, Malcolm (1990), 'The Practice and Theology of the South London Industrial Mission', unpublished PhD thesis, University of London

Turner, Bryan S. (1972), 'The Sociological Explanation of Ecumenicalism', in Mitton, C.L. (ed.), *The Social Sciences and the Churches*, Edinburgh: T. and T. Clark, pp. 233ff.

van Billoen, Etienne (1973), 'Le Modèle d'Authorité dans l'Eglise,' *Social Compass*, **20** (3), 405–17

Weber, Max (1922), 'The Three Types of Legitimate Rule', in Etzioni, Amitai and Lehman, E. (eds) (1980), *A Sociological Reader on Complex Organisations*, 3rd edn, Austin, Texas: Holt, Reinhart and Winston

Weber, Max (1963), *The Sociology of Religion*, Boston: Beacon Press

Williams, Rhys H. (1994), 'Organizational Change in Theological Schools: Dilemmas of Ideology and Resources', *Nonprofit and Voluntary Sector Quarterly*, **23** (2), Summer, 123–37

Williams, Rhys H. (1998), 'Organizational Change in Theological Schools: Dilemmas of Ideology and Resources', in Demerath III, N.J., Hall, Peter Dobkin, Schmitt, Terry and Williams, Rhys H. (eds), *Sacred Companies: Organizational Aspects of Religion and Religious Aspects of Organizations*, New York and Oxford: Oxford University Press, pp. 208ff.

Williams, Rhys H. and Demerath III, N.J. (1998), 'Cultural Power: How Underdog Religious and Nonreligious Movements Triumph Against Structural Odds', in Demerath III, N.J., Hall, Peter Dobkin, Schmitt, Terry and Williams, Rhys H. (eds), *Sacred Companies: Organizational Aspects of Religion and Religious Aspects of Organizations*, New York and Oxford: Oxford University Press, pp. 364ff.

Winter, Gibson (1961), *The Suburban Captivity of the Churches: An Analysis of Protestant Responsibility in the Expanding Metropolis*, New York: Doubleday

Wood, James R. (1972a), 'Unanticipated Consequences of Organizational Coalitions: Ecumenical Co-operation and Civil Rights Policy', *Social Forces*, **50** (4), June, 512–21

Yinger, J. Milton (1967b), 'Religion and Society: Problems of Integration and Pluralism among the Privileged', in Knudten, Richard D. (ed.), *The Sociology of Religion*, Appleton-Century-Crofts, New York, pp. 496ff.

Zaleski, Peter A. and Zech, Charles E. (1997), 'Efficiency in Religious Organizations', *Nonprofit Management and Leadership*, **8** (1), Fall, 3–18

Zech, Charles E. (1998), 'Four Economic Models of Organization Applied to Religious Congregations', in Demerath III, N.J., Hall, Peter Dobkin, Schmitt, Terry and Williams, Rhys H. (eds), *Sacred Companies: Organizational Aspects of Religion and Religious Aspects of Organizations*, New York and Oxford: Oxford University Press, pp. 256ff.

Zygmunt, Joseph F. (1977), 'Jehovah's Witnesses in the USA 1942–1976', *Social Compass*, **24** (1), 45–7

CHAPTER 7

Faith-Based Organizations

A faith-based organization is an organization, the main purpose of which is not religion, but which is related in some way to a religious organization or tradition. Faith-based organizations thus lie between religious organizations and secular organizations. This means that much which has been said about religious organizations will be applicable to faith-based organizations, and that much which has been said about voluntary organizations, commercial organizations and public agencies will also be of relevance.

The term 'faith-based organization' covers an enormously varied field: tiny community development and youth projects run by volunteers from a congregation with the help of a single paid worker; church schools; denomination-founded housing associations; large non-governmental organizations such as Christian Aid, CAFOD, the Red Cross, and the Red Crescent; Jewish elderly care homes; the Children's Society and NCH (founded by the Church of England and the Methodist Church respectively) – and thousands more. They were all differently founded (often by a group of individuals who were members of a particular denomination, more rarely by representative structures of the denomination itself); they have diverse purposes; they relate in different ways to religious traditions and to religious organizations; some are membership organizations, some are service organizations, and some are self-help groups (Blau et al. 1996; Davidson and Koch 1998); and they all relate to different secular organizations.

Recent research in the USA has shown just how broad the spectrum of faith-based organizations is. Sider and Unruh (2004) suggest that there are five types of faith-based organization (though they recognize that the categories are points along a spectrum and that many organizations fall between the categories):

1   Faith-permeated
2   Faith-centred
3   Faith-affiliated
4   Faith-background
5   Faith-secular partnership.

(They also add a sixth type, the 'secular' organization – and probably ought therefore to have added a seventh: the 'religious' organization.)

The organizational and programme characteristics of the different types of organization are tabulated (though again the authors recognize complexity, for it is not easy to measure such characteristics, and what an organization writes about itself is not necessarily what's really happening). Conclusions are drawn for public policy in the USA, and in particular the conclusion that the debate should be about what kinds of faith-based organization should be publicly funded and not about *whether* faith-based organizations should be funded from taxation. This debate is not such a live one in the UK, but where the funding and activity of faith-based organizations is discussed a categorization like that of Sider and Unruh could be helpful.

The diverse nature of faith-based organizations and of their activity means that the study of a faith-based organization must be precisely that: study of that particular faith-based organization.

So what this chapter does *not* offer is a body of theory to which someone managing a faith-based organization might wish to refer. What is always required is a study of the particular organization to discover what kind of organization it is. But what *is* offered is a list of four issues which someone managing a faith-based organization might wish to consider as they seek solutions to management problems.

1   First of all, *is* it a faith-based organization? Netting's view is that if an organization *calls* itself a faith-based organization then it is one (Netting 1984). This is certainly a good place to start, for an organization which states a connection to a religious tradition or to a religious organization is likely to have that connection, even if it isn't quite as strong as a respondent might suggest. But the researcher will need to test out whether there are in fact connections between the organization and a religious tradition or a religious organization in terms of structures, personnel, goals, or values, and not simply connections through one or two individuals who happen to be involved both in a congregation and in the organization under review. If the *only* connection is that the founders were members of a religious organization, then it might not still be a faith-based organization (though it will still be influenced by its founders); and if the trustees *say* that there is a live connection with a religious tradition when in fact the organization is indistinguishable from secular organizations in the same field, then it is not a faith-based organization (ibid.). (This last is the case with a number of housing associations whose trustees think they are something they are not.)

If an organization has a wide diversity of stakeholders then it will exhibit a wide diversity of functions and characteristics. If one of the stakeholders is a religious tradition or organization, then the organization might have one or two religious aspects in the midst of a large number of secular ones (Davidson and Koch 1998). It is still a faith-based organization.

Unlike religious organizations, which are generally not commercial ventures, faith-based organizations might well be commercial organizations. Traidcraft and Tearfund (both fair-trade organizations) are commercial organizations and both are faith-based organizations; and clerical outfitters and religious bookshops are faith-based organizations too. In this case the organization's aim might be profit for shareholders, or it might be the social aims or other purposes of a founding religious organization or individual (Le Barbera 1991); but whatever the aim, research literature on commercial organizations will be as helpful as that on religious organizations (Byrd 1997). Similarly, research literature on schools in general will aid the management of a church school.

2   Once we have decided that an organization *is* a faith-based organization, we can ask how it evolves and how it functions; and we shall find helpful the literature on how other types of organization behave as well as the small amount of literature on how faith-based organizations evolve. For instance, Stone and Wood (1997) find that faith-based service-providers have varied governance structures, with the particular type depending largely on the structure of the founding religious organization. The normal process is then for the purposes and the structures to become more like those in secular organizations in the same field (ibid.), the extent to which this happens depending on the pool of board members: that is, if the board can continue to find new members firmly related to the religious tradition then the secularization process will be slower (Swartz 1998). (It will be *less* slow if the same board members remain for long periods, because they tend to become secularized along with the organization.)

A particularly useful case study is that of an American YMCA (Young Men's Christian Association) which successfully evolved and survived by broadening its goals, retaining local autonomy, unrestricting its clientele, recruiting professional staff with flexible ideologies, and becoming responsive to its users. It became less of an evangelistic organization and more of a service provider, but because the evolution remained in touch both with the organization's original religious goals (though with an altered emphasis), and also with changing circumstances, it still retains a connection with its religious tradition and is still alive and well – at least, it was in 1970 (Zald and Denton 1963; Zald 1970). (And this is a problem: much of the research literature in the field is out of date and thus of questionable relevance in a very different world; and much of the literature is American, which makes it difficult to apply to a more secular United Kingdom.)

3   An important question to ask of any faith-based organization is what *tensions* it experiences.

Jeavons and Cnaan (1997) have found that tensions tend to rise as the organization grows. The reason for this is that growing organizations are often taking on professional staff who have links with other organizations in the same field and thus draw the organization towards more secular ideologies and away from the specifically religious goals of the organization's founders: and frequent lack of clarity as to how the organization relates to the religious tradition or religious organization can increase those tensions (La Barbera 1991). (This process occurred in a particularly clear way in the Carr-Gomm Housing Association in South London during the early 1990s.)

There are *particular* tensions for organizations on the boundary between religious organizations and faith-based organizations (that is, organizations where it is not clear what the main purpose is). The South London Industrial Mission has at times been mainly a service organization for industry and other institutions with little connection with the Christian tradition, and at other times it has been mainly a Christian mission with explicit evangelistic goals; and a theological college has both educational and religious purposes (especially now that many of them take students who have no intention of being ordained into the ministry of any denomination). Williams' study of theological colleges finds tensions related to diverse expectations amongst students and staff, and to a combination of normative and utilitarian compliance structures operating in the same areas of the institution (Williams 1994). These tensions occur in religious organizations, but in faith-based organizations they might be greater because the field of possible expectations is extended into the field of secular expectations, and a religion-related normative compliance structure, if applied to secular expectations, will conflict with the utilitarian or coercive compliance structures which would normally operate amongst them.

Particular tensions can be experienced between the faith-based organization and any religious organization to which it remains attached, especially as denominations become more isolated from a more secular society and as some parts of them become more sectarian as a result. Increasing tensions in such a relationship will often result in a loosening of the bond, which has implications for the denomination because it will then have fewer links into the outside world, fewer opportunities to train staff in secular disciplines and in relating to a wider world, and less possibility of expressing its faith in practical terms. Recruitment to the ministry is likely to suffer as the denomination has fewer links into wider society; and within the denomination spiritual growth is likely to become more important than institutional expression of faith – and is not the modern concern with spirituality a sign of a deepening secularization?

4   A fourth and rather different question which we might want to ask concerns the extent to which commercial and other organizations are becoming like faith-based organizations. The organization MODEM (Managerial and Organizational Disciplines for the Enhancement of Ministry) studies not only what religious organizations might learn from management practices elsewhere, but also what other organizations might learn from religious and faith-based organizations; and there is a slowly growing 'spirituality at work' movement which concerns itself with organizations and not just with the

individuals within them. Bromiley (1998) has identified commercial organizations behaving as religious organizations in terms of preserving and developing a tradition and integrating the different parts of its employees' lives. Such an organization is not a religious organization, but it is a sort of faith-based organization. Faith-based organizations employ a variety of assets not normally available to other organizations, for instance, committed staff and constituents; but they also experience the religious tradition as a constraint and as a source of conflict (La Barbera 1992). Whether other organizations can successfully employ the assets without experiencing the accompanying tension is a matter for further research.

And it is further research which is clearly needed across the whole field of faith-based organizations (Sider and Unruh, 2004: 131ff.), for there is remarkably little of it.

References

Blau, Judith R., Heying, Charles and Feinberg, Joseph R. (1996), 'Second-order Cultural Effects of Civil Rights on Southern Nonprofit Organizations: The Atlanta YMCAs', *Nonprofit and Voluntary Sector Quarterly*, **25** (2), June, 174–89

Bromiley, David G. (1998), 'Transformative Movement and Quasi-Religious Corporations: The Case of Amway', in Demerath III, N.J., Hall, Peter Dobkin, Schmitt, Terry and Williams, Rhys H. (eds), *Sacred Companies: Organizational Aspects of Religion and Religious Aspects of Organizations*, New York and Oxford: Oxford University Press, pp. 349ff.

Byrd, Michael (1997), 'Determining Frames of Reference for Religiously Based Organization: A Case of Neo-Alinsky Efforts to Mobilize Congregational Resources', *Nonprofit and Voluntary Sector Quarterly*, **26** (s), s122–88

Davidson, James D. and Koch, Jerome R. (1998), 'Beyond Mutual and Public Benefits: The Inward and Outward Orientations of Non-Profit Organizations', in Demerath III, N.J., Hall, Peter Dobkin, Schmitt, Terry and Williams, Rhys H. (eds), *Sacred Companies: Organizational Aspects of Religion and Religious Aspects of Organizations*, New York and Oxford: Oxford University Press, pp. 292ff.

Jeavons, Thomas H. and Cnaan, Ram A. (1997), 'The Formation, Transitions and Evolution of Small Religious Organizations', *Nonprofit and Voluntary Sector Quarterly*, **26** (s), s62–84

La Barbera, Priscilla A. (1991), 'Commercial Ventures of Religious Organizations', *Nonprofit Management and Leadership*, **1** (3), Spring, 217–34

La Barbera, Priscilla A. (1992), 'Enterprise in Religious-Based Organizations', *Nonprofit and Voluntary Sector Quarterly*, **21** (1), Spring, 51–67

Netting, F. Ellen (1984), 'Church-related Agencies and Social Welfare', *Social Service Review*, **58** (3), 404–20

Sider, Ronald J. and Unruh, Heidi Rolland (2004), 'Typology of Religious Characteristics of Social Service and Educational Organizations and Programs', *Nonprofit and Voluntary Sector Quarterly*, **33** (1), March, 109–34

Stone, Melissa M. and Wood, Miriam M. (1997), 'Governance and the Small, Religiously Affiliated Social Service Provider', *Nonprofit and Voluntary Sector Quarterly*, **26** (s), s44–61

Swartz, David (1998), 'Secularization, Religion, and Isomorphism: A Study of Large Nonprofit Hospital Trustees', in Demerath III, N.J., Hall, Peter Dobkin, Schmitt, Terry and Williams,

Rhys H. (eds), *Sacred Companies: Organizational Aspects of Religion and Religious Aspects of Organizations*, Oxford and New York: Oxford University Press, pp. 323ff.

Williams, Rhys H. (1994), 'Organizational Change in Theological Schools: Dilemmas of Ideology and Resources', *Nonprofit and Voluntary Sector Quarterly*, **23** (2), Summer, 123–37

Wittberg, Patricia (2000), 'Called to Service: The Changing Institutional Identities of American Denominations', *Nonprofit and Voluntary Sector Quarterly*, **29** (3), 357–76

Zald, Mayer N. (1970), *Organizational Change: The Political Economy of the YMCA*, Chicago and London: University of Chicago Press

Zald, Mayer N. and Denton, Patricia (1963) 'From Evangelism to General Service', *Administrative Science Quarterly*, **8** (2), September, 214–34

CHAPTER 8

Membership in Religious Organizations

Lots of organizations have memberships. A fishing club will have members who pay a subscription and who have the right to elect the committee which manages the club's affairs. The Automobile Association has members who pay differing amounts for differing levels of service. The board of trustees of a charity has members who manage the charity's affairs and elect new trustees. In all of these cases membership is clearly defined both in the sense that it carries defined rights and responsibilities and in the sense that it is clear who is a member and who is not. But in religious organizations things are rarely so clear, and in order to discover what membership might mean in a religious organization I shall ask some questions of the research literature and then study two particular organizations: again, the South London Industrial Mission and the Church of England.

In relation to the literature, I shall ask what the concept of membership means when related to congregations, what membership's characteristics are, what members' motives for membership might be, and finally whether there is any difference between members and volunteers in religious organizations.

First of all: the definition of congregational membership: Bruce (1995: 44) discusses the way in which different methods of gathering statistics reveal different definitions of membership. Church membership is here defined in terms of church attendance. Ammerman et al. (1997) discusses 'membership growth' amongst religious organizations in a context in which it appears that there is some clarity about whether someone is a member – though as the issue is not explicitly addressed it is not clear who is being counted as members of the congregations she is studying and who is not. Penny Edgell Becker posits a variety of congregation types (1999: 195) and offers us material on how congregations behave, but the congregation is understood as a relatively stable body of people which satisfies its members' needs; there is no discussion of either explicit or implicit criteria for membership. Similarly, Hopewell (1987: 12) defines a congregation as 'a group that possesses a special name and recognized members who assemble regularly to celebrate a more universally practised worship but who communicate with each other sufficiently to develop intrinsic patterns of conduct, outlook, and story'. Again, there is no discussion of the definition of 'member'. The most thorough definition of membership I have found is in Cnaan (2002). The dilemma is well presented, for example: Should children of members be counted as members? Should attenders or just communicants be counted? These options are then offered:

1 all on official rolls
2 active members (attending once a month)
3 active non-members (that is, those who don't fulfil religious membership criteria but who attend), and
4 average attendance at non-holiday services.

For the congregations in his dataset Cnaan finds respectively 1235, 492, 87 and 387. He decides to use the figure 2 + 3 (so, people who attend at least once a month) to determine a congregation's membership (Cnaan 2002).

As for the motivations of members: Jenkins (2004: 119) suggests that 'people go to church ... both to embody a form of public good, and [to] publicly sustain the claim to represent that public good'; Douglass (1967) and Coleman (2004) find that people shop around for a congregation which they feel suits them; Buchanan finds that people turn up for worship (for some reason or other), feel welcome, and stay (Buchanan 2002: 12–14); Blaikie (1972) finds value-commitment and behavioural differences between people who decide to join churches and people who don't; Clark (1970) suggests that congregations are more likely to recruit from locally-orientated people than from more cosmopolitan people; Mayer and Sharp (1967) show how social class is related to different types of membership; and Barker (1983) suggests that sect membership is a phase through which many people pass. Thus already we find diverse motivations for joining congregations.

There is also literature on the satisfaction and utility which members of religious organizations experience once they are members. Bouma (1980) finds that people remain members because of commitment both to the ideology and to the community; Munters (1971) shows how successful the Jehovah's Witnesses' socialization techniques are at satisfying members' needs; Reed (1972; 1978) discusses what some of those needs are; and Blau et al. (1998) and Iannaccone (1998) study churches which make high demands on members and find that such churches are likely to grow because members benefit psychologically from the high demands. (Cf. Lelkes (2002) on the satisfaction which congregation membership gives to people in a stressful political situation, and Knoke (1990: 186) on the enhancement in involvement experienced by members of collective action organizations when extensive communication networks enable them to participate in decision-making.) Coleman (2004) finds that, even though evangelical religion is often associated with growing congregations, it can cause decline if it denies the importance of long-nurtured expectations and if authority-figures ridicule social norms. By employing an economic model, Iannaccone (1994) concludes that members allocate resources rationally to maximize overall utility, and Crittenden et al. (1988) tell how organizations set out to satisfy members' aspirations at the same time as extracting necessary resources from them. Ashbrook (1966) distinguishes between instrumental activity (making things happen) and expressive activity (participation in worship), and finds that both provide the satisfaction which members seek and which keeps them in the congregation; and Hougland and Wood (1982) find that recruitment and retention correlate positively with the extent to which members are in control of a congregation's activity. There is thus a variety of factors which determine whether people first of all join a congregation and then whether they stay in it, and the needs-based content of their membership is clearly both important and diverse.

As for different types of membership within a congregation, Beckford (1975a; 1978), Becker (1998) and Harris and Rochester (2001a) all discuss the diversity of them; and Himmelfarb (1975) shows how many different ways there are of measuring individual commitment to a religious organization. A particularly interesting piece of research is Nelson's, into the membership of a chapel in a poor area of Charleston, South Carolina. He finds that in terms of time commitment demanded, the costs of joining are high for higher socio-economic groups but relatively low for lower socio-economic groups; that the benefits are considerable for lower socio-economic groups (because high expectations help members to reject the negative alternatives to membership); that the members' loyalty is to the church and not to one another; and that a lowering of the level of commitment demanded of members caused a decline in membership (Nelson 1997: 181–6).

The overwhelming impression is of diversity – of reasons for joining, of reasons for staying, and of types of membership – and that membership is motivated by a 'curious mixture of selflessness and self-interest' (Knoke 1990: xi). The consequence of this is that rational choice theory is far from sufficient for understanding membership of religious and faith-based organizations, because 'normative and affective motivations, incentives, and objectives' are all in play (ibid.: xi).

A particularly significant characteristic of most members of religious organizations is that they are voluntary, that is, that they can walk away tomorrow (Brannon 1971). Significant for our purposes is the fact that both volunteers and members are voluntary but are not the same. The difference and the difference's consequences are explored by Cameron (1999), and it is in this difference that a possible negative definition of membership begins to emerge. Rochester (1999) discovers four models of voluntary involvement in voluntary organizations: the service delivery model; the support role model; the member/ activist model; and the co-worker model. Cameron explores the difference between the first and third models and suggests that 'the most significant difference [between members and volunteers] is that engaging in unpaid work is seen as the essence of volunteering, whereas it is an optional element within membership' (Cameron 1999: 55). She quotes Harris (1998a):

1 'Members are more committed to organizational values than volunteers are, and ... This can lead some members to over-commit themselves and suffer from burnout' (Harris 1998a: 13; quoted Cameron 1999: 56);

2 'Members expect their views to be taken into account more than volunteers
   do' (Harris 1998a: 17; quoted Cameron 1999: 56);
3 'In congregations, members have religious expectations of the clergy that
   give those clergy added authority' (Harris 1998a: 17; quoted Cameron 1999:
   56).

Cameron suggests three further distinctions:

1 'Members have a greater sense of reciprocity than do volunteers ...
   members see their relationship with the congregation as an exchange where
   their contribution builds up an organization on which they themselves
   rely';
2 'Members have a better overview of the organization than volunteers and
   will try to make helpful connections, whether or not it is their 'job' to do so.
   Members seem to show a sense of responsibility for the organization as a
   whole rather than purely for the work they undertake';
3 'Members distinguish less between their private and public roles than
   volunteers do. The work they do for the organization is seen in the context
   of all those aspects of their life that are involved in church membership.
   This includes not only a public commitment to the values of the church but
   also family ties and longstanding friendships' (Cameron 1999: 57).

(Similar distinctions are found between guiders and unit helpers in the Guides;
Nichols and King 1998.)
   Cameron employs Billis's theory that voluntary organizations lie between
the association and the bureaucracy (Billis 1993: ch. 11). Associations have
members who set and aim to meet the organization's goals through voluntary
labour, whereas bureaucracies have paid staff and are rule-based. Voluntary
agencies can have both. Volunteers are in a similarly ambiguous zone: they
receive no pay (like members) and their activity must enable the organization
to meet its objectives (like staff). Some voluntary agencies are more like
associations and some are more like bureaucracies; similarly, some volunteers
operate more like paid staff and some more like members.
   The theory explains the six differences between volunteers and members:

1 volunteering doesn't imply the same degree of assent to goals;
2 members govern an association;
3 religious values reinforce the authority of leaders, so members, committed
   to the values, give respect to clergy etc.;
4 membership implies a primary commitment to the organization, whereas
   volunteers give commitment to beneficiaries;
5 members govern so have a better overview, and commitment means they
   will act on it;

6   an association lies between the private realm/family and bureaucracies, so joining an association is a decision of the individual which affects their private realm; whereas bureaucracies distinguish between the private and the public, and rules govern participation, so the private realm can remain relatively unaffected. It is therefore not surprising that members (who consider themselves to be in the associational world) find their private lives affected by their membership whereas volunteers (between the associational and bureaucratic worlds) do not to the same extent.

There are clear implications as to how religious organizations should relate to members and volunteers. For instance, volunteers might value job descriptions, and members might resent them. Similarly, Harris (1998a: 115–17) suggests that 'management' isn't going to be a word attractive to members. They can choose what they do and still remain members. So there is a problem when members perform poorly when the work is essential to the organization; and when a member performs well a reward can embarrass them. Recognition must match the person's expectations. In her study of churches and synagogues Harris found that 'attempts to become "more businesslike" were usually resisted as alien to the ethos of the Church ... Organising the work of members seemed to require a thorough knowledge of the constitution and an ability to interpret it sensitively' (ibid.: 62). For paid work, management organizes the work, monetary reward is expected, and recruitment is for competence. For members, work is managed co-operatively and there is no financial reward. Volunteers lie between members and paid staff so will sometimes behave and be treated like members and will sometimes behave and be treated like paid staff (see Rochester 1999). Cameron (1999: 62) concludes: 'I would argue that the need for volunteers to conform in some respect to the requirements of the work as determined by the organization will set them apart in some ways from members.' Complications arise, of course, when members become volunteers in projects organized by their organizations, leading to paid staff expecting to manage their work and volunteers resenting members' attempts to control the project.

   It might well be true, as Cnaan (2002: 211) suggests, that 'volunteerism is strongly associated with membership in a religious organization and that personal religious faith alone is a weaker explanation for the decision to volunteer', but our discussion suggests that we need to be careful to distinguish between volunteerism and membership. It might be true, as Cameron suggests, that voluntary work is not a necessary part of membership, but given the diversity of types of membership in a religious organization it is highly likely that there will be overlap between volunteering and some of those types; and it does appear to be true that membership of a religious organization is closely correlated with voluntary work (as opposed to membership) in a religious, faith-based or secular organization, and that members of religious organizations are simply more active generally in their communities (Putnam 2000: 66f.). Membership of religious organizations thus provides benefits both to the members and to their communities.

We have not succeeded in discovering from the literature a robust definition of membership in religious organizations, but we have distinguished membership from volunteering and have discovered some of the diverse characteristics and motivation of membership. The total impression suggests that 'membership' has a diverse definition and can mean different things in different contexts. It is a many-layered affair, and each religious organization should thus be said to have categories of membership (in the plural) rather than a single category of membership. Wilson (1970) asks a particularly interesting question: Are the children of members members? The answer is clearly yes: and that there is a category of membership related to members' children. A broader question is: How connected with each other are the (diverse and fluid) membership criteria at different levels in a religious organization? We have already discussed membership of a congregation, and at the end of this chapter we shall discuss membership in the Church of England. Whilst many people will be members of both the Church of England and of a congregation, those memberships will have different meanings: and there will be people belonging to a Church of England congregation who are not members of the Church of England, and members of the Church of England who are not members of a congregation.

The South London Industrial Mission

We have already related a brief history of the South London Industrial Mission in Chapter 6. The story of its formal membership begins in 1952 when the Bishop of Southwark's Industrial Advisory Council was appointed by the Bishop to support the chaplains' activity. In 1956, this turned into the South London Industrial Mission (SLIM) which had a constitution that gave subscription-paying members (mainly shop stewards and managers) the responsibility for electing part of the Council; in 1966, the constitution became entirely member-based (the Bishop losing the right to appoint the Council); and in 1989, SLIM became a company limited by guarantee, the Council again became advisory, and members elected a Board of Directors.

In 1967, following a survey of the members of SLIM, the Senior Chaplain suggested that 'Associate' was more appropriate than 'member', because 'SLIM' was its influence on the relationship between Christian faith and the world of work, and was not a particular group of people. From then on, 'Associates' meant people who paid subscriptions and elected the Council at the Annual General Meeting, and 'associate' meant anyone who related in any way to SLIM's work.

In 1974, a survey of paid-up Associates showed that 68 were ordained, 11 were from the professions, 34 were from management, 5 were in clerical jobs, 2 were trade union officers, 4 were from the shop floor, and 3 were housewives. They met just once a year, at the Annual General Meeting, and requests for reports on their work went largely unheeded. There was a policy of no active recruitment.

Also by 1974 there was a large full-time team of chaplains who largely determined SLIM's direction and activity. (In 1969 there was a serious suggestion that SLIM should avoid industrial themes at its conferences and instead hold conferences on subjects in which the chaplains were expert.) From the mid-1970s the number of full-time and part-time chaplains declined, and now there are no chaplains with sufficient time to spare to meet regularly at SLIM's headquarters at Christ Church, Blackfriars Road, and the team has ceased to exist.

Thus SLIM had a *variety* of memberships: members of the Council, members of the executive committee or board, members of the chaplains' team, Associates, associates, and members for the purpose of electing the board. If, as we have suggested previously, the part of the organization actually connected to SLIM's work was the chaplains' team, then that particular membership might be regarded as a particularly important kind; but they are all membership types, and characteristics of each would need to be studied separately.

From the beginning, SLIM was its chaplains, and originally these were volunteers who were paid honoraria. When a full-time team evolved, a 'General Team' continued in existence, consisting of parish clergy visiting industry in their own parishes; and throughout SLIM's history volunteer chaplains (though often only a handful of them) have visited industry in South London. (The author is such a chaplain.) The General Team used to meet, and so the volunteer chaplains were members of that Team, but they were not invited to other meetings unless they were also paid-up Associates or members (and some of them were of course). Such chaplains are therefore volunteers, and only members if by some means other than their chaplaincy work or their membership of the General Team.

As for the members of the chaplains' team: the 1989 Memorandum, Articles and Rules tell us about a chaplains' team, and they state that it should be represented on the Board and should report to the Board; but no criteria are offered to enable us to know what sort of person can be a member of the chaplains' team, how they are chosen, for how long they remain members, or how they might cease to be members. The same is true of previous constitutions. This is because SLIM evolved out of parochial clergy and Cathedral staff visiting factories in their parishes, and because appointments of chaplains were always individually negotiated between denominations, industries, and SLIM (usually in the person of the Senior Chaplain).

So this particular membership, which is in fact the most active kind, is without clear boundaries, and there have never been consistent qualifications for this membership, suggesting that the heart of the organization has been a loose association of interested individuals. The team has now disappeared, and the constitutional members who remain are not active participants. If an organization has only non-active memberships then the question has to be faced as to whether it still exists as an organization. All the time the board has members and holds meetings it probably does: but it is a somewhat tenuous kind of existence (Torry 1990).

The Church of England

Any study of the Church of England must distinguish between membership of a congregation and membership of the Church of England. Both notions are problematic.

There is no definition of membership in the Canons of the Church of England. Canon 15A tells us who can be admitted to Holy Communion: 'members of the Church of England who have been confirmed . . .' along with a variety of other categories. There are canons about baptism (nos 21 to 26), but given that there is no statement that baptism admits to membership of the Church, and that according to Canon B28 'reception into the church of England' requires Confirmation (or submission to a Form of Reception if the person is already confirmed), it is impossible to regard baptism as admitting to membership of the Church. It is also impossible to regard Confirmation as admission to membership because in March 1997 the Bishops issued guidelines enabling children to be admitted to communion before Confirmation. Similarly, someone can ask to put their name on the Electoral Roll if they are baptized, are over 16, and declare themselves to be 'a member of the Church of England', without 'member' being defined and without Confirmation being mentioned. But being on the Electoral Roll cannot be regarded as equivalent to membership because a condition of membership would then be membership, which is circular; and being on the Electoral Roll cannot in any case be the same as membership as the March 1997 regulations allow children aged seven to receive communion and they are not eligible to be on the Electoral Roll.

The Church of England has evolved out of a situation in which everyone was assumed to be a member unless they declared themselves otherwise. As society has changed and decisions have been required (for instance, about who can and who can't receive communion, or over who can and who can't vote for the Parochial Church Council at the Annual Parochial Church Meeting – it is these elections which gave birth to the Electoral Roll), the Church has caused boundaries to be drawn, but no consistent definition of membership has emerged. Is a child who receives communion a member? Is someone who was baptized as an infant but who has never been near a church since a member? The answer could be yes or no in both cases.

If we turn our attention to *congregations* of the Church of England, new questions arise: Is someone who always comes but was never baptized a member? Is a Roman Catholic who comes regularly a member? Is the choir member who was never confirmed and never receives communion but who is on the Parochial Church Council a member? In all three cases the answer is probably yes.

The Diocese of Southwark (which pays clergy stipends) collects money from parishes on the basis of a formula which relies on an estimate by the parish of the number of people who attend at least once a month (a figure which is tested against a congregational count over several Sundays during the autumn). This suggests that the Diocese of Southwark believes attendance once a month to constitute membership of the congregation – that is, it demonstrates sufficient commitment to suggest that such people should be contributing financially to the Church's activity. The system for collecting money from the parishes has the confidence of the parishes, which suggests that attendance once a month is generally believed to constitute membership. In the absence of any other agreement as to who is a member of a congregation, 'attendance at least once a month' might be a useful working definition of membership – and it is certainly true that this statistic is taken more seriously than the congregational count, the number of children baptized, or the number of people who receive communion at Easter.

This is important because, in our pluralistic society, *congregational* belonging is a realistic definition of membership of the Church of England. (The fact that people belong to a congregation and not, in their own minds, to the Church of England, is evidenced by the fact that many people who move house cease to attend church, attend a church of another denomination, or travel back to the church which they had previously attended.) This suggests that a count of the number of people who attend at least once a month is the best measure we're likely to get of the membership of the Church of England – which in turn suggests that its membership is rather small; that it's time this figure was collected and published nationally, as the figure for Electoral Roll membership is (The Church of England Year Book 2001: liii); and that the Church of England's claim to be the national church is wearing rather thin.

Conclusion

'Membership' is clearly a problematic concept in relation both to the South London Industrial Mission and to the Church of England. There are, of course, religious organizations in which membership is not quite so problematic, but even here (for instance, in independent Evangelical churches) there will be different *kinds* of membership, and there will be different *degrees* of membership as people join and leave: where, even if there *is* a strict *definition* of membership relating to a personal declaration or some other action or set of actions, ceasing to participate actively would call that membership into question.

In one sense, all this chapter can be is a call for further research on membership in religious organizations; but it also carries a strong suggestion that one of the characteristics of a religious organization is likely to be a hazy definition of membership, and that we are likely to find several different kinds of membership (of both explicit and implicit kinds) in any one organization. It also emphasizes the point made in the Introduction and in Chapter 6 on governance that all organizations, and particularly religious and faith-based organizations, are communities of persons; which is why only a management which includes governance within its definition is appropriate (Selznick 1992: 290). As Selznick goes on to say:

> A vital part of governance is that it has the care of a community or quasi-community. People subject to managerial direction may be thought of as interchangeable, deployable, expendable units, to be used or discarded as efficiency may require. They are not objects of care or of moral concern. In [fulfilling the tasks of governance], on the contrary, leaders (or systems) have a basic commitment to participants *as persons*. (ibid.: 290f.; italics in the original)

References

Ammerman, Nancy Tatom, Farnsley II, Arthur E. et al. (1997), *Congregation and Community*, New Brunswick, New Jersey: Rutgers University Press

Ashbrook, James B. (1966), 'The Relationship of Church Members to Church Organization', *Journal for the Scientific Study of Religion*, **5** (3), 397–419

Barker, Eileen (1983) 'New Religious Movements in Britain: The Context and the Membership', *Social Compass*, **30** (1), 33–48

Becker, Penny Edgell (1998), 'Congregational Models and Conflict: A Study of How Institutions Shape Organizational Process', in Demerath III, N.J., Hall, Peter Dobkin, Schmitt, Terry and Williams, Rhys H. (eds), *Sacred Companies: Organizational Aspects of Religion and Religious Aspects of Organizations*, New York and Oxford: Oxford University Press, pp. 231ff.

Becker, Penny Edgell (1999), *Congregations in Conflict: Cultural Models of Local Religious Life*, Cambridge: Cambridge University Press

Beckford, James A. (1975a), 'Organization, Ideology and Recruitment: The Structure of the Watch Tower Movement', *Sociological Review*, **23** (4), 893–909

Beckford, James A. (1978), 'Sociological Stereotypes of the Religious Sect', *Sociological Review*, **26** (1), 109–23

Billis, David (1993), *Organising Public and Voluntary Agencies*, London and New York: Routledge

Blaikie, Norman W.H. (1972), 'What motivates Church Participation? Review, Replication and Theoretical Reorientation in New Zealand', *Sociological Review*, **20** (1), 39–58

Blau, Judith R., Redding, Kent and Land, Kenneth C. (1998), 'Ethnocultural Cleavages and the Growth of Church Membership in the United States, 1860–1930', in Demerath III, N.J., Hall, Peter Dobkin, Schmitt, Terry and Williams, Rhys H. (eds), *Sacred Companies: Organizational Aspects of Religion and Religious Aspects of Organizations*, New York and Oxford: Oxford University Press, pp. 132ff.

Bouma, Gary D. (1980), 'Keeping the Faithful: Patterns of Membership Retention in the Christian Reformed Church', *Sociological Analysis*, **41** (3), 259–64

Brannon, Robert C.L. (1971), 'Organizational Vulnerability in Modern Religious Organizations', *Journal for the Scientific Study of Religion*, **10** (1), 27–32

Bruce, Stephen (1995), *Religion in Modern Britain*, Oxford: Oxford University Press

Buchanan, Colin (2002), *Mission in South-East London: The Practice and Calling of the Church of England*, London: Diocese of Southwark

Cameron, Helen (1999), 'Are members volunteers? An exploration of the concept of membership drawing upon studies of the local church', *Voluntary Action*, **1** (2), 53–66

Church Representation Rules (2001), London: Church House Publishing

Clark, David B. (1970), 'Local and Cosmopolitan Aspects of Religious Activity in a Northern Suburb', in Martin, David (ed.), *A Sociological Yearbook of Religion in Britain*, vol. III, London: Student Christian Movement, pp. 45ff.

Cnaan, Ram A. (2002), *The Invisible Caring Hand: American Congregations and the Provision of Welfare*, New York and London: New York University Press

Coleman, Simon (2004), ' "Conference People": Congregational Studies in a Globalizing World', in Guest et al. (2004), pp. 39ff.

Crittenden, William E., Crittenden, Vicky L. and Hunt, Tammy G. (1988), 'Planning and Stakeholder Satisfaction in Religious Organizations', *Journal of Voluntary Action Research*, **17** (2), 60–73

Douglass, Truman B. (1967), 'Ecological Change and the Church', in Knudten, Richard D. (ed.), *The Sociology of Religion*, New York: Appleton-Century-Crofts, pp. 147ff.

Guest, Mathew, Tusting, Karin and Woodhead, Linda (eds) (2004), *Congregational Studies in the UK: Christianity in a Post-Christian Context*, Aldershot: Ashgate

Harris, Margaret (1998a), *Organizing God's Work: Challenges for Churches and Synagogues*, London: Macmillan

Harris, Margaret, and Rochester, Colin (2001a), *Governance in the Jewish voluntary sector*, London: Institute for Jewish Policy Research: Planning for Jewish communities, report no. 1

Himmelfarb, Harold S. (1975), 'Measuring Religious Involvement', *Social Forces*, **53** (4), 606–18

Hopewell, James F. (1987), *Congregation: Stories and Structures*, London: SCM Press

Hougland, James G. and Wood, James R. (1982), 'Participation in Local Churches: An Exploration of its Impact on Satisfaction, Growth and Social Action', *Journal for the Scientific Study of Religion*, **21** (4), 338–52

Iannaccone, Laurence R. (1994), 'A Formal Model of Church and Sect', *American Journal of Sociology*, **94** (s), s241–69

Iannaccone, Laurence R. (1998), 'Why Strict Churches Are Strong', in Demerath III, N.J., Hall, Peter Dobkin, Schmitt, Terry and Williams, Rhys H. (eds), *Sacred Companies: Organizational Aspects of Religion and Religious Aspects of Organizations*, New York and Oxford: Oxford University Press, pp. 269ff.

Jenkins, Timothy (2004), 'Congregational Cultures and the Boundaries of Identity', in Guest et al. (2004), pp. 113ff.

Knoke, David (1990), *Organizing for Political Action: The Political Economies of Associations*, New York: Aldine de Gruyter

Lelkes, Orsolya (2002), *Tasting Freedom: Happiness, religion and economic transition*, London: Centre for Analysis of Social Exclusion

Mayer, Albert J. and Sharp, Harry (1967), 'Religious Preferences and Worldly Success', in Knudten, Richard D. (ed.), *The Sociology of Religion*, Appleton-Century-Crofts, New York, pp. 332ff.

Munters, Q.J. (1971), 'Recruitment as a Vocation', *Sociologica Neerlandica*, 7 (2), 88–100

Nelson, Timothy J. (1997), 'The Church and the Street', in Becker, Penny Edgell and Eisland, Nancy L. (eds) (1997), *Contemporary American Religion: An Ethnographic Reader*, Walnut Creek, London and New Delhi: Altamira Press

Nichols, G. and King L. (1998), 'Volunteers in the Guide Association: Problems and Solutions', *Voluntary Action*, 1 (1), 21–32

Putnam, Robert (2000), *Bowling Alone: The Collapse and Revival of American Community*, New York: Simon and Schuster

Reed, B.D. (1972), 'The Local Church as Institution', in Mitton, C.L. (ed.), *The Social Sciences and the Churches*, Edinburgh: T. and T. Clark, pp. 39ff. and 51ff.

Reed, Bruce (1978), *The Dynamics of Religion: Process and Movement in Christian Churches*, London: Darton, Longman and Todd

Rochester, Colin (1999), 'One size does not fit all: Four models of involving volunteers in small voluntary organisations', *Voluntary Action*, 1 (2), 7–20

Selznick, Philip (1992), *The Moral Commonwealth: Social Theory and the Promise of Community*, Berkeley: University of California Press

The Canons of the Church of England (2000), 6th edn, London: Church House Publishing

The Church of England Year Book 2001 (2001), London: Church House Publishing

Torry, Malcolm N.A. (1990), 'The Practice and Theology of the South London Industrial Mission', unpublished PhD thesis, University of London

Wilson, Bryan (1970), *Religious Sects: a sociological study*, London: World University Library/ Weidenfeld and Nicolson

CHAPTER 9

The Clergy: Priests or Professionals?

We have identified the importance of Weber's traditional authority-structure (Weber 1922) and Etzioni's normative compliance structure to religious organizations and their governance (Etzioni 1980), and in this chapter we study the clergy, who, as we have already seen in our work on governance, exercise a variety of types of authority and possess roles in a variety of compliance structures. The clergy operate within the bureaucratic structures in the parish and in the denomination, and we shall return to these roles. The clergy sometimes possess charismatic authority: an issue which we shall barely touch as there is so little research literature on it, presumably because charismatic authority by its nature is difficult to define and categorize. One issue which we shall treat at some length is the question as to whether the clergy are a profession. But the most important difference between the clergy and other functionaries is that, at the same time as operating within bureaucratic structures and utilitarian compliance structures, they operate within a traditional authority-structure and within normative compliance structures.

In relation to *traditional* authority, the clergy are an example of 'objectivation': they are authority-figures who put into practice the values of a religious tradition, so that they themselves become part of the plausibility structure (Berger 1977) not only within the congregation but also in the wider community, particularly in the context of such 'occasional congregations' as funeral and memorial services (Davies 2004), where the priest mediates a relationship between the individual and the wider community in much the same way as he or she mediates a relationship between the individual and the congregation. The clergy will thus often be granted high status in the organization (Kane 1967), relatively small changes in the priest's behaviour can cause a considerable effect on the congregation (Ward 2004: 133), seniority will be an important influence on who is chosen to fill senior posts because in a normative organization long service implies commitment to the organization's values and thus suitability for leadership positions (Peterson and Schoenheir 1978), and it will seem natural to the clergy to develop strategies to control the congregation's direction because they feel their own authority to be of divine origin, and will not feel it a contradiction if the strategies they employ rely on bureaucratic structures and utilitarian compliance structures rather than on traditional authority structures and normative compliance structures (Falbo et al. 1987). Such tactics have, of course, caused questions to be asked about the roots of the clergy's influence. Nelson and Maguire study rural congregations and find that they are largely made up of locally-oriented members, but that their clergy are generally cosmopolitan in outlook (Nelson and Maguire 1980; cf. Clark 1971), meaning that the minister will generally be more liberal than their congregations, often better educated, and often better connected to resources and to where decisions are made, thus giving the minister power over the congregation: power which has little to do with traditional authority.

Blizzard has also studied rural clergy and found that the congregation's conservative expectations can cause stress for the minister as he or she tries to take on new roles in relation to new situations (Blizzard 1967b). He also studies urban clergy and finds that emphases are changing: from preaching, scholarship and the administration of the sacraments, to counselling, social action, administration and recruitment. He again finds differences between ministers' and congregations' expectations (Blizzard 1967a). Butterworth finds similar changes and stresses amongst Imams (Butterworth 1969: 150ff), and Sharot (1973) finds similar conflicts amongst rabbis, who expect to be scholars and are expected to be pastors and administrators. He calls this a tendency to become 'ministers' rather than 'rabbis' (Sharot 1975; cf. Bulka 1986). (This chapter is able to consider religious traditions other than the Christian because there is research literature available on the clergy of a variety of traditions because sociologists have found them interesting.) To extend the same terminology to the Christian clergy would suggest that we should use 'priest' to refer to the religious functionary operating in traditional, normative, liturgical and scholarly mode, and 'minister' to refer to the functionary operating in bureaucratic, utilitarian and administrative mode. We shall not do this consistently, but shall leave a certain ambiguity in our use of terminology, because in the Christian tradition the pastoral role is an expectation shared by the priest and by the congregation and is an aspect of both the priestly and the ministerial roles – and I suspect that the same is in fact true of most rabbis, suggesting that Sharot's distinction, based on older research, is a little clearer than it would be if based on more recent research. Warren identifies five models for Christian clergy: the representative, the pastor, the servant, the shepherd, and the teacher; and on the basis of interviews with 60 clergy finds that most identify with the representative and pastor models, that a few identify themselves with the servant and shepherd models, but that no one identifies themselves as a teacher (Warren 2002: 75).

Whilst differences in expectations might sometimes cause stress, the clergy have resources to draw on as they cope with the conflict, and particularly resources built up during their formation (usually at a theological college) during which they have internalized values from their denomination's polity and theology (Shupe et al. 1973). But such resources are not always decisive in a contest with a laity which does not possess the resources to the same degree, because the clergy's authority can be contested from within the tradition (Harris 1998a: 174; Cameron 2001), especially as congregation members might be more likely to appeal to traditional authority than would be the more cosmopolitan minister, or they might be able to appeal both to charismatic and traditional authority at the same time (as has happened in the case of the charismatic movement in the mainstream denominations: an issue over which clergy and denominational structures have exerted no control, mainly because they couldn't; Moore 1972). The Brahmin's authority is supposed to be by birthright, but he can in fact only exercise authority by consent of the congregation (Hertel 1977), and similarly, except where the priestly role is guaranteed by ecclesiology (such as the priest's prerogatives in relation to the sacraments), congregation members can contest any clerical action or idea and, if they are not heard, they can exercise the ultimate sanction and leave the congregation. Where the laity *could* contest a minister's authority they often don't because they are aware of the potential for divisive conflict and decide not to exercise the power they know they have (Homan 1982–83). (Sklare (1967) suggests that in orthodox synagogues there is little division of function between rabbi and laity, and there is much lay control, because the fundamental division is between male and female roles and thus all the men perceive themselves as sharing a set of religious duties.)

There is some disagreement in the research literature as to whether clergy and laity roles should be regarded as clearly distinguishable. Dempsey (1969) finds a lack of definition and thus conflict, especially over the organizational structure of the congregation, expectations of the minister, and theology, whereas Harrison (1967) believes roles to be clear-cut, particularly in relation to the minister's involvement in a denominational bureaucracy, which enables the minister to dominate the laity – though because the laity are better involved in the secular environment the minister's status in the congregation is not as high as it might otherwise be (Harrison 1967). The discrepancy of viewpoint is evidence of a complex situation. From the laity's point of view, the clergy have some highly visible roles which only they can perform, and the clergy belong to both traditional and bureaucratic structures not available to the laity. (The traditional structure is particularly difficult for the laity to tackle because, even though it is available to them as it is to the clergy, its diffuse nature means that the minister, often with deeper experience of interpretational possibilities, is frequently better able to employ this type of authority.) Some of the congregation's structures are bureaucratic and here the clergy's power can be contested more easily and conflict can occur. From the minister's point of view, the minister possesses roles which the laity do not, and the minister has a traditional authority which they do not; but the minister knows that in the end the congregation can leave next week: hence a perception of weakness in an unpredictable situation, and the resulting stress. It is thus in the minister's interests to resist the bureaucratization of the congregation (Ingram 1980): hence the denomination's and the minister's resistance to elected church councils and their tendency to dominate them and/or subvert them when they do exist.

Conflict can be particularly acute when it comes to the laity's belief-systems and actions. In a traditional authority-structure the office-holder might expect to have some say as to how the congregation's members behave and believe; but there is of course no such control, except a residual psychological control: and tensions are particularly acute in the Roman Catholic Church where there is now a substantial gulf between the Church's stipulations and the laity's behaviour, a gulf so wide that clergy often think silence preferable to alienating the laity or revealing their own ambivalence. The laity are now so used to society's flexible and democratic forms that the Church's traditional authority-structure is feeling like a foreign country (Kokosalakis 1971).

Hoge et al. are not so sure that the differences between the laity and the clergy are about authority-structures at all: they think they have much more to do with theological differences, for they notice that there are few differences between clerical and lay opinion on the religious education of children or the priest's pastoral tasks and that differences appear over such issues as social action, evangelism, and administrative detail (Hoge et al. 1978). But whatever the roots of the differences, they can, as we have seen, be sources of conflict and stress, and Dubach (1972) identifies role uncertainty as a reason for Roman Catholic clergy leaving the priesthood. (We shall see below why his suggestion that a greater professionalization amongst the clergy, and hence seeing the Church as a modern service-provider, isn't necessarily a useful response.) Towler and Coxon (1979) identify a series of secularizations as the roots of the problem, as these marginalize the clergy, and, even though their analysis is flawed in that it isolates the minister from the congregation, there might still be some truth in their allocation of a primary role to secularization. Warren (2002) agrees that a changing world in which the Church no longer receives the public respect it once did is a source of stress for the clergy, but her research reveals a complex picture in which the priest's personality, background and support networks are important factors in determining whether the priest experiences stress in their particular situation. One element of the clergy's position which will often be a source of stress is the minister's knowledge that they have to satisfy the whole of a congregation containing diverse expectations at the same time as following their own conscience in relation to theology, social action, individual lifestyle, and so on; and, unsurprisingly, Campbell and Pettigrew find that ministers tend only to conform to their own values and those of other clergy if those values are also those of their congregations – though they also find that the situation is different for Roman Catholic clergy (for whom a conservative hierarchy is a brake on social action and theological innovation), for Jews (where the congregation's own sense of marginalization might support radical social action), and for some ministers who will act according to their consciences and not concern themselves too much over falling congregational membership (Campbell and Pettigrew 1967).

An issue which receives very little attention (though some in Warren 2002) is the relationship between religious conviction and employment. Whilst clergy are often counted as office-holders rather than as employees, their office involves their time, their energy, their payment, their home, their family and their relationships: and a necessary qualification each time they are appointed to a particular office is an affirmation of faith; and continuance in that office requires (at least implicitly) a continuance in that expressed faith. But the roots of religious faith are complex, and not entirely under the control of the minister. Thus clergy can find themselves living in a difficult psychological position, continuing with the role and its functions but no longer believing the faith on which their role is supposed to be based (ibid.: 194ff.). Some find this a source of stress: some don't.

We thus find a complex picture. Clergy are intimately bound up with their congregations, but their distinctive position within a variety of faith, authority and compliance structures gives them distinctive roles and imposes on them distinctive pressures. Amongst those pressures is being accountable to a *very* broad range of individuals and institutions: the denomination, a particular theological tradition, normative texts, hierarchical authority-structures, congregational office-holders, congregational members, civic leaders, civil institutions, local residents – and God. I make no apology for this final theological word. As we saw in Chapter 4, it is the existence of an authority beyond the social and institutional boundaries of the organization which gives to the congregations' members and to the congregation as a whole their autonomy in relation to other individuals and institutions. The same is true of the clergy. The fact that they and others recognize that the clergy are subject to an authority beyond *every* institutional boundary gives to the priest or minister a relative autonomy in relation to any other authority-structure. This has an important effect: it means that under normal circumstances no single authority can trump any other; so the diversity of accountability structures can expand without limit. The priest or minister thus has to handle a wide variety of authorities (which can be stressful), but it also means that under normal circumstances no one authority can have the final say, thus giving to the minister or priest a certain amount of freedom of action. I say 'under normal circumstances' because in many situations it is open to one particular authority or to authorities acting together to remove a priest or minister from the situation by ejecting him or her from their post. If other relevant authority-structures haven't been involved in this decision (for instance, local office-holders if a minister has been removed by denominational authorities), then anger is the inevitable result.

So an important theological question to ask is: Is the minister's mandate from God, from the federation, or from the congregation? The answer is: from all three – so not only does the minister belong to a variety of authority-structures, but there is support for this diverse belonging from the core-values of the religious organization, values which both minister and congregation to some extent internalize.

Given that the minister's position is thus fairly unusual relative to that of post-holders in other types of organization, the obvious next question is: Is the minister a professional?

Professionalization

We call a group of people 'professionals' if they have a body of expertise (a 'technology'; Hasenfeld 1992: 10ff.; Hasenfeld and English 1974: 12) which, because others don't have it, gives them the ability to regulate their own work and to some extent the conditions under which they work, particularly where their work is essential to the organization they work for (Hasenfeld and English 1974: 12ff.). Thus doctors are clearly a profession, and teachers ambiguously so (as the technology is not so extensive and not so difficult to acquire for those with the natural capacity to acquire it). Professionals tend to undergo training which initiates them into their profession as well as teaching them what they need to know; they normally have predictable career patterns; and the professions tend to have boundaries which they themselves police. Other marks of a profession are occupational choice (that is, people primarily choose to be doctors rather than to work for a particular health authority), a profession's members tend to have high social status, and social relationships tend to be within the profession.

During the nineteenth century the clergy of the European and American denominations became more like other professionals. They began to be trained in theological colleges rather than being ordained on the basis of academic study (though the colleges were often an induction into a particular tradition of biblical interpretation or into a particular ritual tradition rather than being mainly about practical pastoral skills); they began to meet for further education and for discussion of their role; and rational selection processes were put in place, managed by clergy. This was a time when other professions, such as medicine and the law, were developing tighter structures; and both then and now it is contact between the clergy and members of other professions which encourages the clergy to develop and to maintain their own professional structures (Dunstan 1967).

One of the means of determining whether a body of people is a profession is that body's ability to prevent interference with its work. Whilst the medical profession is becoming more accountable, there is a limit to how far this can go, because in the end only doctors can judge how good a doctor's medical judgment is. The situation is clearly not the same for the clergy, and so non-interference has to be argued for (often successfully) in relation to traditional authority and to the clergy's special position within a traditional authority-structure, and it is by this means that the clergy's normal monopoly of Eucharistic presidency is maintained. As Braude (1961) points out, non-interference remains by permission of the laity, who in practice rarely question clerical monopolies, rather than by possession of a technology.

As to whether the clergy have careers in the way in which other professionals do (Bryman 1974), the situation is complex. Clergy will move from one post to another, but any sense of progression in a career (apart from those few who become Archdeacons or Bishops or their equivalents) is tenuous. This is basically because denominations are federations of congregations and not of bureaucratic structures, so moving from one task to another is moving from one voluntary organization to another rather than moving within a single rational structure or within a small group of related structures. Thus it is only in the context of the denominational structures that career patterns emerge: and once a minister has taken a post in a denominational umbrella organization he or she is likely to develop a career like other professionals' careers, and to become distanced from the denominations' other congregational and bureaucratic structures – thus giving us a variant of Benson's conclusion that in bureaucracies professionalization and bureaucratization are not compatible (Benson and Dorsett 1971) and supporting Struzzo's finding that because a professionalized priest is less likely to follow hierarchical norms (because professions develop their own norms) the Roman Catholic church actively resists the professionalization of its clergy, causing loss of status and thus departures from the priesthood (Struzzo 1970).

Clergy meet other clergy, not only within their denomination but also ecumenically: so what develops is a *single* clerical profession, not a separate one for each denomination (another reason for the Roman Catholic Church's resistance to a professionalized priesthood; Bryman and Hinings 1974). Within this single profession social relationships develop, training is often ecumenical and thus into an ecumenical profession, and social status shifts (though not necessarily upwards). However, occupational choice usually *is* of the individual denomination, so there are still some boundaries *within* the single profession (Fichter 1961). Such boundaries are particularly clear for more sectarian denominations, and a Pentecostalist minister will experience conflict between a gradual socializing into the clerical profession, as he or she meets clergy from other denominations, and the expectations of their congregations – and they can find themselves marginalized both within the profession and within their denomination (Wilson 1967c). Similarly, when a sect starts to pay its minister, the whole sect starts to build bridges into the social environment as the minister does, and inconsistencies in belief, in practice, and between practice and belief, are slowly rationalized – because that's what the minister finds other clergy enabling to happen. In addition to the ecumenical profession, there is now a growing interfaith clerical profession as leaders of various faith communities relate to each other (Wind and Lewis 1994).

The one basic ingredient missing from the clerical profession is, of course, an exclusive technology. Yes, most clergy will be educated in theology, but so are many people who are not clergy; and the clergy no doubt develop pastoral expertise – but so do other people. The clergy resist such activities as data collection (Berlinger and Te'eni 1999), but this merely raises the question as to what the boundaries of the clerical technology might be, rather than denying that there is a technology – a suggestion borne out by the impossibility of measuring the effectiveness of activity which both clergy and laity regard as the primary role of the clergy. The reason Nauss finds resistance to measuring clergy performance is not only that this can be threatening but because what is measured is either secondary activity or the consequences of primary activity, consequences which depend as much on the situation within which the minister operates as it depends on the effectiveness of the minister. Nauss suggests that it *is* important to measure effectiveness and that it *is* possible to do so (and not simply to measure consequences), and he develops four measures which enable him to suggest what might be optimum lengths of pastorates in different situations (Nauss 1972; 1974); but such measurement will always be contentious, as it is in other professions, such as teaching – where again it is easier to measure consequences (especially if differences between situations are ignored) than it is to measure the effectiveness of the professional's work. The fact that it is often impossible for a priest or anyone else to determine what is work and what is not when they examine a priest's diary (an interesting consultancy exercise) rather suggests that, if we have here a profession at all, then it is rather a strange one; and the fact that the same priest might be highly effective in one post and hopelessly ineffective in another, and that two different clergy will behave very differently in any one post, rather suggests that trying to measure effectiveness in what we have seen are individual voluntary organizations is extremely difficult.

It is still normal for clergy to be educated at theological colleges, though part-time courses are becoming more common, thus suggesting that what is being educated for is a role in a voluntary organization rather than a profession. The colleges are clearly designed to socialize clergy into particular traditions within the denominations, as they possess elements of a religious community (to enable the candidate to master a tradition and to receive a spiritual formation), of a vocational college (for practical and spiritual formation), and of a university (to enable mastery of a tradition and of secular awareness). Different colleges contain these different elements to different degrees, and thus produce clergy with different emphases (Carroll 1971) – though it must also be true that candidates choose colleges in relation to their own preferences. (Kahane (1981) finds that Brahmin are now seeking higher educational attainment in order to give their tradition new secular meaning and greater status – though because their example is encouraging others to be more highly educated, the Brahmin's position in the social order is in fact weakening.)

So what we have here is a *partial* and *diverse* professionalization, with different elements of professionalization in different places, but with nowhere the broad spectrum of characteristics of professionalization which we find for instance in the medical profession. But still, the connection with other professions contributes to a partial professionalization, to a secularization, and to an accommodationist rather than an exclusivist attitude (Aldridge 1994), and the process of partial professionalization has probably enhanced the *abilities* of the clergy at the same time as leaving sufficient room for traditional authority and for the diversity and flexibility necessary to enable the minister to serve a religious organization. (The larger numbers of non-stipendiary clergy who now constitute a growing proportion of the clergy are both a symptom and a cause of reduced social status, and are helping to reduce the extent to which the clergy are professionalized (Fuller and Vaughan 1986; Coxon 1967).)

In one sense the clergy were the *first* professionals: they could often read and write when other people couldn't; they were teachers, doctors and scientists – and then the state took over health-care, education, social work, and other fields in which the church's clergy had exercised professional roles: and now that the clergy are *not* clearly professionals, even in their own field, they have been *de*professionalized, their status has fallen, they are often not as well-educated as people in a wide variety of occupations, and their progressive secularization has left them insecure in a secular and impersonal society, insecure within more bureaucratic and more democratic denominations, and with too little idea as to how a historic religious tradition might relate to a rapidly changing society (Goldner et al. 1973; Dolan 1994).

The clergy have only ever been partially professionalized and now the level of professionalization is declining further. The clergy are the servants of small religious voluntary organizations and of their federations, and whatever else they have been in the past, servants of voluntary religious organizations is what they are going to be in the foreseeable future. Their role will be one of listening as well as telling, of narrative knowledge as well as of rational knowledge: in fact, the kind of 'professionalism' which medical practitioners are now learning. So perhaps, once again, the clergy are out ahead, offering a kind of professionalism which other professions are now beginning to understand. The important task will be to enact this new professionalism with the utmost skill, and to develop the kinds of expectations, commitment and infrastructure which will make this possible.

Payment and Authority

Does the route by which the clergy are paid make any difference to their roles? Margaret Harris's work on religious congregations discusses the ambiguous role of the clergy and asks the question: Are they employees of the congregation, or are they in authority over it? (Harris 1995b) She might also have asked: Is the 'authority' which the clergy possess simply a particular instance of 'professionalization', or is it a function of how the clergy are paid? No doubt the roots of the clergy's authority are mixed, but it might be that precisely who is the employing authority is a significant question to ask.

In a community group, the management committee employs the staff member (Figure 9.1a); in a campaigning or service organization the same applies. In the Church of England, the Diocese (rather than the congregation) is the employer (Figure 9.1b) – and this presumably makes a difference to the minister's relationship to the congregation. It means that the staff member is less accountable to the congregation and thus has greater authority within it. Ministers paid by their congregations, on the other hand, are what Luke Smith calls 'client-controlled'. (He calls priests in episcopal, hierarchical churches and paid by the Diocese 'manager-controlled', which makes the point about the difference but might not be the best term to use; 'federation-controlled' would be better.) He finds that the client-controlled minister moves more often and is likely to join occupation-wide organizations or to create institutions within the congregation, both tactics designed to increase his or her own security (Smith 1953).

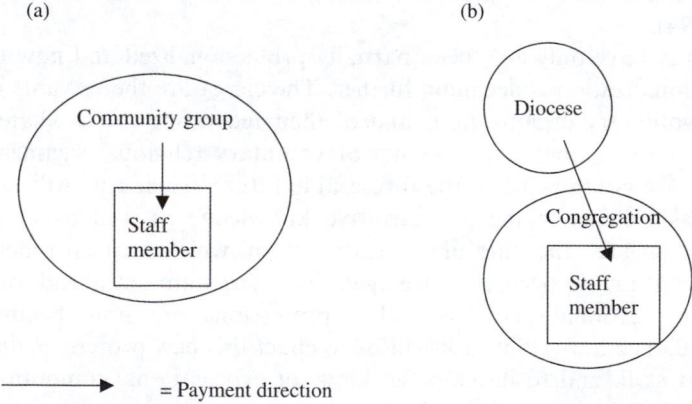

(a)   (b)

Community group

Staff member

Diocese

Congregation

Staff member

⟶ = Payment direction

Figure 9.1   Payment of staff members of community groups (a) and of clergy of congregations (b)

Harris recognizes that more research is needed as 'it is not clear from research to date how appropriately we can view the position of a religious functionary in a congregation as equivalent to the position of a senior staff officer in a secular non-profit organization' (Harris 1995b: 270). Payment by a body exterior to the congregation suggests that the minister is *not* in the same position as the senior staff officer, and the variety of authority-structures within which the minister operates would suggest the same. The minister who is paid by the congregation would be in a position far more similar to that of the staff officer.

Just as it makes a difference whether the minister is paid by the congregation or by an outside body, so it makes a difference as to *which* outside body does the paying. Roman Catholic parochial clergy belong either to the Diocese or to a religious order charged with providing a priest for a particular parish. Gannon has discovered differences in behaviour between the two categories, and also differences within each category. This is hardly surprising. The differences *between* the categories presumably stem from the religious order's clergy having two authority-figures, the Bishop and the provincial authority, so they can be relatively independent of both. The Diocesan priest has only the Bishop, so accountability is relatively clear (Gannon 1979).

Similar issues can arise in a community group if an outside body is the employer of a worker, as is often the case with youth workers: the Borough being the employer, but the community organization being expected to manage the youth project. The worker expects an authority within the group by virtue of their external line management, but the group expects the worker to be accountable to them. Conflict is inevitable. Conflict is less inevitable in a congregation because there is an agreed traditional authority-structure which coheres with the authority which a minister is able to exercise by virtue of their payment by an outside body.

A broader question than *how* the minister is paid is, of course, the question as to whether the minister *should* be paid. During the Middle Ages there was some debate as to whether a rabbi should be paid: some rabbis thought they should be, as the scholarly task was the highest vocation possible and a scholarly élite set free from other concerns was therefore required; others thought the idea close to blasphemous (Sacks 2002: 95f.). Similar debates have gone on the Christian Church since the matter was debated in Paul's letters, in which he gives permission for ministers to be paid but makes it clear that he will continue to support himself by tent-making.

We have discussed the position of the paid priest. The unpaid priest carries a Diocesan authority by virtue of their licensing, but they are less set apart from the congregation than a priest paid by the Diocese would be, because they are in practice one voluntary member amongst others and they, like other members of the congregation, can decide not to turn up next week; and, as we have suggested, the non-stipendiary minister is likely to be less professionalized than the paid minister, because part of the normal definition of professionalization is that being a professional involves payment. But the minister is still an ordained minister, and still exercises a traditional authority – and sometimes bureaucratic and charismatic authorities too. Here is clearly an issue deserving of further research.

Priest or Professional?

In 1964, Paul wrote a report in which he suggested that it is problematic calling the clergy a profession (Paul 1964: 93) – and he then went on to treat them as one. He also treated the Church of England as a rational, national organization, and suggested that rational deployment of clergy was what was required (ibid.; 1972). In 1965, Wilson wrote a critique of the report, suggesting that the Church is a voluntary and sacred organization and should not be treated as a bureaucratic and secular one (Wilson 1965), that the clergy's role is too diffuse for them to be regarded as a profession, and that pastoral care and spirituality won't be served by organizational efficiency. (Wilson unfortunately saw the Church as one large voluntary organization rather than as a federation of smaller ones, but this doesn't affect the force of his argument.)

Russell's conclusion, after reviewing the nineteenth-century professionalization of the clergy *and* the fact that the Church is a voluntary organization, suggests that the Church is a voluntary organization, and that we ought *not* to regard the clergy as professionals (Russell 1984); and McSweeney reminds us that Weber treated the priest as a priest rather than as a religious specialist: that is, the priest as a servant of institutionalized magic (Weber 1922; 1963). For the Roman Catholic priest, the priest's person is still where ritual, myth and discipline are focused, and the priest's authority has a direct relationship with the source of spiritual power rather than that authority being mediated by the congregation (McSweeney 1974). Ammerman, on the basis of her research, suggests that congregations need both lay decision-making and effective clerical leadership in order to be able to adapt to a changing environment (Ammerman et al. 1997). This is probably because a diverse mixture of authority and compliance structures can be brought to bear on complex situations, thus giving the congregation greater ability to negotiate a rapidly changing environment.

Bruce (1995) suggests that a more involved laity needs *more* clergy, not less, but also recognizes that the clergy's role will remain uncertain and that the clergy really aren't a profession; and Towler (1968) suggests that they aren't even an occupation because the role is too diffuse. He also suggests that possible futures for the denominations are sect-like congregations with paid organizers, full-time clergy serving denominations, or more non-stipendiary clergy – or a mixture of all three (ibid.). He thinks that the clergy should *not* attempt to (re)professionalize, but should instead seek more radical roles and statuses in order to tackle increasing secularization (Towler 1972).

Whatever changes evolve for the clergy or are imposed on them, great care will need to be taken. To professionalize will reduce the scope of traditional and charismatic authority and of normative compliance structures, and in a changing environment what is needed is plenty of diversity in the authority and compliance structures available.

What we need is priests, and we need them because what congregations are for is the production of the sacred (Wuthnow 1994). The focal task is the priest or minister presiding at worship, not the priest or minister in a business meeting deciding on budget priorities. The liberal education which clergy receive, whilst it enriches them and their congregations, runs the risk of distancing both clergy and congregation alike from their religious roots; and the loss of the clergy's role as cultural producers in the wider community means that they and their congregations need to work harder to create public religion: religion which has some kind of influence on society at large and at the same time remains definitely religious (ibid.: 58).

One particular strength which the clergy have is that they definitely belong to an organization. Whilst there remains some doubt as to whether a congregation is an organization (because its membership is hard to determine), it *is* clear that any denomination's clergy form an organization. The membership is clear (at least relatively so), there are means of joining – and of leaving, there are prescribed activities, there are rules of behaviour, there are prescribed ways of making decisions, and there are agreed purposes: the ministry of word and sacrament in the Christian case, the interpretation of the Torah in the Jewish case, the leading of Friday and other prayers in the case of Islam, and so on. So, to call ordination as a minister 'going into the church' might mean more than we sometimes think it does.

And this organization of clergy is, whether we like it or not, the crucible within which change occurs: within which the ideas and energy are generated for reform. And if congregations are to continue to 'produce the sacred' (Wuthnow 1994), then the clergy are going to need to take their responsibility in the matter with the utmost seriousness – and the first part of this responsibility is the task of keeping the congregation in existence. If it is true that 'it is important that the sacred be proclaimed, but [also that] the proclamation must be enacted by the presence and the gathered community of the congregation' (ibid.: 60f.), then the clergy need to do all they can to keep that enactment in being. Only if they fulfil their focal role in this task will the congregation survive and be effective in its environment.

References

Aldridge, Alan (1994), 'Women Priests: From Exclusion to Accommodation', *British Journal of Sociology*, **45** (3), 501–10

Ammerman, Nancy Tatom, Farnsley II, Arthur E. et al. (1997), *Congregation and Community*, New Brunswick, New Jersey: Rutgers University Press

Benson, J. Kenneth and Dorsett, James H. (1971), 'Toward a Theory of Religious Organizations', *Journal for the Scientific Study of Religion*, **10** (2), 139–51

Berger, Peter L. (1977), *Facing up to Modernity*, New York: Basic Books

Berlinger, Lisa and Te'eni, Dov (1999), 'Leaders' Attitudes and Computer Use in Religious Congregations', *Nonprofit Management and Leadership*, **9** (4), 399–412

Blizzard, Samuel W. (1967a), 'Role Conflicts of the Urban Protestant Parish Minister', in Knudten, Richard D. (ed.), *The Sociology of Religion*, New York: Appleton-Century-Crofts, pp. 212ff.

Blizzard, Samuel W. (1967b), 'Role Conflicts of the Rural Protestant Parish Minister', in Knudten, Richard D. (ed.), *The Sociology of Religion*, New York: Appleton-Century-Crofts, pp. 240ff.

Braude, Lee (1961), 'Professional Autonomy and the Role of the Layman', *Social Forces*, **39** (3), March, 297–301

Bruce, Stephen (1995), *Religion in Modern Britain*, Oxford: Oxford University Press

Bryman, Alan (1974), 'Sociology of Religion and Sociology of Élites', *Archives de Sciences Sociales des Religions*, **38**, 1974, pp. 109ff.

Bryman, Alan and Hinings, C. Robin (1974), 'Participation, Reform and Ecumenism: The Views of Laity and Clergy', in Hill, Michael (ed.), *A Sociological Yearbook of Religion in Britain*, vol. VII, London: Student Christian Movement, pp.13ff.

Bulka, Reuven P. (1986), 'Characteristics of Rabbinic Leadership: A Psychological View', in Sacks, Jonathan (ed.), *Tradition and Transition: Essays presented to Chief Rabbi Sir Immanuel Jakobovits to Celebrate Twenty Years in Office*, London: Jews College Publications, pp. 87ff.

Butterworth, Eric (1969), 'Muslims in Britain', in Martin, David (ed.), *A Sociological Yearbook of Religion in Britain*, vol. II, London: Student Christian Movement, pp. 137ff.

Cameron, Helen (2001), 'A perspective from the study of religious organisations', in Anheier, Helmut K. (ed.), *Organisational Theory and the Non-profit Form*, report no. 2, London: Centre for Civil Society, London School of Economics

Campbell, Ernest Q. and Pettigrew, Thomas F. (1967), 'Racial and Moral Crisis: The Role of Little Rock Ministers', in Knudten, Richard D. (ed.), *The Sociology of Religion*, New York: Appleton-Century-Crofts, pp. 228ff.

Carroll, Jackson W. (1971), 'Structural Effects of Professional Schools on Professional Socialization: The Case of Protestant Clergymen', *Social Forces*, **50** (1), September, 61–74

Clark, David B. (1971), 'Local and Cosmopolitan Aspects of Religious Activity in a Northern Suburb', in Martin, David (ed.), *A Sociological Yearbook of Religion in Britain*, vol. IV, London: Student Christian Movement, pp. 141ff.

Coxon, Anthony P.M. (1967), 'Patterns of Occupational Recruitment: The Anglican Ministry', *Sociology*, **1** (1), 73–9

Davies, Douglas (2004), 'Priests, Parish and People: Reconceiving a Relationship in Guest et al. (2004), pp. 153ff.

Dempsey, Kenneth C. (1969), 'Conflict in Minister/Lay Relations', in Martin, David (ed.), *A Sociological Yearbook of Religion in Britain*, vol. II, Student Christian Movement, London, pp. 58ff.

Dolan, Jay P. (1994), 'Patterns of Leadership in the Congregation', in Wind and Lewis (1994), vol. II, pp. 225ff.

Dubach, Alfred Th. (1972), 'Entre la Résistance et l'Adaptation: Situation Professionelle du Prêtre en Suisse', *Social Compass*, **19** (2), 291–307

Dunstan, G.R. (1967), 'The Sacred Ministry as a Learned Profession', *Theology*, **70** (568), October, 433–42

Etzioni, Amitai (1980), 'Compliance Structures', in Etzioni, Amitai and Lehman, E. (eds), *A Sociological Reader on Complex Organisations*, 3rd edn: Austin, Texas: Holt, Reinhart and Winston, pp. 87ff.

Falbo, Toni, New, B. Lynn and Gaines, Margie (1987), 'Perceptions of Authority and the Power Strategies used by Clergymen', *Journal for the Scientific Study of Religion*, **26** (4), 499–507

Fichter, Joseph H. (1961), *Religions as an Occupation: A Study in the Sociology of Professions*, Notre Dame, Indiana: University of Notre Dame Press

Fuller, John and Vaughan, Patrick (eds) (1986), *Working for the Kingdom*, London: SPCK

Gannon, Thomas M. (1979), 'The Impact of Structural Differences on the Catholic Clergy', *Journal for the Scientific Study of Religion*, **18** (4), 350–62

Goldner, Fred H., Ference, Thomas P. and Ritti, R. Richard (1973), 'Priests and Laity: A Profession in Transition', *The Sociological Review Monograph no.20: Professionalization and Social Change*, 199–237

Guest, Mathew, Tusting, Karin and Woodhead, Linda (eds) (2004), *Congregational Studies in the UK: Christianity in a Post-Christian Context*, Aldershot: Ashgate

Harris, Margaret (1995b), 'The Organisation of Religious Congregations: Tackling the Issues', *Nonprofit Management and Leadership*, **5** (3), Spring, 261–74

Harris, Margaret (1998a) *Organizing God's Work: Challenges for Churches and Synagogues*, London: Macmillan

Harrison, Paul M. (1967), 'Church and the Laity among Protestants', in Knudten, Richard D. (ed.), *The Sociology of Religion*, New York: Appleton-Century-Crofts, pp. 250ff.

Hasenfeld, Yeheskil (ed.) (1992), *Human Services as Complex Organisations*, London: Sage

Hasenfeld, Yeheskil and English, Richard A. (eds) (1974), *Human Service Organisations: A Book of Readings*, Ann Arbor: University of Michigan Press

Hertel, Bradley R. (1977), 'Church, Sect and Congregation in Hinduism: An Examination of Social Structure and Religious Authority', *Journal for the Scientific Study of Religion*, **16** (1), 15–26

Hoge, Dean R., Perry, Everett L. and Klever, Gerald L. (1978), 'Theology as a Source of Disagreement about Protestant Church Goals and Priorities', *Review of Religious Research*, **19** (2), 116–38

Homan, Roger (1982–83), 'Liturgical Change and the Clerisy in Crisis', *Faith and Worship*, no. 13, Winter, 10–14

Ingram, Larry C. (1980), 'Notes on Pastoral Power in the Congregational Tradition', *Journal for the Scientific Study of Religion*, **19** (1), 40–48

Kahane, Reuven (1981), 'Priesthood and Social Change: The Case of the Brahmins', *Religion*, **11**, 353–66

Kane, John J. (1967), 'Church and Laity among Catholics', in Knudten, Richard D. (ed.), *The Sociology of Religion*, New York: Appleton-Century-Crofts, pp. 261ff.

Kokosalakis, N. (1971), 'Aspects of Conflict between the Structure of Authority and the Beliefs of the Laity in the Roman Catholic Church', in Martin, David (ed.), *A Sociological Yearbook of Religion in Britain*, vol. IV, London: Student Christian Movement, pp. 21ff.

McSweeney, Bill (1974), 'The Priesthood in Sociological Theory', *Social Compass*, **21** (1), 5–23

Moore, John (1972), 'The Catholic Pentecostal Movement', in Hill, Michael (ed.), *A Sociological Yearbook of Religion in Britain*, vol. VI, London: Student Christian Movement, pp. 73ff.

Nauss, Allen (1972), 'Problems in Measuring Ministerial Effectiveness', *Journal for the Scientific Study of Religion*, **11** (2), 141–51

Nauss, Allen (1974), 'The Relation of Pastoral Mobility to Effectiveness', *Review of Religious Research*, **15** (2), 80–86

Nelson, Hart M. and Maguire, Mary Ann (1980), 'The Two Worlds of Clergy and Congregation: Dilemma for Mainline Denominations', *Sociological Analysis*, **41** (1), 74–80

Paul, Leslie (1964), *The Deployment and Payment of the Clergy*, London: Church Information Office

Paul, Leslie (1972), 'The Role of the Clergy Today: An Organizational Approach: Problems of Deployment', in Mitton, C.L. (ed.), *The Social Sciences and the Churches*, Edinburgh: T. and T. Clark

Peterson, Robert W. and Schoenheir, Richard A. (1978), 'Organizational Status Attainment of Religious Professionals', *Social Forces*, **56** (3), March, 794–822

Russell, Anthony (1984), *The Clerical Profession*, London: Society for Promoting Christian Knowledge

Sacks, Jonathan (2002), *The Dignity of Difference: How to Avoid the Clash of Civilizations*, London and New York: Continuum

Sharot, Stephen (1973), 'Religious Change in Native Orthodoxy in London, 1870 to 1914: Rabbinate and Clergy', *The Jewish Journal of Sociology*, **15** (2), December, 167–87

Sharot, Stephen (1975), 'The British and American Rabbinate: A Comparison of Authority Structures, Role Definitions and Role Conflicts', in Hill, Michael (ed.), *A Sociological Yearbook of Religion in Britain*, vol. VIII, London: Student Christian Movement, pp. 139ff.

Shupe, Jr., Anson D. and Wood, James R. (1973), 'Sources of Leadership Ideology in Dissident Clergy', *Sociological Analysis*, **34** (3), Fall, 185–201

Sklare, Marshall (1967), 'Church and the Laity among Jews', in Knudten, Richard D. (ed.), *The Sociology of Religion*, New York: Appleton-Century-Crofts, pp. 270ff.

Smith, Luke M. (1953), 'The Clergy: Authority Structure, Ideology, Migration', *American Sociological Review*, **18** (3), 242–8

Struzzo, John A. (1970), 'Professionalization and the Resolution of Authority Conflicts among the Catholic Clergy', *Sociological Analysis*, **31** (2), Summer, 92–106

Towler, Robert (1968), 'The Changing Status of the Ministry', *Crucible*, May, pp. 73ff.

Towler, R. (1972), 'The Role of the Clergy of Today', in Mitton, C.L. (ed.), *The Social Sciences and the Churches*, Edinburgh: T. and T. Clark, pp. 151ff.

Towler, Robert and Coxon, A.P.M. (1979), *The Fate of the Anglican Clergy: A Sociological Study*, London and Basingstoke: Macmillan

Ward, Frances (2004), 'The Messiness of Studying Congregations Using Ethnographic Methods', in Guest et al. (2004), pp. 125ff.

Warren, Yvonne (2002), *The Cracked Pot: The State of Today's Anglican Parish Clergy*, Stowmarket: Kevin Mayhew

Weber, Max (1922), 'The Three Types of Legitimate Rule', in Etzioni, Amitai and Lehman, E. (eds) (1980), *A Sociological Reader on Complex Organisations*, 3rd edn: Austin, Texas: Holt, Reinhart and Winston

Weber, Max (1963), *The Sociology of Religion*, Boston: Beacon Press

Wilson, Bryan (1965), 'The Paul Report Examined', *Theology*, **68** (536), February, 89–97

Wilson, Bryan (1967c), 'The Pentecostalist Minister: Role Conflicts and Contradictions of Status', in Wilson, Bryan (ed.), *Patterns of Sectarianism: Organization and Ideology in Social and Religious Movements*, London: Heinemann, pp. 138ff.

Wind, James P. and Lewis, James W. (eds), (1994), *American Congregations*, Chicago and London: University of Chicago Press

Wuthnow, Robert (1994), *Producing the Sacred: an essay on public religion*, Urbana and Chicago: University of Illinois Press

Young, Frank W. (1967), 'Adaptation and Pattern Integration of a California Sect', in Knudten, Richard D. (ed.), *The Sociology of Religion*, New York: Appleton-Century-Crofts, pp. 136ff.

CHAPTER 10

Religious and Faith-Based Organizations: Their Contribution to Civil Society

In 1995, Robert Putnam wrote an article entitled 'Bowling Alone: America's Declining Social Capital' (Putnam 1995). This was an examination of changing American habits: away from corporate voluntary activity and towards individual interests. As Putnam saw it, this was gutting society of its mediating structures. Whilst Putnam's research is on the USA (though some of his earlier research was on Italy), much the same applies to the UK, where those institutions between the state and the family (Sacks 1997) which hold society together in ways in which the state on its own cannot do are neither as numerous nor as large as before, leaving us with a lack of moral order, unstructured individual lives (Berger 1977), and markets and states without morality (Sacks 2002: 152). What Edmund Burke called the 'little platoons' (Burke 1993: 198), Alexis de Tocqueville 'habits of association' (de Tocqueville 1968) and Putnam 'social capital' (Putnam 1993; 1995; 2000) is a vital component of our society and has historically been vital to the health of democracy (Skocpol 2003); but modernization is causing its decline, and religious and faith-based organizations, which have long been important sources of social capital, therefore have an increasingly important role to play. It is by doing things together that trust is built up (Uslauer 1999: 144ff.; Farnell et al. 2003) and, whilst the state bears some responsibility for the building of trust and for creating an environment within which corporate voluntary activity can flourish (Cohen 1999: 223), and must remain responsible for the large-scale social safety nets which can only be provided on a national scale (Skocpol 1998: 40; 2003), *only* voluntary activity can build the social trust which the polity and the economy need (Putnam 1993: 164, 176), so the voluntary sector is going to have an increasingly important part to play in creating trust (Rochester 1998) and within that sector religious and faith-based organizations have a particular responsibility.

In this chapter we study the relationship between religious organizations and civil society. Most attention is on how congregations relate to the building of social capital, mainly because there is sufficient research literature on this issue. Faith-based organizations in the USA will receive a mention now and then, because there is some literature available on these (though even in the United States, where they are such an important subgroup of voluntary organizations, they are often neglected in studies of voluntary organizations: Knoke 1990).

There is remarkably little literature on faith-based organizations in the UK, which is a pity, because now that so much of the voluntary sector is government-influenced, if not actually government-controlled, religious organizations might come to have an even more important role in civil society. As Wuthnow recognizes, 'religion is a somewhat protected zone in which issues can be debated in ways that may be critical of established government policies or may simply defy the logic of bureaucratic norms in either the political or economic sectors' (Wuthnow 1994: 17, 199ff.). It is by *being religious* that religious organizations contribute to civil society, for the sacred contributes to the carving out of an autonomous public realm (that is, one not completely controlled by private or public organizations: and it can do this because its authority-structure extends beyond the boundaries of all institutions), and for the same reason the sacred's prophetic aspect can promote justice in ways in which self-interested organizations cannot. It is certainly true that the sacred is not clearly defined, but this is a strength and not a weakness, for it means that congregations have to debate activities in the context of a diversity of values, and this debate is itself a contribution to civil society (ibid.: 55).

There are three major ways in which congregations contribute to the stock of social capital: by simply being congregations with links into communities; by encouraging volunteering; and by organizing social action.

The Congregation in the Community

Simply by being social institutions, by having memberships, by having memberships with unclear boundaries, by having recognized office-holders, and by having links into the communities in which they are set, congregations increase the sum total of social capital: for within the congregation, and in relationship with the congregation, social contacts are made, social skills are learnt, and moral frameworks evolve and are communicated – and that is apart from the benefits to the community of rites of passage and celebratory and other events which a congregation might host. As communities change, congregations have a particularly important role to play, as they are institutions which change but which do not change in the same way as the rest of the community and thus can provide a sense of perspective; and they often still do what they have always done, and that is to give birth to new voluntary organizations as new needs arise. Indeed, the very existence of a congregation as a structured organization makes it possible for needs to be identified, resources to be gathered, and plans to be laid and carried out (Ammerman et al. 1997; Cormode 1994; Demerath and Schmitt 1994; Farnell et al. 2003).

Not that congregations usually make immediate or substantial differences to their communities. As Brannon shows, the impact is generally low-key and long-term, and more to do with attitudes than structural changes (Brannon 1971) because congregation members are generally there for their own diverse reasons and these will often have little to do with creating social capital. But there *is* an effect, for the congregation creates and transmits a religious tradition with a world-directed element (Farnell et al. 2003), and the congregation is more than the sum of its parts – so individual motivations, when put together in a congregation, can generate significant long-term social effects, particularly in deprived communities where the congregation can provide the 'glue' which the community needs in order to develop out of its deprivation (Deakin 2001: 70).

Different congregations, of course, will contribute differently to social capital. There are those which, because they are sectarian and world-denying in their views, will contribute little (Jeavons 2000), and there are those – such as some New Religious Movements (NRMs) – which, because they require social control, absorb social and individual emotional and organizational effort, and therefore deprive society of social capital rather than contributing to it (Beckford 1985a). Some NRMs, however, because in the end they need social acceptance if they are to continue to recruit (as they need to do, as for many people membership is a phase rather than a long-term commitment), will begin to build positive links with wider society (Barker 1982; 1983; Richardson et al. 1979).

Most of the influence we are here discussing is exercised locally, but it all adds up, and both nationally and globally society benefits from the presence of religious and faith-based organizations. Not only do congregations and their federations contribute to the political process by simply being institutions which are not state institutions, and thus by being fora for evaluation of social and political trends from within conceptual frameworks which might be different from those prevalent within state institutions; but globally they represent a critique of the marketization and globalization of culture (Deakin 2001), a critique sometimes manifested in corporate action, such as during the Jubilee 2000 campaign on Third-World debt: a campaign mainly organized by congregations, by denominations, and by faith-based organizations.

In some countries, for example in the USA, the culture represented by congregations is a prevailing culture and one consistent with the culture of government; religious organizations in these contexts rarely offer anything very distinctive in terms of critique (though their leaders might do so sometimes). In other parts of the world the situation is very different, and congregations and denominations have represented significant opposition to the government's culture, to the prevailing culture, or to both.

So it is already clear that, by their activity and by simply being organizations with links into the world around them, congregations contribute to social capital: which raises the question as to how this process occurs and thus how it can be encouraged.

Chang et al. (1994) have found that black-led congregations are more likely to refer people to community health agencies if the congregation already relates to the agency, and that such existing relationships are often individual-to-individual. Similarly, it was through individuals that the civil rights movement related to denominations, mainly because individuals were often less insulated from their social environments than congregations were – for congregations have to take account of the prejudices of their members and are therefore less likely to take contentious action or raise contentious ideas (Wood 1972b). What Benson (1971) finds, interestingly, is that if a congregation is diverse then it is more rather than less likely to be socially involved. Wood's and Benson's conclusions can only be reconciled by supposing that in the congregations Benson studied it is subgroups which are socially active, leaving us with the conclusion that a congregation will be more socially active if it develops subgroups with sufficient autonomy to carry out projects without a mandate or approval from the congregation as a whole.

The Jewish community recognizes that it is a 'community of communities' (Commission on Representation of the Interests of the British Jewish Community 2000: 3), meaning that its representation of itself to the wider world must be multi-faceted, and also meaning that its different groupings can relate to society in different ways. Hager et al. (1997) find that, whilst in the USA smaller faith-based organizations are declining in favour of larger ones, the smaller ones fulfil diverse social functions and are therefore essential to the sector's contribution to social capital. This suggests that the Jewish community and any other religious tradition will have greatest effect by working in a diverse fashion and by encouraging diversity of thought and action.

We have thus seen that the contributions to social capital made by congregations and other religious and faith-based organizations will be enhanced by individuals and subgroups having the freedom to relate to communities and to secular agencies, a suggestion backed up by Benson's conclusion that bureaucratized religious organizations are *not* good at integrating with wider society (Benson and Dorsett 1971). (However, Hall (1998) points out that in institution-to-institution relationships in higher education the larger bureaucratic religious organizations can make a contribution.)

Because leaders are often institutionally insecure, and because they have few sanctions available to them, leaders are not always the best placed people to encourage new links outside the religious organization. It is *always* difficult to introduce unwanted change into congregations (for instance, racial integration in the USA: Wood and Zald 1966), and it is no surprise that Hall has found that the congregation's typical action is response to change rather than instigation of it (Hall 1992). Hall also finds, again unsurprisingly, that where a congregation *does* sponsor social change in its community, the congregation itself is changed, as Wineburg has found in a study of congregations involved in welfare provision, congregations in which social action has led from a civic religion to a more activist stance because new relationships with society, and thus a more positive image in society, have led them into work for social justice based on a newly-felt need and on the opportunity which social acceptance offers (Wineburg 1994).

Since the end of the nineteenth century, voluntary organizations have been declining in the UK (Yeo 1973), a process which has included religious and faith-based organizations; but religious and faith-based organizations are still significant inventors of voluntary organizations and of other ways of building social capital – and one of those ways is the encouragement which congregations give to volunteering.

Volunteering

Lukka and Locke's survey data shows that a regular churchgoer is two or three times more likely to do voluntary work than someone who doesn't go to church. It isn't the presence of any particular belief-system which is the important factor: rather, it is belonging to a congregation. (The researchers recognize the complexity of the relationship between believing and belonging.) Belonging to a congregation introduces people to others who are already volunteers, thus encouraging them to volunteer too (most volunteers have initially become involved through personal contact); and belonging to a congregation increases social skills and is thus likely to motivate people to use those skills – though it might also be that particular personality-types are both likely to join congregations and to volunteer for purposeful activity elsewhere (Lukka and Locke 2000; Harris 1995a). This last possibility is consistent with Jackson's finding that someone who belongs to a subgroup within a congregation is more likely to do voluntary work than someone who doesn't (Jackson et al. 1995): but that finding is also consistent with the hypothesis that it is through meeting existing volunteers while attending the subgroup that encouragement is given to volunteer.

Cnaan et al. (1993) find supporting evidence for the conclusion that strength of religious belief does not affect the likelihood of volunteering, but also find that if the voluntary activity is *connected* to the congregation then strength of belief *does* affect the likelihood of volunteering – presumably because congregation-linked voluntary work functions as a direct expression of faith in ways in which other voluntary work does not. The researchers therefore suggest that voluntary activity linked to a congregation is an efficient way to provide social welfare. In the USA, congregations are the single biggest source of volunteers (DiIulio 1998), and Cnaan's major piece of research (Cnaan 2002: 211ff.) shows just how substantial that contribution is.

Social Action

In Germany and in the USA the denominations are responsible for a wide range of social welfare provision. In the UK and in other European countries the volume is not so great, but the denominations' contribution of welfare provision (often through organizations supported by a variety of congregations) is still substantial. Cnaan's research reveals just how different American congregations are from those of other developed countries, and it charts their enormous contribution to welfare provision (Cnaan 2002: 296ff.; cf. Cnaan 1997); and Wineburg shows how this contribution has risen in importance as government commitment to social welfare has dropped (Wineburg 1992; 1993). Gibbs and Ewer have found that in the United States the level of response to social issues depends on the congregation's size, its educational composition, and the leadership resources available (Gibbs and Ewer 1969), and the same might be true for the UK.

Kosmin and Ritterband (1991) have found that for synagogues and for Jews individually, support for traditional Jewish causes is falling, suggesting a greater degree of assimilation; but they also find that support for alternative Jewish causes is rising, suggesting more political awareness amongst Jews. Generally, the more congregations are involved in wider society the more they become politically active (Lenski 1961), mainly because they come to see that their welfare goals can only be met by political means (Choe 1980) and because, unless they are funded by government, they have a position of independence and are thus able to make a distinctive contribution.

Religious organizations which involve themselves in social action encounter a number of problems, particularly in relation to work funded by government or carried out in partnership with secular organizations. Religious groups can be socially reactionary, they can speak a religious language which it is difficult for secular authorities to engage with, and they are often not representative of the societies in which they are set and have only rudimentary representative structures, if any (Farnell et al. 2003). There is often little work which is distinctive, because isomorphism occurs, and the religious organization can often find itself as a junior and marginal partner to a secular organization (Hammonds-Smith and Malone-Atkins 2001) – and in these circumstances elements within the religious organization might begin to question the work's value (Finneron 1993) at the same time as secular power distances the organization from its religious roots and motivations (Farnell et al. 2003). But there *is* something distinctive if the welfare work is based in the congregation, for Chaves and Tsitsos (2001) have found that here the work tends to be of the short-term emergency variety rather than the longer-term development work provided by other types of organization – a distinction not necessarily true of community development projects sponsored by urban congregations in the UK. Farnell et al. have found that in the UK religious and faith-based organizations are important partners in many urban regeneration projects. For these organizations, religious faith is

> a source of motivation and direction in community activity...and many make strong connections between the spiritual and the social...Many in faith communities apply critical and challenging perspectives to official regeneration programmes. These derive both from their theologies and values and from their long-term local experience, often informed by substantial informal regeneration activity and by their participation in formal programmes...Across Britain there are thousands of social initiatives which faith organizations and their members provide or host for their own members, and in many cases, the wider population. Together, these activities reflect strong commitment to social care and often to a wider civic social and political engagement. Much of this work is informal and self-funded. However, members of faith communities are often prominent in more official regeneration programmes and many religious organizations contribute to the development and implementation of policy. (Farnell et al. 2003: 20, 29)

The researchers call for long-term engagement between secular authorities and religious and faith-based organizations so that they can be enabled to 'bring to regeneration activity [their] distinctive and strong motivations for social action, a particular long-term presence, the provision of informal settings and activities, and a commitment to listening to local people' (ibid.: 41).

But there are always problems, and funding is often one of them (Billis 2001: 46), either because it is not available or because the application process is complex. (This last has been found the case in the USA by congregations applying for funding under the new Charitable Choice legislation, which no longer requires a clear distinction between religious and welfare activity (Farnsley 2001), and in the UK by congregations involved in applications for Single Regeneration Budget money (Farnell et al. 2003).) Particularly difficult to maintain are projects funded by denominations, because welfare projects never seem like the organization's core business and are thus easy to shed when finances are problematic (Finneron 1993). Ecumenical projects are even more difficult to organize and to fund because different denominations will have different social aims (Tamney and Johnson 1990) and no denomination will regard itself as responsible for funding future work; but if ecumenical or multifaith projects do get off the ground then they can be a source for new understanding between different religious traditions (Farnell et al. 2003) and faith communities' involvement in practical projects can cause those communities to become less sectarian (ibid.).

A drawback with much congregation-based work is that it is run by small groups or by individuals and is thus likely to relate to individuals in need rather than to society's institutions: and it is in society's institutions and structures that the problem will often lie. Unusual amongst religious organizations are the industrial and urban missions, which have regarded institutions as important (Torry 1990; Choe 1980) and have seen one of their roles as relating religious institutions to secular institutions for the sake of the world of work, the environment, society, individuals, and the Kingdom of God (Davidson et al. 1979).

The industrial mission movement's strengths bring us to other important strengths of welfare activity managed by religious organizations. Because religious organizations are legitimated socially by their social action projects, they are able to gain acceptance for their relationships with secular organizations; and because they remain marginal organizations, they can serve the marginalized. This is an important combination, enabling religious organizations to mediate between different parts of our society (Cameron 1998). Chaves and Higgins find that in the USA black congregations are generally *less* active socially than white ones, but that where they are active they are active amongst the underprivileged, and also that they are more likely to be active if they are long-established – presumably because they then have the energy to put into the work and because their involvement is socially acceptable (Chaves and Higgins 1992).

As Harris shows, congregation-based social welfare work tends to be of the 'quiet care' variety and to be short-term. The motivation is religious, and benefits accrue to the volunteer, to the congregation, and to the person cared for, and in easily graspable fashion: which is not always the case for longer-term development projects (Harris 1995a; 1996). Moberg shows that more liberal Christians are more likely to involve themselves in social structures than conservative Christians are (Moberg 1970), so either there are innate connections between types of theology and types of social engagement, or people in different socio-economic classes are being drawn towards both conservative theology and personal care or towards both liberal theology and concern with social justice and society's structures.

So there might or might not be theological motives for involvement in welfare provision, and, if there are, different theologies might or might not lead to different results. (Lohmann (1995) suggests that the Buddhist tradition has given birth to particular kinds of community organization.) The greater social legitimation which the religious organization might receive might also be a motive for welfare work (Cameron 1998) (though legitimation and involvement bring demands for greater social accountability, which organizations might experience as constraining; Harris 1997); welfare work can be an active expression of a religious faith and can thus strengthen that faith (Mares 1994); involvement in an external piece of work can sometimes help a congregation or groups within it to handle change within the congregation (Zald and McCarthy 1998); and to be involved in person-to-person care can reduce the need felt to be involved in society's larger processes: for religious organizations are now less involved in civic life and might have taken up therapy, education, social work and leisure provision as a displacement activity (Martin 1977: 132).

An important consequence of social welfare work of all kinds is new networks formed which benefit both the community and the congregation, especially when a good balance is kept between a welfare project's relationship with the congregation which set it up and its relationship with the community: a balance which must be maintained through extending networks of involved people both into the congregation and into the community. This gives the congregation new social understanding and provides a route into the community for the social capital which the congregation can contribute (Schneider 1999).

Social Capital

Whilst much of this chapter has been about welfare projects, volunteering, and the congregation in the community, the message throughout has been about the contribution which religious and faith-based organizations can make to a society's social capital. In his *Making Democracy Work: Civic Traditions in Modern Italy* (1993) and his original article entitled 'Bowling Alone' (1995), Putnam worried about a loss of social capital being brought about by social changes. His later book entitled *Bowling Alone* (2000) is subtitled *The Collapse and Revival of American Community*, and in this substantial work he recognizes the membership of religious organizations as an important source for new social capital. Churches engender 'civic skills, civic norms, community interests and civic recruitment' (Putnam 2000: 66); church members learn to 'give speeches, run meetings, manage disagreements, and bear administrative responsibility' (ibid.: 66); and members of congregations are more likely than non-members to be involved in secular organizations and they are more likely to engage in such small-scale community-building tasks as visiting friends (ibid.: 67). In a survey of voluntary association membership 'it was membership in religious groups that was most closely associated with other forms of civic involvement, like voting, jury service, community projects, talking with neighbours, and giving to charity' (ibid.: 67). (Causality is probably bi-directional, particularly amongst black Americans, because the churches were the only black-controlled institutions (ibid.: 68).) Putnam concludes that 'religious people are unusually active social capitalists' (ibid.: 67) – which is why he is so concerned about increasing secularization (ibid.: 79).

The connection between membership of a religious organization and involvement in other organizations and in the wider community is an issue of which governments are now very much aware. Having attempted to tap the voluntary sector in general for its finances and its voluntary labour, the government is now turning to particular types of organizations (for instance, black and ethnic minority community groups for the contribution they can make to social harmony). One of the types of organization which the government and local authorities are now looking to is faith-based organizations. Harris et al. (2003) employ the results of their research on the financing and governance of Jewish educational and welfare organizations to study the viability of current expectations of an enhanced role for faith-based organizations. They conclude that, whilst Jewish organizations attract considerable amounts of voluntary labour and money, these resources are given in relation to the particular community which will benefit from the organization's work. This suggests that a wider role for such organizations will not necessarily be either welcome or possible to fulfil. Additionally, faith-based organizations are not necessarily located where needs are greatest, their priorities are not necessarily those of government, their financial base and their source of voluntary labour are both fragile, and it might not be possible to turn their motivation towards the needs of those outside the community which they normally serve. The researchers conclude:

> In sum, our studies suggest that faith communities may well be providing a good service for their own adherents and may also be contributing to the development of civil society by drawing together their own members in associational and voluntary activities. Yet, many of the characteristics which have drawn them to the attention of social-policy-makers reflect the fact that they have, up to now, been free to set their own strategic objectives and to govern themselves in ways which suit the wishes and culture of their community funders and volunteers. Partnerships with government which threaten their independence may not only be [inimical] to sustaining civil society and democracy ... but may also undermine the commitment of those who currently donate time and money to their own faith communities. The scope for *expanding* the role of [faith-based organizations] to meet broader, government-defined, social policy objectives appears to be limited. (Harris et al. 2003: 109)

Congregations and faith-based organizations make a substantial contribution to civil society by encouraging volunteering, by quiet care, and simply by being organizations in their communities. To expect them to take on additional activities might mean that they are less able to do what they're good at, that social capital might therefore decline, and the organizations might suffer, contributing to the general decline in religious and faith-based organizations and their links into other institutions. If religious organizations decline or become more inward-looking then volunteering will decline (Wuthnow et al. 1990: 112), trust will decline, social networks will decline, and social capital generally will decline. There are a number of religious reasons for religious and faith-based organizations to survive and thrive. There are clearly some good social reasons too.

References

Ammerman, Nancy Tatom, Farnsley II, Arthur E. et al. (1997), *Congregation and Community*, New Brunswick, New Jersey: Rutgers University Press

Barker, Eileen (ed.), (1982), *New Religious Movements: A Perspective for Understanding Society*, New York and Toronto: Edwin Meller Press

Barker, Eileen (1983), 'New Religious Movements in Britain: The Context and the Membership', *Social Compass*, **30** (1), 33–48

Beckford, James A. (1985a), *Cult Controversies: The Societal Response to New Religious Movements*, London and New York: Tavistock

Benson, J. Kenneth and Dorsett, James H. (1971), 'Toward a Theory of Religious Organizations', *Journal for the Scientific Study of Religion*, **10** (2), 139–51

Berger, Peter L. (1977), *Facing up to Modernity*, New York: Basic Books

Billis, David (2001), 'Tackling Social Exclusion: The contribution of voluntary organisations', in Harris and Rochester (2001b), pp. 37ff.

Brannon, Robert C.L. (1971), 'Organizational Vulnerability in Modern Religious Organizations', *Journal for the Scientific Study of Religion*, **10** (1), Spring, 27–32

Burke, Edmund (1993), *Reflections on the Revolution in France*, Oxford: Oxford University Press

Cameron, Helen (1998), 'The Social Action of the Local Church: Five Congregations in an English City', Unpublished PhD thesis, London School of Economics

Cameron, Helen (1999) 'Are members volunteers? An exploration of the concept of membership drawing upon studies of the local church', *Voluntary Action*, **1** (2), Spring, 53–66

Cameron, Helen (2001), 'A perspective from the study of religious organisations', in Anheier, Helmut K. (ed.), *Organisational Theory and the Non-profit Form*, report no. 2, London: Centre for Civil Society, London School of Economics

Chang, Patricia M.Y., Williams, David R., Griffith, Ezra E.H. and Young, John (1994), 'Church–Agency Relationships in the Black Community', *Nonprofit and Voluntary Sector Quarterly*, **23** (2), Summer, 91–105

Chaves, Mark and Higgins, Lynn M. (1992), 'Comparing the Community Involvement of Black and White Congregations, *Journal for the Scientific Study of Religion*, **31** (4), 425–40

Chaves, Mark and Tsitsos, William (2001), 'Congregations and Social Services: What They Do, How They Do It, and With Whom', *Nonprofit and Voluntary Sector Quarterly*, **30** (4), December, 660–83

Choe, Jae-Hyeon (1980), 'The Range of Voluntary Association Activity in Dependent Capitalism: The Case of Urban Industrial Mission in South Korea', *Journal of Voluntary Action Research*, **9** (1–4), 124–30

Cnaan, Ram (1997), *Social and Community Involvement of Religious Congregations Housed in Historic Religious Properties: Findings from a Six-City Study Program for the Study of Organized Religion and Social Work*, Philadelphia: University of Pennsylvania

Cnaan, Ram A. (2002), *The Invisible Hand: American Congregations and the Provision of Welfare*, New York: New York University Press

Cnaan, Ram A., Kasternakis, Amy and Wineburg, Robert J. (1993), 'Religious People, Religious Congregations, and Volunteerism in Human Services: Is there a Link?' *Nonprofit and Voluntary Sector Quarterly*, **22** (1), Spring, 33–51

Cohen, Jean (1999), 'Trust, voluntary association and workable democracy: the contemporary American discourse of civil society', in Warren, Mark E. (ed.), *Democracy and Trust*, Cambridge: Cambridge University Press, pp. 208ff.

Commission on Representation of the Interests of the British Jewish Community (2000), *A Community of Communities*, London: Institute for Jewish Policy Research

Cormode, D. Scott (1994), 'Review Essay: Religion and the Nonprofit Sector', *Nonprofit and Voluntary Sector Quarterly*, **23** (2), Summer, 171–82

Davidson, James D., Elly, Ronald, Hull, Thomas and Need, Donald (1979), 'Increasing Church Involvement in Social Concern: A Model for Urban Ministries', *Review of Religious Research*, **20** (3), pp. 291ff.

Deakin, Nicholas (2001), *In Search of Civil Society*, Basingstoke: Palgrave

Demerath III, N.J. and Schmitt, Terry (1994), 'Transcending Sacred and Secular: Mutual benefits in analyzing religious and nonreligious organizations', in Bromiley, David G., Greil, Arthur L. and Robbins, Thomas (eds), *Religion and the Social Order*, vol. 4, Greenwich, Connecticut: Jai Press

De Tocqueville, Alexis (1968), *Democracy in America*, London: Fontana

DiIulio, John J. (1998), 'The Lord's Work: The Church and Civil Society', in Dionne (1998), pp. 50ff.

Dionne, E.J. (ed.) (1998), *Community Works: The Revival of Civil Society in America*, Washington DC: Brookings Institute Press

Farnell, Richard, Furbey, Robert, Hills, Stephen Shams Al-Haqq, Macey, Marie and Smith, Greg (2003), *'Faith' in Urban Regeneration? Engaging faith communities in urban regeneration*, Bristol: Policy Press

Farnsley II, Arthur E. (2001), 'Can Faith-Based Organizations Compete?' *Nonprofit and Voluntary Sector Quarterly*, **30** (1), March, 99–111

Finneron, Doreen (1993), *Faith in Community Development: Case Studies of Church Based Community Development Projects in Urban Priority Areas*, Manchester: University of Manchester

Gibbs, James O. and Ewer, Phyllis A. (1969), 'External Adaptation of Religious Organizations: Church Response to Social Issues', *Sociological Analysis*, **30** (4), Winter, 223–34

Hager, Mark A., Pins, Joel J. and Jorgensen, Cheryl A. (1997), 'Unto Thy Maker: The Fate of Church-Based Nonprofit Clinics in a Turbulent Health Care Environment', *Nonprofit and Voluntary Sector Quarterly*, **26** (s), s85–100

Hall, Leda McIntyre (1992), 'A Commission to Change: the United Methodist Church in Detroit, Michigan, 1950–1980', *Nonprofit and Voluntary Sector Quarterly*, **21** (1), Spring, 39–49

Hall, Peter Dobkin (1998), 'Religion and the Organizational Revolution in the United States', in Demerath III, N.J., Hall, Peter Dobkin, Schmitt, Terry and Williams, Rhys H. (eds), *Sacred Companies: Organizational Aspects of Religion and Religious Aspects of Organizations*, New York and Oxford: Oxford University Press, pp. 99ff.

Hammonds-Smith, Maxine and Malone-Atkins, Dottie (2001), 'Volunteers and the 3C Model (Campus, Church, Community)', *Voluntary Action*, **3** (2), Spring, 47–56

Harris, Margaret (1995a), 'Quiet Care: Welfare Work and Religious Congregations', *Journal of Social Policy*, **24** (1), 53–71

Harris, Margaret (1996), '"An Inner Group of Willing People": Volunteering in a Religious Context', *Social Policy and Administration*, **30** (1), 54–68

Harris, Margaret (1997?), *The Jewish voluntary sector in the United Kingdom: its role and its future*, London: Institute for Jewish Policy Research

Harris, Margaret (1998a) *Organizing God's Work: Challenges for Churches and Synagogues*, London: Macmillan

Harris, Margaret and Rochester, Colin (eds) (2001b), *Voluntary Organisations and Social Policy in Britain*, Basingstoke: Palgrave

Harris, Margaret, Halfpenny, Peter and Rochester, Colin (2003), 'A Social Policy Role for Faith-based Organizations? Lessons from the UK Jewish Voluntary Sector', *Journal of Social Policy*, **32** (1), 93–112

Ingram, Larry C. (1980), 'Notes on Pastoral Power in the Congregational Tradition', *Journal for the Scientific Study of Religion*, **19** (1), 40–48

Jackson, Elton F., Bachmeier, Mark D., Wood, James R. and Craft, Elizabeth A. (1995), 'Volunteering and Charitable Giving: Do Religious and Associational Ties Promote Helping Behavior', *Nonprofit and Voluntary Sector Quarterly*, **24** (1), 59–78

Jeavons, Thomas H. (2000), 'Understanding Congregations as Voluntary Organizations: New Insights for the Nonprofit Sector', *Nonprofit Management and Leadership*, **10** (4), Summer, 457–62: a review of Ammerman, Nancy Tatom (1997), *Congregation and Community*, New Brunswick, N.J.: Rutgers University Press, and Harris, Margaret (1998), *Organizing God's Work: Challenges for Churches and Synagogues*, New York: St Martin's Press, and London: Macmillan

Knoke, David (1990), *Organizing for Political Action: The Political Economies of Associations*, New York: Aldine de Gruyter

Kosmin, Barry A. and Ritterband, Paul (eds) (1991), *Contemporary Jewish Philanthropy in America*, New York: Rosman and Littlefield

Lenski, Gerhara (1961), *The Religious Factor: A Sociological Study of Religions' Impact on Politics, Economics and Family Life*, New York: Doubleday

Lohmann, Roger A. (1995), 'Buddhist Commons and the question of a third sector in Asia', *Voluntas*, 6 (2), 140–58

Lukka, Priya and Locke, Michael (2000), 'Faith, voluntary action and social policy: a review of research', *Voluntary Action*, **3** (1), Winter, 25–42

Mares, Alvin S. (1994), 'Housing and the Church', *Nonprofit and Voluntary Sector Quarterly*, **23** (2), Summer, 139–57

Martin, David (1977), *Reflections on Sociology and Theology*, Oxford: Clarendon Press

Moberg, David O. (1970), 'Theological Position and Institutional Characteristics of Protestant Congregations: An Exploratory Study', *Journal for the Scientific Study of Religion*, **9** (1), 53–8

Putnam, Robert (1993), *Making Democracy Work: Civic Traditions in Modern Italy*, Princeton, New Jersey: Princeton University Press

Putnam, Robert (1995), 'Bowling Alone: America's Declining Social Capital', *Journal of Democracy*, **6**, January, 65–78

Putnam, Robert (2000), *Bowling Alone: The Collapse and Revival of American Community*, New York: Simon Schuster

Richardson, James T., Simmonds, Robert B. and Stewart, Mary W. (1979), 'The Evolution of a Jesus Movement Organization', *Journal of Voluntary Action Research*, **8** (3–4), October–December, 93–111

Rochester, Colin (1998), *Social Benefits: Exploring the value of community sector organisations*, West Malling: Charities Aid Foundation

Sacks, Jonathan (1997), *The Politics of Hope*, London: Jonathan Cape

Sacks, Jonathan (2002), *The Dignity of Difference: How to Avoid the Clash of Civilizations*, London and New York: Continuum

Schneider, Jo Anne (1999), 'Trusting that of God in everyone: Three examples of Quaker-based social service in disadvantaged communities', *Nonprofit and Voluntary Sector Quarterly*, **28** (3), 269–95

Skocpol, Theda (1998), 'Don't Blame Big Government: America's Voluntary Groups Thrive in a National Network', in Dionne (1998), pp. 37ff.

Skocpol, Theda (2003), *Diminished Democracy: From Membership to Management in American Civil Life*, Norman, Oklahoma: University of Oklahoma Press

Tamney, Joseph B. and Johnson, D. (1990), 'Religious Diversity and Ecumenical Social Action', *Review of Religious Research*, **32** (1), 16–26

Torry, Malcolm N.A. (1990), 'The Practice and Theology of the South London Industrial Mission', unpublished PhD thesis, University of London.

Uslauer, Eric M. (1999), 'Democracy and Social Capital', in Warren, Mark E. (ed.), *Democracy and Trust*, Cambridge: Cambridge University Press, 121–50

Williams, Jr., Charles (1984), 'Contemporary Voluntary Associations in the Urban Black Church: The Development and Growth of Mutual Aid Societies', *Journal of Voluntary Action Research*, **13** (4), October–December, 19–30

Wind, James P. and Lewis, James W. (eds) (1994), *American Congregations*, Chicago and London: University of Chicago Press

Wineburg, Robert J. (1992), 'Local Human Service Provision by Religious Congregations: A Community Analysis', *Nonprofit and Voluntary Sector Quarterly*, **21** (2), Summer, 107–18

Wineburg, Robert J. (1993), 'Social Policy, Community Service Development, and Religious Organizations', *Nonprofit Management and Leadership*, **3** (3), Spring, 283–97

Wineburg, Robert J. (1994), 'A Longitudinal Case Study of Religious Congregations in Local Human Services', *Nonprofit and Voluntary Sector Quarterly*, **23** (2), Summer, 159–69

Wood, James R. (1972b), 'Personal Commitment and Organizational Restraint: Church Officials and Racial Integration', *Sociological Analysis*, **33** (3), Fall, pp. 142ff.

Wood, James R. and Zald, Mayer N. (1966), 'Aspects of Racial Integration in the Methodist Church: Sources of Resistance to Organizational Policy', *Social Forces*, **45** (2), December, 255–65

Wuthnow, Robert (1994), *Producing the Sacred: an essay on public religion*, Urbana and Chicago: University of Illinois Press

Wuthnow, Robert, Hodgkinson, Virginia A. et al. (1990), *Faith and Philanthropy in America: Exploring the Role of Religion in America's Voluntary Sector*, San Francisco and Oxford: Jossey Bass

Yeo, Stephen (1973), 'A Contextual View of Religious Organisation', in Hill, Michael (ed.), *A Sociological Yearbook of Religion in Britain*, vol. VI, London: Student Christian Movement, pp. 207ff.

Yeo, Stephen (1976), *Religion and Voluntary Organisations in Crisis* (London: Croom Helm)

Zald, Mayer N. and McCarthy, John D. (1998), 'Religious Groups as Crucibles of Social Movements', in Demerath III, N.J., Hall, Peter Dobkin, Schmitt, Terry and Williams, Rhys H. (eds), *Sacred Companies: Organizational Aspects of Religion and Religious Aspects of Organizations*, New York and Oxford: Oxford University Press, pp. 24ff.

CHAPTER 11

Leadership in Religious and Faith-Based Organizations

All of the other chapters in this book have been as descriptive as possible and have drawn tentative conclusions. This chapter is rather different: it is prescriptive, with its prescriptions backed up by the literature. This is in keeping with the literature on leadership (for example, Bennis 2000), and is presumably because any definition of 'leadership' must be either axiomatic or a definition in the form of a hypothesis (and whilst hypotheses can be supported they cannot be proved). In a book which is intended to be practical, a final chapter on leadership seems appropriate, even if it argues in the other way round from the other chapters. I can only claim in defence that all science is in fact hypothesis seeking support and giving rise to new questions (Popper 1959; 1962).

Much of what we said on governance in Chapter 6 is relevant here, for an important function of a leader in a religious or faith-based organization is to ensure that governance structures are working and that their own work serves the organization through those structures rather than conflicting with them (which does not mean that there will be no conflict, as we shall see below).

Here we outline some tasks which any successful leader will be undertaking: The leader will:

1 understand the organization's structure and the organization's values and work with them;
2 structure the organization according to its values;
3 develop goals in line with the organization's values and will ensure that the goals are met;
4 manage change in ways coherent with the organization's values;
5 manage conflict in accordance with the organization's values; and
6 in their own lives give expression to the organization's values.

The tasks will require the leader to exhibit particular qualities and skills:

1 understanding and working with the organization's values will require communication skills and also personal qualities and a spirituality which can relate to the ethics and spirituality of the organization;
2 structuring the organization according to its values will require leadership, interpersonal, communication and management skills appropriate to the organization;

3   developing goals in line with the organization's values and ensuring that
    they are met will require the same combination of skills;
4   and   5   the management of change and of conflict in ways coherent with
    the organization's values will require leadership and management skills
    appropriate to the organization and also considerable interpersonal skills;
    and
6   giving expression in the leader's own life to the organization's values will
    require a spirituality and personal qualities coherent with the spirituality
    and qualities of the organization.

In research carried out amongst congregations and faith-based organizations, Bill Allen has discovered considerable consensus as to the skills required
of church leaders, all of which fall into the six 'core quality and skill areas' of
spirituality, personal qualities, leadership, management, communication skills
and interpersonal skills (Allen 2004: 36). Allen's conclusion is that leadership
training needs to address all of these quality and skill areas if good church
leaders are to be the result.

1   Knowing the Organization's Structure and Values

The first leadership task is a clear-eyed evaluation of the structures of the
particular organization and of the ideologies, theologies and other value-
systems operating within it. (I shall here use 'values' to denote all ideological,
theological, ethical, political, social and other values underlying the organization's structures and activities.)

   In previous chapters we have studied the structures of religious and faith-
based organizations in general and of a few such organizations in particular.
There is no need to repeat that material here. What is essential to the leadership
task is to understand how the organization works, how it changes, and how it
makes decisions. The organization, if it is religious or faith-based, will be to a
large extent like a community, and might be best described *as* a community;
and if it is religious or faith-based then it will have goals related to its religious
tradition and will be 'a device for mobilizing energies and achieving purposes'
(Selznick 1992: 289). The leader will need not only to balance these two
characteristics of the organization but also to assist the organization in
fashioning these two characteristics into a complementary pair rather than a
confrontational duality.

   An equal objectivity will be needed in relation to the organization's values.
So if 'the American way of life' happens to be one of the sets of values
underlying an organization's activity, then that fact has to be recognized
(whatever the leader might think about that fact; Glock 1967); and if values
attached to a particular social class are controlling the organization's direction,

or if the voluntary principle determines members' attitudes to membership, or if a professionalization of the clergy is having an impact on their behaviour, then all of this must be brought into the open, both for the leader and for the organization: for it is only in the context of understood values that a leader can help an organization to formulate goals and meet them; and it is only if existing values are recognized that they can be changed (Dolan 1994). The values together constitute a 'culture', which often has little to do with the stated culture of a denomination or of a faith-based organization, and so the connections between values are as important as the values themselves (Anderson 1971). Franklin points out that attention to values, and to maintaining them, is what makes a leader: no amount of charismatic leadership will substitute for this – though charismatic leadership will sometimes be channelled into maintaining a culture, as it often is in black-led congregations through a preaching tradition (Franklin 1994). As we shall see, it is in fact attention to the whole culture, with all its inter-connections and all its connections beyond the organization, which is what makes a leader.

In a religious or faith-based organization, authority is maintained by enacting and articulating values, rather than through the kind of rational means which commercial organizations employ: so what a leader is doing is operating within a traditional authority-structure and enabling a normative compliance structure to operate (Cameron 2001) – something which those reshaping the Church of England's central structures never understood (Archbishops' Commission 1995). Such authority, based on organizational values, is by no means static, as the values develop as the environment changes: and the leader's role is to help this process to happen – always with an eye on values from the past as well as on ways in which they might need to change.

Amongst the authoritative structure of values there will be values at various levels. At deeper levels the values will change slowly – for instance, the 'institution', 'mystical communion', 'sacrament', 'herald', 'servant' and 'community of disciples' theological values underlying denominations and the Church as a whole (Dulles 1988). A secondary layer will change faster – for instance, values related to the position of the clergy; and they will change in such a way that the organization will thrive if they change in accordance with the deeper values. The leader will need to understand this process and to work with it, allowing the organization's values to shape goals, structures, resources sought and means employed, always recognizing that the values will themselves be changed by the organization's activities (Hinings and Foster 1973). In religious organizations, leadership itself is legitimated by values rather than by any position in a bureaucratic structure, and the leader will need to understand the traditional and the bureaucratic aspects of their organization, how these relate to each other, how they relate to the organization's values, and how they impinge on the leadership task (Bartholomew 1981).

In most voluntary organizations, as Dane (1998) shows, statute law defines a great deal of what is done and how it is done because it defines the organization's structure. In religious and faith-based organizations, religious and other values fulfil this role, leaving law to mediate between the organization's values and the wider society. Thus the organization and society negotiate a mutual understanding, and one of the leader's tasks is to ensure that this happens to the benefit both of society and of the organization.

It is also the leader's task to understand the consequences of an organization's values. For instance: the Jehovah's Witnesses' very definite core values enable them to recruit to a single unified organization at the same time as allowing cultural diversity (Munters 1971), whereas severe membership problems can be caused by the rather less definite values of humanist societies (Budd 1967), of Israel's now pluralist voluntary sector (a pluralism itself fostered by the voluntary sector; Gidren 1997), and of American Liberal Protestant denominations (where again the values have contributed to attitudes which have caused organizational decline; Demerath 1998) – especially in a context of social acceptance of the organization. In such a situation, the leader's task is to bring the values to consciousness, to enable the organization to evaluate their effects, and to draw up strategies – which might, of course, include doing nothing and allowing institutional decay.

2 Creating Structures and Practices

An important leadership role, once the values have been understood, is to enable the organization's structures and practices to conform to these values. Good organization *is* the key to survival, for enthusiastic movements as well as for any others (Beckford 1985b), and 'good' organization here means organization consistent with the organization's values; but this isn't always easy to arrange, especially when appropriate resources are not available. For instance, recruiting staff who share an organization's values is important to shaping the organization's practices according to those values, and this can be difficult (Jeavons 1994b; Valins 2002). Not only must a faith-based organization's staff be treated according to the organization's values (Jeavons 1992), but as the environment changes this care for staff must be maintained at the same time as ensuring that the staff represent the organization's values in their work: not always possible when everything around them is changing (Jeavons 1993; 1994a). To the organization, the values represent a technology (McCann 1993) in which the staff must become expert so that they can ensure that not only the organization's goals but also the means employed to obtain them are consistent with those values (Jeavons 1994a).

3   Creating Goals and Meeting Them

There is no shortage of goals around religious organizations, because every member has their own, and unless all of these goals are met the organization will lose members. Similarly, faith-based organizations will survive if they meet the personal goals of staff and users, but not necessarily if they meet only organizational goals (Bibby and Mauss 1974). Because leaders are only rewarded if religious organizations have members or if faith-based organizations have staff and users, this leaves leaders insecure and with little control over the organization's direction (Brannon 1971). Thung (1978) suggests that the leader's task is therefore to reduce individuals' value-commitments and to enable organizational goals to be formulated and met. The other possibility, of course is to develop a range of organizational goals both to meet individuals' goals and to enable the organization to do useful work consistent with its values. This is a complex process and it requires constant decision-making as the environment changes: and this decision-making can become particularly difficult when a faith-based organization needs to decide whether to serve the religious organization which set it up or to serve users' needs, or whether to let activity follow funding or to develop a mission and hope that funding will follow (Jeavons 1994a). The hardest decisions need to be made when it is not possible to maintain foundational values and at the same time survive.

Rooney offers an interesting case study of a rescue mission, the goal of which had become to employ staff but the stated goal of which was still to rescue young people from addictions: for only by maintaining the semblance of a social purpose would further funding be forthcoming (Rooney 1980). The combination of failure and survival is not uncommon, and it demands difficult leadership decisions. Another interesting case is the religious organization apparently without goals. If a religious organization is meeting individual members' personal goals, and it has traditional and bureaucratic authority-structures which function, then it can survive whilst appearing to have no organizational goals (Scalf et al. 1973). But there *is* a goal here – that is, to meet members' religious and other needs – and for many congregations this is in fact the organizational goal.

There always are organizational goals, even if it is merely the goal to survive. The leader's task, particularly where organizational goals are minimal, is to scour the organization's values, its potential resources, and its opportunities, and to enable the organization to set and meet goals. In the process of meeting goals it is more likely that the organization will survive than that it would do so without setting goals for itself, and this is something which most memberships understand, however much they might wish to resist change to their organization. Thus, a religious order will generally thrive if it has a leader who concentrates on organizational goals as well as on personal ones, who is able to express the order's values in everyday affairs, who is able to help the whole membership to own decisions, and who is able to consult – for that way the decisions are more likely to be owned by the order as a whole (Nygren et al. 1994).

4 Managing Change

No organization stands still. Members change and the environment changes, and the leader's task is therefore to manage change in such a way that the organization thrives at the same time as remaining true to its values.

Religious organizations have changed ever since their religious traditions were founded, but today's changing is more complex than change used to be because communication is easier, so the environment has become more plural; and every religious organization knows itself to be one organization amongst many and subject to a larger number of unpredictable pressures (Martin 1977: ch. 10). In this situation, the leader's first task is to ensure that change is always on the agenda, for simply trying to change will encourage adaptation and thus more appropriate behaviour in new environments (Ammerman et al. 1997).

Particularly interesting changes in the environment are new ideas or new combinations of ideas. Religious organizations are partly theology-driven, so when new theology emerges the organization's values will start to change, either in line with the new ideas or in reaction to them. Provided the new theology won't derail the tradition, it will be integrated into the organization's values (Berger 1977); but where integration might prove impossible, the ideas will be rejected – though if there are integrable elements then they will be taken on board if that is necessary for maintaining links with other organizations. The leader's task is to help the difficult integration or rejection decision to be made: a decision which will in fact be made as much on the grounds of the organization's social reality (including the views of its members and its status amongst other organizations) as on purely theological grounds (Berger 1969a). The good leader will probably prefer integration of new ideas if that is at all possible, for that will tend to maintain necessary networks; and the leader will be encouraged in this view by the knowledge that theological ideas are readily adaptable and that the same idea can often fit into apparently opposed conceptual frameworks with relatively little difficulty (Berger 1969b). The leader will also be encouraged by the knowledge that organizations change ideas, so to build relationships with new ideas will change those ideas and will change other organizations which have made relationships with them (Wilson 1967b).

In this process, and in general as religious or faith-based organizations negotiate change, the leader will be a 'boundary-spanner', someone who makes links in order to gather new cultural and other resources. Religious organizations are open systems, so success will relate to keeping good connections with a variety of networks, communities, organizations, ideas, practices and values; and spanning the boundaries with new values will not only change an organization's goals and activities, it will also change the values underlying the organization's structures and activities (Milofsky 1997).

Such leadership is exploratory in nature, and in religious and faith-based organizations it is such exploration which is just as necessary to good leadership as is any ability to set goals and meet them, to manage change, or to manage conflict.

5   Managing Conflict

There *will* of course be conflict, especially if the organization is changing, as it needs to do if it is to thrive in a changing environment. Thus leaders must be positive about conflict and not deny its importance (Ammerman et al. 1997).

There will be conflict over values, particularly if they are changing; there will be conflict between people with different roles (for instance, between clergy and laity), particularly as those roles change as the organization changes and previous accommodations no longer function (Kokosalakis 1971); there will be conflicts between structures and values (as sometimes they reinforce each other and sometimes they don't) and such conflict will cause conflict between people more attached to values and people more attached to structures (Stout and Cormode 1998); there will be conflict over symbols, for these represent important values – and the importance of such symbol-conflicts should never be minimized (Thompson 1973: 293); and there will be conflicts generated by wider social conflicts, such as class or ethnic conflicts, where changes in religious or faith-based organizations cause previously submerged conflicts to come to the surface – as, for instance, when leaders' relationships with social élites prevent them from mediating between élites and other groups when the community or the congregation might expect them to do so (Allcock 1968).

Leaders are problem-solvers, and this is no more clearly their role than when they are trying to resolve conflicts (Butler and Herman 1999: 229).

6   Objectivating

Above all, the leader's task is objectivation: the putting into practice of the organization's values so that they themselves become part of the organization's plausibility structure. (The converse is deobjectivation, where the leader's actions and values oppose the organization's values and both their own plausibility and the organization's plausibility suffer (Berger 1977; Cameron 2001).)

It is in this sense that the leader of the religious organization or of the faith-based organization will be somewhat different from leaders of other types of organization. The managing director of a furniture manufacturing company might or might not be passionate about furniture – and there might be an argument that it would be better if they weren't. The leader of a religious or faith-based organization, on the other hand, must share the organization's values to a considerable extent (more so in the case of the religious organization, less so in the case of the faith-based organization) *and* must put them into practice; and their own lives must at least not contradict those values.

This is one final complication to add to what we have seen is already a complex leadership task: a complication because as the environment and the organization change the leader must change too, and must change their values, in order to remain a good leader of their religious or faith-based organization. The good leader will be one who knows their organization's narrative (Hopewell 1987; Wuthnow 1994: 61), inhabits it and develops it as the world around changes. There will be challenges to face. If a congregation takes on staff members who are not members, then their own interests might conflict with those of the congregation – and the leader's role will be to retell the narrative so that everyone involved can know that it's theirs; or an achievement ethos might be imposed from outside the congregation, threatening the congregation's narrative and the religious tradition's core commitments with relativism – and again, the leader's role is to retell the narrative so that it remains the congregation's story and at the same time adapts to a changing world; or the congregation might take on new activities which threaten to change its ethos and alienate some of its members – and again the leader will need to retell the congregation's story in a way which is both new and recognizable. If the story is not retold in such new ways then it will stagnate, the activity will stagnate, and the leader's role will be to listen to the possibilities and to tell the next instalment of the congregation's narrative before it is too late.

A good leader of a religious or faith-based organization is, above all, a good story-teller.

References

Allcock, J.B. (1968), 'Voluntary Associations and the Structures of Power', *Sociological Review*, **16** (1), March, 59–81

Allen, Bill (2004), 'Pathways to Leadership', in Adair, John and Nelson, John (eds), *Creative Church Leadership*, Norwich: Canterbury Press, pp. 32ff.

Ammerman, Nancy Tatom, Farnsley II, Arthur E. et al. (1997), *Congregation and Community*, New Brunswick, New Jersey: Rutgers University Press

Anderson, William H. (1971), 'The Local Congregation as a Subculture', *Social Compass*, **18** (2), 287–91

Archbishops' Commission (1995), *Working as One Body: The Report of the Archbishops' Commission on the Organisation of the Church of England* [The Turnbull Report], London: Church House Publishing

Bartholomew, John Miles (1981), 'A Sociological View of Authority in Religious Organizations', *Review of Religious Research*, **23** (2), 118–32

Beckford, James A. (1985b), 'Religious Organizations,' in Hammond, Philip E. (ed.), *The Sacred in a Secular Age: Towards Revision in the Scientific Study of Religion*, Berkeley, Los Angeles and London: University of California Press, pp. 125ff.

Berger, Peter L. (1969a), *The Social Reality of Religion*, London: Faber

Berger, Peter (1969b), *The Sacred Canopy*, New York: Doubleday

Berger, Peter L. (1977), *Facing up to Modernity*, New York: Basic Books

Bibby, Reginald W. and Mauss, Armand L. (1974), 'Skidders and their Servants: Variable Goals and Functions of the Skid Road Rescue Mission', *Journal for the Scientific Study of Religion*, **13** (2), pp. 421ff.

Brannon, Robert C.L. (1971), 'Organizational Vulnerability in Modern Religious Organizations', *Journal for the Scientific Study of Religion*, **10** (1), Spring, 27–32

Budd, Susan (1967), 'The Humanist Societies: The Consequences of a Diffuse Belief System', in Wilson, Bryan (ed.), *Patterns of Sectarianism: Organization and Ideology in Social and Religious Movements*, London: Heinemann, pp. 377ff.

Butler, D. Martin and Herman, Robert D. (1999), 'Effective Ministerial Leadership', *Nonprofit Management and Leadership*, **9** (3), Spring, 229–39

Cameron, Helen (2001), 'A perspective from the study of religious organisations', in Anheier, Helmut K. (ed.), *Organisational Theory and the Non-profit Form*, report no. 2, London: Centre for Civil Society, London School of Economics

Dane, Perry (1998), 'The Corporation Sole and the Encounter of Law and Church', in Demerath III, N.J., Hall, Peter Dobkin, Schmitt, Terry and Williams, Rhys H. (eds), *Sacred Companies: Organizational Aspects of Religion and Religious Aspects of Organizations*, New York and Oxford: Oxford University Press, pp. 50ff.

Demerath III, N.J. (1998), 'Snatching Defeat from Victory in the Decline of Liberal Protestantism: Culture versus Structure in Institutional Analysis', in Demerath III, N.J., Hall, Peter Dobkin, Schmitt, Terry and Williams, Rhys H. (eds), *Sacred Companies: Organizational Aspects of Religion and Religious Aspects of Organizations*, New York and Oxford: Oxford University Press, pp. 154ff.

Dolan, Jay P. (1994), 'Patterns of Leadership in the Congregation', in Wind, James P. and Lewis, James W. (eds), *American Congregations*, vol. II, Chicago and London: University of Chicago Press, pp. 225ff.

Dulles, Avery (1988), *Models of the Church*, 2nd edn, Dublin: Gill and Macmillan

Franklin, Robert Michael (1994), 'The Safest Place on Earth: The Culture of Black Congregations', in Wind, James P. and Lewis, James W. (eds), *American Congregations*, vol. II, Chicago and London: University of Chicago Press, pp. 257ff.

Gidren, Benjamin (1997), 'The Evolution of Israel's Third Sector: The Role of Predominant Ideology', *Voluntas*, **8** (1), 11–38

Glock, Charles Y. (1967), 'Religion and the Integration of Society', in Knudten, Richard D. (ed.), *The Sociology of Religion*, New York: Appleton-Century-Crofts, pp. 72ff.

Hinings, C. Robin and Foster, Bruce D. (1973), 'The Organization Structure of Churches: A Preliminary Model', *Sociology*, **7** (1), 93–106

Hopewell, James F. (1987), *Congregation: Stories and Structures*, London: SCM Press

Jeavons, Thomas H. (1992), 'When the Management is the Message: Relating Values to Management Practices in Nonprofit Organizations', *Nonprofit Management and Leadership*, **2** (4), Summer, 403–17

Jeavons, Thomas H. (1993), 'The Role of Values: Management in Religious Organizations', in Young, Dennis R., Hollister, Robert M. and Hodgkinson, Virginia A. (eds), *Governing, Leading and Managing Nonprofit Organizations*, San Francisco: Jossey-Bass Publishers, pp. 52ff.

Jeavons, Thomas H. (1994a), *When the Bottom Line is Faithfulness*, Bloomington and Indianapolis: Indiana University Press

Jeavons, Thomas H. (1994b), 'Stewardship Revisited: Secular and Sacred Views of Governance and Management', *Nonprofit and Voluntary Sector Quarterly*, **23** (2), Summer, 107–22

Kokosalakis, N. (1971), 'Aspects of Conflict between the Structure of Authority and the Beliefs of the Laity in the Roman Catholic Church', in Martin, David (ed.), *A Sociological Yearbook of Religion in Britain*, vol. IV, London: Student Christian Movement, pp. 21ff.

McCann, Joseph F. (1993), *Church and Organization: A Sociological and Theological Enquiry*, Scranton, Pennsylvania: University of Scranton Press

Martin, David (1977), *Reflections on Sociology and Theology*, Oxford: Clarendon Press

Milofsky, Carl (1997), 'Organization from Community: A Case Study of Congregational Renewal', *Nonprofit and Voluntary Sector Quarterly*, **26** (s), s139–60

Munters, Q.J. (1971), 'Recruitment as a Vocation', *Sociologica Neerlandica*, **7** (2), 88–100

Nygren, David J., Ukeritis, Miriam D., McClelland, David C. and Hickman, Julia L. (1994), 'Outstanding Leadership in Nonprofit Organizations: Leadership Competencies in Roman Catholic Religious Orders', *Nonprofit Management and Leadership*, **4** (4), Summer, 375–91

Popper, Karl (1959), *Logic of Scientific Discovery*, London: Hutchinson

Popper, Karl (1962), *Conjectures and Refutations*, London: Routledge and Kegan Paul

Rooney, James F. (1980), 'Organizational Success through Program Failure: Skid Row Rescue Mission', *Social Forces*, **58** (3), 904–24

Scalf, John H., Miller, Michael J. and Thomas, Charles W. (1973), 'Goal Specificity, Organizational Structure and Participant Commitment in Churches', *Sociological Analysis*, **34** (3), Fall, pp. 169ff.

Selznick, Philip (1992), *The Moral Community: Social Theory and the Promise of Commonwealth*, Berkeley: University of California Press

Stout, Harry S. and Cormode, D. Scott (1998), 'Institutions and the Story of American Religion: A Sketch of a Synthesis', in Demerath III, N.J., Hall, Peter Dobkin, Schmitt, Terry and Williams, Rhys H. (eds), *Sacred Companies: Organizational Aspects of Religion and Religious Aspects of Organizations*, New York and Oxford: Oxford University Press, pp. 62ff.

Thompson, Kenneth A. (1973), 'Religious Organizations: The Cultural Perspective', in Salaman, Graeme and Thompson, Kenneth (eds), *People and Organizations*, Harlow: Longman, pp. 293ff.

Thung, Mady A. (1978), 'An Alternative Model for a Missionary Church: An Approach of the Sociology of Organizations', *The Ecumenical Review*, **30**, 18–31, Geneva: World Council of Churches

Valins, Oliver (2002), *Facing the future: the provision of long-term care facilities for older Jewish people in the United Kingdom*, London: Institute for Jewish Policy Research

Wilson, Bryan (1967b), 'The Exclusive Brethren: A Case Study in the Evolution of a Sectarian Ideology', in Wilson, Bryan (ed.), *Patterns of Sectarianism: Organization and Ideology in Social and Religious Movements*, London: Heinemann, pp. 287ff.

Wuthnow, Robert (1994), *Producing the Sacred: an essay on public religion*, Urbana and Chicago: University of Illinois Press

CHAPTER 12

Conclusion

We have explored the emerging new field of religious and faith-based organizations and their management; we have offered working definitions of religious and faith-based organizations; and we have discussed how such organizations should be studied. We have studied the congregation, the fundamental religious organization; we have discussed different kinds of federation; we have discussed the governance of these organizations; and we have asked how faith-based organizations fit into the picture. Of particular issues which face religious and faith-based organizations and their management we have studied the concept of membership, the secularization process, and the position of the clergy. Finally, we have located religious and faith-based organizations in civil society and shown their importance to it, and we have made suggestions as to how religious and faith-based organizations should be led. There would be a long list of the things which we have not done. In particular, we have not submitted our material to theological analysis, and we have not drawn detailed conclusions about how religious and faith-based organizations should be managed. What we have done is to lay the foundations on which both of these tasks might be attempted. Both tasks are essential, for religious and faith-based organizations need to be appropriately managed if they are to be effective, and because religious organizations 'produce the sacred' (Wuthnow 1994) theological analysis of our material and social science analysis of any theology of religious organizations are both both appropriate and necessary.

I shall make no attempt here to summarize the content of the somewhat diverse material in this book. I merely wish to draw attention to two hypotheses which might help future study of this emerging field.

1   We have found helpful Weber's three authority-types: the traditional, the bureaucratic, and the charismatic (Weber 1922); and we have also found helpful Etzioni's three compliance structures: the normative, the utilitarian and the coercive (Etzioni 1980). We have already identified connections (though certainly not equivalence) between the traditional authority type and normative compliance structure, the bureaucratic authority type and the utilitarian compliance structure, and the charismatic authority type and the coercive compliance structure (it is this last pairing which is the least legitimate).

Of the different types of congregations and federations, the denominational tends to the bureaucratic, the church-type tends to the traditional, and the sectarian tends to the charismatic; though, as we have seen, there are strong traditional elements to the sect, and all three exhibit bureaucratic structures at federation level.

As we suggested in our first chapter, faith-based organizations lie between religious organizations and secular organizations and exhibit characteristics of both. Since secular organizations experience the bureaucratic authority-type and sometimes the charismatic authority-type, but the traditional type to a lesser degree, we should expect faith-based organizations to experience the complete mixture of authority-types and also the complete mixture of compliance structures.

We can therefore construct a diagram (Figure 12.1), whilst recognizing of course that is a highly simplified picture and that many organizations won't fit into it.

2   In Chapter 4 on congregations and in Chapter 9 on the clergy we recognized that the existence of an authority structure beyond institutional and social boundaries (leaving to one side the question of the independent existence of such an authority) was a major reason for congregations behaving as they do and for clergy behaving as they do. It might therefore be possible to represent the difference between secular and religious organizations as in Figure 12.2.

Two very different authority patterns emerge. Whether these diagrams have explanatory power will only become clear as the field develops. If they do, then they suggest that faith-based organizations, caught between the two authority

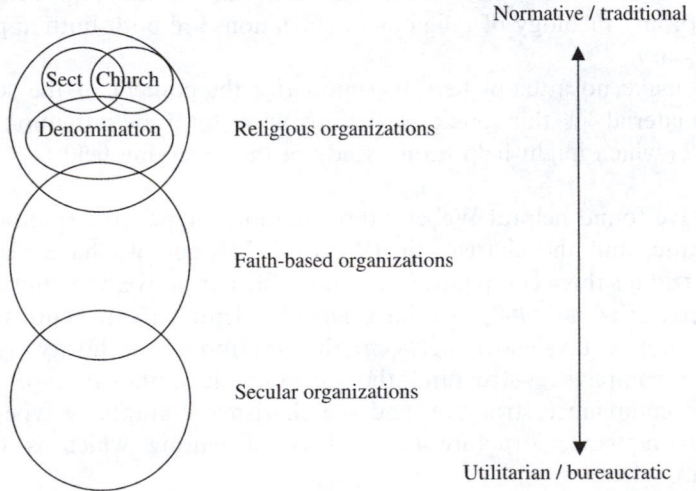

Figure 12.1   Organizational, authority and compliance-structure types

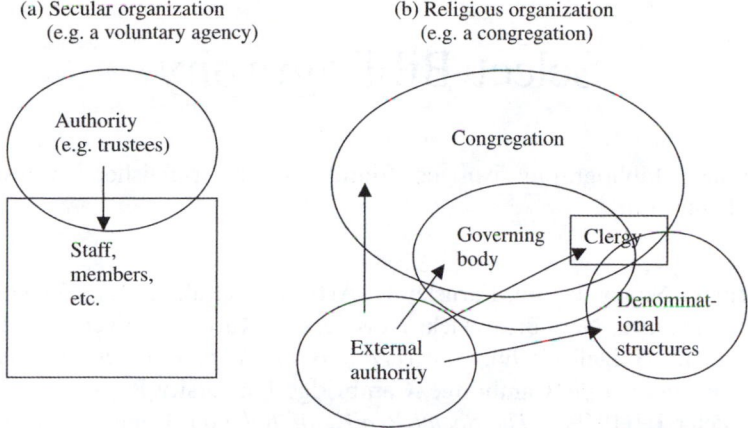

Figure 12.2   Authority structures in secular and religious organizations

patterns, are bound to find life difficult as they try to operate within two very different patterns at the same time. They will inevitably drift towards the simpler secular structure.

Whether or not future exploration of the field will find these hypotheses and diagrams helpful I don't know; but two things do need to be said in conclusion: that if the field is to develop then a great deal more research is going to be required to improve our understanding of these important and fascinating organizations; and that if religious and faith-based organizations are to be managed appropriately then their difference from other kinds of organizations will need to be translated into kinds of management and leadership appropriate to the organizations concerned.

References

Etzioni, Amitai (1980), 'Compliance Structures', in Etzioni, Amitai and Lehman, E. (eds), *A Sociological Reader on Complex Organisations*, 3rd edn: Austin, Texas: Holt, Reinhart and Winston

Weber, Max (1922), 'The Three Types of Legitimate Rule', in Etzioni, Amitai and Lehman, E. (eds) (1980) *A Sociological Reader on Complex Organisations*, 3rd edn: Austin, Texas: Holt, Reinhart and Winston

Wuthnow, Robert (1994), *Producing the Sacred: an essay on public religion*, Urbana and Chicago: University of Illinois Press

Select Bibliography

A complete bibliography can be found on the publisher's website at www.ashgate.com

Ammerman, Nancy Tatom, Farnsley II, Arthur E. et al. (1997), *Congregation and Community*, New Brunswick, New Jersey: Rutgers University Press

Becker, Penny Edgell (1999), *Congregations in Conflict: Cultural Models of Local Religious Life*, Cambridge: Cambridge University Press

Berger, Peter L. (1969a), *The Social Reality of Religion*, London: Faber

Billis, David (1993), *Organizing Public and Voluntary Agencies*, London and New York: Routledge

Billis, D. and Harris, M. (eds) (1996), *Voluntary Agencies*, Basingstoke: Macmillan

Brown, Callum G. (2001), *The Death of Christian Britain: Understanding secularization 1800–2000*, London and New York: Routledge

Bruce, Stephen (1995), *Religion in Modern Britain*, Oxford: Oxford University Press

Caplow, Theodore, Bahr, Howard M. and Chadwick, Bruce A. (1983), *All Faithful People: change and continuity in Middletown's religion*, Minneapolis: University of Minnesota Press

Chadwick, Owen (1975), *The Secularisation of the European Mind in the Nineteenth Century*, Cambridge: Cambridge University Press

Clarke, Peter and Byrne, Peter (1993), *Religion Defined and Explained*, Basingstoke and London: St Martin's Press/Macmillan

Cnaan, Ram A. (2002), *The Invisible Hand: American Congregations and the Provision of Welfare*, New York: New York University Press

Davie, Grace (1994), *Religion in Britain since 1945: Believing without Belonging*, Oxford: Blackwell

Davie, Grace (2002), *Europe: The Exceptional Case: Parameters of Faith in the Modern World*, London: Darton, Longman and Todd

Demerath III, N.J., Hall, Peter Dobkin, Schmitt, Terry and Williams, Rhys H. (eds) (1998), *Sacred Companies: Organizational Aspects of Religion and Religious Aspects of Organizations*, New York and Oxford: Oxford University Press

Guest, Mathew, Tusting, Karin and Woodhead, Linda (eds) (2004), *Congregational Studies in the UK: Christianity in a Post-Christian Context*, Aldershot: Ashgate

Harris, Margaret (1998a) *Organizing God's Work: Challenges for Churches and Synagogues*, London: Macmillan

Harris, Margaret and Torry, Malcolm (2000), *Managing Religious and Faith-based Organisations: A Guide to the Literature*, Birmingham: University of Aston Business School

Harris, Margaret and Rochester, Colin (eds) (2001b), *Voluntary Organisations and Social Policy in Britain*, Basingstoke: Palgrave

Hopewell, James F. (1987), *Congregation: Stories and Structures*, London: SCM Press

Hornsby-Smith, Michael P. (1989), *The Changing Parish: A Study of Parishes, Priests and Parishioners after Vatican II*, London and New York: Routledge

Jeavons, Thomas H. (1994a), *When the Bottom Line is Faithfulness*, Bloomington and Indianapolis: Indiana University Press

McCann, Joseph F. (1993), *Church and Organization: A Sociological and Theological Enquiry*, Scranton, Pennsylvania: University of Scranton Press

MacIntyre, Alasdair (1967), *Secularization and Moral Change*, Oxford: Oxford University Press

Martin, David (1978), *A General Theory of Secularization*, Oxford: Blackwell

Mason, David E. (1984), *Voluntary Nonprofit Enterprise Management*, New York and London: Plenum Press

Mitton, C.L. (ed.) (1972), *The Social Sciences and the Churches*, Edinburgh: T. and T. Clark

O'Dea, Thomas F. (1969), *Sociology and the Study of Religion: Theory, Research, Interpretation*, New York and London: Basic Books Inc.

Powell, Walter W. and DiMaggio, Paul J. (1991), *The New Institutionalism in Organizational Analysis*, Chicago and London: University of Chicago Press

Putnam, Robert (2000), *Bowling Alone: The Collapse and Revival of American Community*, New York: Simon Schuster

Ranson, Stewart, Bryman, Alan and Hinings, Bob (1977), *Clergy, Ministers and Priests*, London, Henley and Boston: Routledge and Kegan Paul

Reed, Bruce (1978), *The Dynamics of Religion: Process and Movement in Christian Churches*, London: Darton, Longman and Todd

Roberts, Richard H. (2002), *Religion, Theology and the Human Sciences*, Cambridge: Cambridge University Press

Rochester, Colin (1998), *Social Benefits: Exploring the value of community sector organizations*, West Malling: Charities Aid Foundation

Rudge, Peter F. (1976), *Management in the Church*, London: McGraw Hill

Russell, Anthony (1984), *The Clerical Profession*, London: Society for Promoting Christian Knowledge

Saliba, John A. (1995), *Perspectives on New Religious Movements*, London: Geoffrey Chapman

Scherer, Ross P. (ed.) (1980), *American Denominational Organization: A Sociological View*, Pasadena, California: William Carey Library

Towler, Robert and Coxon, A.P.M. (1979), *The Fate of the Anglican Clergy: A Sociological Study*, London and Basingstoke: Macmillan

Van Til, Jon (2000), *Growing Civil Society*, Bloomington, Indiana: Indiana University Press

Warner, R. Stephen (1988), *New Wine in Old Wineskins: Evangelicals and Liberals in a Small-Town Church*, Berkeley: University of California Press

Warren, Yvonne (2002), *The Cracked Pot: The State of Today's Anglican Parish Clergy*, Stowmarket: Kevin Mayhew

Wilson, Bryan (1982a), *Religion in Sociological Perspective*, Oxford: Oxford University Press

Wind, James P. and Lewis, James W. (eds) (1994), *American Congregations*, Chicago and London: University of Chicago Press

Wuthnow, Robert (1994), *Producing the Sacred: an essay on public religion*, Urbana and Chicago: University of Illinois Press

Wuthnow, Robert, Hodgkinson, Virginia A. et al. (1990), *Faith and Philanthropy in America: Exploring the Role of Religion in America's Voluntary Sector*, San Francisco and Oxford: Jossey Bass

Yeo, Stephen (1976), *Religion and Voluntary Organisations in Crisis*, London: Croom Helm

Zald, Mayer N. (1970), *Organizational Change: The Political Economy of the YMCA*, Chicago and London: University of Chicago Press

Zuckerman, Phil (1999), *Strife in the Sanctuary: Religious Schism in a Jewish Community*, Walnut Creek, California: Altamira Press

Index